BUSINESS REPORT WRITING

BUSINESS REPORT WRITING

Phillip V. Lewis
Oklahoma State University

William H. Baker
Brigham Young University

Grid, Inc., Columbus, Ohio

CONTENTS

PART II
BUSINESS RESEARCH METHODOLOGY

9 INTERPRETING THE INFORMATION GATHERED   81

Analysis and Interpretation as the Basis of Every Activity
Processing the Data
Summary
Discussion Questions and Exercises

PART III
THE PROCESS OF REPORT WRITING

10 BASIC COMPOSITION OF RESEARCH REPORTS   89

Readability
Sentence Construction
Emphasis
Paragraph Development
Organization of the Report
Summary
Discussion Questions and Exercises
Endnote

11 ORGANIZING YOUR REPORT FOR PRESENTATION   101

Preparing an Outline
Writing the Major Divisions
Summary
Discussion Questions and Exercises

12 VISUAL COMMUNICATION TECHNIQUES   117

Tables
Graphs
Summary
Discussion Questions and Exercises

13 PREFATORY AND APPENDED SECTIONS   133

The Prefatory Sections
The Appended Sections
Summary
Discussion Questions and Exercises
References for Bibliography Preparation

PART IV
THE PROCESS OF ORAL REPORTING

PART V
CASE STUDIES FOR REPORT WRITING

PART VI
READINGS

x

PREFACE

Some of the most commonly heard words in business and industry are, "Send me a report. . . ." Reports are part of the system of business organization and communication, and to a large degree every worker is judged on the basis of the reports submitted to upper management. This text is concerned primarily with the written or spoken report which results from some form of research.

COMPETENCY IN RESEARCHING AND REPORTING

Research, or data gathering, is infinitely important in our world of increasing populations, changing societies and cultures, overconsuming and polluting, and mushrooming technology. Business managers must rely on research as an important base on which to analyze their current situation and to initiate change. Research is only part of the story, however. After the data have been gathered, they must be recorded, organized, analyzed, and presented in a useful format. In fact, the ability to present clear, concise reports may be the foundation for other managerial skills.

Evidence that competency in business communications is a skill needed by potential managers has been well documented. For example, studies have shown:

1. California business executives indicate that effective communication is a significant factor in moving people to top management positions. (7)
2. Two thousand executives show communication a most significant factor in influencing promotions. (12)
3. There is a definite relationship between communication and employee productivity. (57)
4. Over 70 percent of personnel officers of one hundred companies indicate that business writing is preceded in importance only by accounting and economics. (44)

5. Twenty-seven personnel executives of leading firms in the St. Louis metropolitan area rank written English and public speaking number one and three respectively in the five most important courses for preparing a person for a business career. (92)
6. In ranking fifty business courses senior managers chose business letter writing number one and English composition number two. (41)
7. Eighty percent of American business executives place writing skills at the top of their list of essential business skills. (85)

Studies of the skills needed by successful executives and of the recommended preparations for business students position communication effectiveness at or very near the top of the list. A large proportion of business knowledge finds its communicative potency in reports. For this reason, learning cannot advance unless someone is trained to "put it together" in an acceptable report format.

Give attention to what employers say because there is evidence that many students are being graduated from colleges and universities without the ability to express themselves clearly and concisely. One study shows that the inability of college graduates to communicate either orally or in written form is a weakness frequently named by personnel officers. (92) The ability to express yourself successfully is even more important as you advance into more responsible positions. Even if you are intellectually capable in your chosen career, you will be judged by your reporting ability. Without this ability you may remain in a mediocre role.

TEXTUAL DESIGN

This text proposes to develop research and reporting techniques by guiding you through the nature of reports, research methodology in business, and the writing process. We are aware that occasionally the word "research" triggers a negative attitude, but research is the only proven method for ascertaining the "why." Thus at each major juncture there will be practice exercises to demonstrate your learning, researching, writing, and reporting skills. By the end of the book you should be able to research and present effective reports (either formally or informally) based on the needs of those requesting the report. You will know *why* the research and reporting processes are important and *why* your skills are vital to your future success.

Some of the specific advantages for using this textbook are:

1. Alternate chapter readings
2. Multidisciplinary cases
3. Emphasis on both written and oral reports
4. Fresh, unique approach to problem solving
5. Exhaustive list of books and periodicals from numerous business areas. (Numbers in parentheses throughout text refer to the bibliography following the last reading.)
6. Traditional techniques of data gathering
7. Readable treatment of basic writing characteristics

8. Thorough report checklist
9. Student-oriented, step-by-step guide through the complete problem-solving and report-writing process

ACKNOWLEDGMENTS

This book is the product of suggestions offered by students, colleagues, friends, and editors. We thank each person. We also thank our editors at Grid Publishing for their patience in getting this work published.

We also thank Doris Sponseller whose critical reviews were helpful in making this textbook meet the demands of the classroom. Our colleagues, Harold Coonrad, Lloyd Garner, Herb Jelley, and John Williams also offered valuable insights about the content.

Naturally we owe a debt of thanks to our wives and children whose love and constant devotion helped in moments of writing frustration.

Part I

The Nature of
Researching and
Reporting

The Function of the Business Report

Business is more complex and competition is more vigorous than ever; improved communication has become a compelling need in the last decade and a half. A steadily increasing flood of information demands greater control and coordination of work forces. However, the degree to which any organization achieves coordination is usually related to the success or failure of communication—communication in the form of an oral or a written report.

The need for reports has intensified proportionally with the entanglement of organizations and individuals. Clear and concise reports are a major factor in the success of any enterprise. Illogical, poorly written reports cause the loss of thousands of manhours and perhaps millions of dollars in information. If you are not already aware, you soon will discover that effective reports are necessary to all but the most minor business decisions. Your future advancement in management will, to a very large degree, depend upon your reporting skills.

THE REPORT PROCESS

There is a steady flow of information down, up, and across organizational lines. The larger a firm is, the more necessary are written records, and good written records (reports) require ideas, researchers, reporters, and readers. Any breakdowns along the line can lead to serious loss of information. To begin this study, you need a workable definition of a business report.

DEFINITIONS OF "REPORT"

Several definitions are available:

1. A written or oral message which (*a*) conveys information about research or status from one area of business to another to assist a manager's decision-making function or (*b*) presents a solution to a business problem. (40)

2. An orderly and objective communication of factual information which serves some basic business purpose—solving problems or presenting information needed in the conduct of business. (56)
3. A creative communication between two people, an interaction which sets up a dynamic equilibrium between writer and reader. (91)
4. Any communication aimed primarily at conveying facts or generalizations purportedly based on fact. (89)

The basis used in defining "report" should relate to the purpose of a report; it provides managers with information that will allow the solving of problems or the making of decisions. *A report is any record that helps people understand the business environment of which they are a part.* To be useful, however, a report must contain information for decision and action.

THE NATURE OF REPORTS

Because a report is conceptually no more than a presentation of data, it may be either useful or worthless. If a report contains vague ideas, opinions, or prejudices, the information will be of little use to the receiver. However, if a report documents the past, present, or future state of events, relations, objects, persons, or things, it should be effective. Thus a business report may be viewed on a continuum from an informal, personally oriented document to a highly specialized technical form of communication; it may range from a fairly restricted perspective to a very broad one.

Other basic characteristics of reports are: although reports may differ in aim, they are written to be read. All reports convey facts of some kind, and some also interpret those facts and make recommendations. Reports may be carried by a variety of media and differ in length and form—from a very brief, informal memo to a very formal, many-paged document. Each report is tailored for a specific reader or audience.

A CLASSIFICATION SYSTEM FOR BUSINESS REPORTS

There are certain general functions of reports that may be agreed upon, but a universally accepted report classification system apparently is unavailable. A report usually has a limited audience because it is directed to an individual or group to whom the writer feels a definite responsibility. The report presented is the end result of research and consists of notes, statistics, tables, charts, figures, or quoted material. What is presented is a permanent record of research activity and the selection of material may determine whether the information receives acceptance or rejection.

A report generally is preceded by considerable research. It tends to be longer, more complex, and more detailed than a letter and requires careful analysis and investigation. Emphasis is on presenting facts that will accomplish a specific purpose; therefore, facts must be practical and clearly stated. The language of the report must meet the needs of the receiver. In essence, *a basic classification system for business reports* may be based on a report's *direction, context, function,* and *format.* Reports should be factual, objective, and specific; they must be planned and presented according to the reader and the nature and purpose of the material.

THE DIRECTIONAL CLASSIFICATION

Communication is usually presented as a flow of information in upward, downward, or horizontal directions. These directional designations are widely accepted, although there is some justification for believing that communication seldom follows these patterns. Actually, it is more *radial* in nature, cutting across the managerial levels of authority, flowing both within (internal) and without (external) the organization.

Vertical Reports

Vertical reports occur between superiors and subordinates. The subordinate sends a report *upward* to a superior, containing either requested or nonsolicited information. The primary purpose is to furnish management with useful information (feedback) for intelligent decision making. Specific types of information relayed upward might include accomplishments, problems, plans, attitudes, or feelings. The manager who encourages upward communication usually improves the morale and attitude of employees.

In turn, a manager also sends reports *downward* to a subordinate. Usually this flow of information is the giving of instructions for carrying out policies and procedures. Typically the most-used channel in organizations, downward communication also may be the most misused because of its one-way nature.

Two basic types of vertical reports set the tempo of day-to-day operations and keep an administrative finger on the pulse of the organization:

1. *Reports designed to standardize performance* tell people where, when, and how; they bring a degree of consistency to organizational performance by providing a foundation of procedures or methods.
2. *Reports designed to control performance* primarily flow up the lines of communication in a hierarchy; they allow the receiver to make a decision either to accept performance as is or to take corrective action. (74)

Horizontal Reports

Horizontal reports flow between levels of equal authority; they provide colleagues with information needed to carry out assignments and make intelligent decisions. Although horizontal communication probably is the strongest of all flows in an organization, it may not be satisfactory. People on the same level, who work together daily, usually understand one another; yet people on the same level seldom listen to instructions ("commands") from their peers. A better use of horizontal communication is to coordinate performance.

Internal and External Reports

Internal and external reports are both concerned with the operational and administrative details of an organization. *Internal reports* move vertically between managers and subordinates or horizontally between levels of equal authority. They are written by and for persons in the same organization. *External reports* are prepared for readers outside the enterprise. A typical function of an external report is selling the company and its products or informing a specified group about the company and its products. These reports are intended principally for stockholders, customers, government agencies, or the general public.

THE CONTEXTUAL CLASSIFICATION

One of the best systems for classifying business reports is based on the nature of a report or its subject matter (sometimes classified as *field* research). Reports under this classification may be either technical and nontechnical and convey information both internally and externally. Contextual reports typically are classified according to their subject matter—accounting, financial, marketing, sales, production, personnel, insurance.

Accounting and Financial Reports

One of the functions of an accountant is to serve management through the reporting process. Management and investors need to know "how are we doing?" and periodic financial statements provide an answer. In the past, accountants were satisfied with accumulating and reporting historical data; however, in today's complex business world, this information has little applicability to decision making. Now there is an emphasis on integrating nonfinancial data into an organization's record-keeping and reporting systems.

Sales Reports

Salesmen, in their daily routine, accumulate a great deal of information about what is happening in the market place. Unless they communicate this to management, however, a company may not gauge accurately the progress of business and competition. Thus sales reports can convey several types of relevant information for managers—status of the company's accounts, sales performance, complaints, current trends, and new product ideas. Based on these inputs, management can then make decisions about future production, advertising, and marketing.

Personnel Reports

An important time to record data accurately, objectively, uniformly, and completely is when personnel reports are prepared for management. Since the future of an applicant or employee may be at stake, personnel reports especially should avoid human error. For example, based on reports of interviews, 1) employers can decide whether to hire an applicant, 2) counselors can give the correct advice to an employee, or 3) supervisors can improve a subordinate's job performance. Obtaining, recording, and communicating data are critical steps in personnel reports.

THE FUNCTIONAL CLASSIFICATION

The basic function of any report is to inform or to analyze; however, there are many types of reports that may be used. For example:

1. *Informational reports* are usually concerned with *fact-finding;* they present data but omit comments. Financial statements, minutes of meetings, abstracts and digests of published material, and business records would fit this category.
2. *Research reports* are concerned with *knowledge* (basic research) and any *practical consequences of knowledge* (applied research).
3. *Analytical reports* not only present information but also *interpret and analyze facts.* These reports generally are prepared on request and analyze present and past conditions to determine a future course of action.
4. *Recommendation reports* consist principally of *recommendations for present and future action;* for example, an advertising agency's suggestion for a new advertising campaign, a labor arbitrator's proposal for settling a strike, or a government commission's plan for slum renovation.

Other designations could be provided for *advisability, feasibility, proposal, justification, investigation, inspection,* and *progress* reports. Hence the functional classification is one of the broadest categories for special types of reports. However, there are three primary report processes which contribute to the decision process: information, interpretation, and analysis (Exhibit 1-1). Fact finding leads to interpretation, which leads to analysis, which leads to a decision.

Informative Reports

Informative reports are sometimes called periodic reports because they present information at regular intervals (Exhibit 1-2) to keep the reader informed of the status of operations. In the decision-making pyramid, informational reports merely present facts. No attempt is made to analyze, interpret, draw conclusions, or make recommendations. A bank statement is a common informational report. Other information reports include readership surveys, sales reports, policy statements, and credit reports.

Although the information report is the lowest in status, in some respects it is the most difficult to handle effectively because the researcher and writer must distinguish between raw, unevaluated information and data evaluated for a specific purpose. The difference between knowledge which represents general-use data and knowledge which is significant to the immediate specific situation must be spotted.

Interpretive Reports

The second level of the decision-making pyramid is concerned with reports which not only inform but interpret, which explain unusual sales

8

EXHIBIT 1-1
Report Status Hierarchy in Decision Making

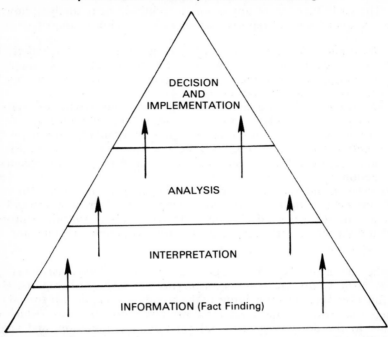

Source: Adopted from Jessamon Dawe and William J. Lord, Jr. *Functional Business Communication* (Englewood Cliffs, N.Y.: Prentice-Hall, Inc., 1968) pp. 282, 283 .

slumps or upsurges. As with informative reports, however, no attempt is made to reach a conclusion or make a recommendation. Such reports are generally prepared on written request.

Analytical Reports

The third level of the decision-making pyramid concerns the entire nature of research and report writing. It breaks the whole into parts and shows how they relate to each other. An analytical report 1) formulates an issue or identifies a problem; 2) analyzes, synthesizes, and interprets pertinent data; and 3) presents conclusions and recommendations for appropriate action. However, depending on the wishes of the person assigning the report, an analytical report may not contain recommendations. Examples of analytical reports are marketing surveys, product analyses, employee attitude surveys, improvement reports, and justification reports.

THE FORMAT CLASSIFICATION

Classifications according to format are principally concerned with formal/informal or long/short designations. These distinctions have little to do with content but are more concerned with method of presentation. The

EXHIBIT 1-2
Example of an Informational (Periodic) Report

AARDVARK, INC.

FIRST QUARTER REPORT

The First Quarter in Brief	This Year	Last Year
FINANCIAL		
Total revenues	$5,000,000,000	$4,500,000,000
Net income	$ 342,000,000	$ 314,000,000
Net income per share	$ 5.00	$ 4.50
Dividends paid	$ 160,000,000	$ 159,000,000
Dividends paid per share	$ 2.00	$ 2.00
Capital and exploration expenditures	$ 720,000,000	$ 713,000,000
Total assets	$5,651,000,000	$5,397,000,000
Shareholders' equity per share	$ 51.00	$ 49.00
Working capital	$ 698,000,000	$ 484,000,000
OPERATING		
Crude oil and natural gas liquids, barrels per day—		
Net production	769,000	744,000
Refinery input	990,000	977,000
Natural gas sold, thousand cubic feet per day	3,600,000	3,500,000
Refined products sold, barrels per day	1,100,000	1,000,000
Chemicals, plastics, and fertilizers sold	$ 482,000,000	$ 392,000,000

choice of an informal, short report or a formal, long report depends on how the report is to be used.

Formal Versus Informal Reports

Precise distinguishing characteristics between formal and informal are at times difficult. *Informal* denotes a casual, easy-going, offhand style of writing. *Formal* denotes the development of a report according to certain prescribed rules. The form is often predetermined and carries the connotation of ritual, stiffness, and sometimes stuffiness. Variables which will influence the choice are the complexity of the problem being researched and the status, needs, and temperament of the reader. The report should be constructed so it does not convey an attitude contrary to the purpose.

Short Versus Long Reports

The short/long decision is similar to the formal/informal one. Obviously, a distinguishing criteria is length; however, the overriding principle should be providing the information the reader is seeking. The short report ranges from extreme brevity to moderate length (one-half to ten pages). The two most common models of short reports are the memorandum report and the letter report. The style of the long report is more one of prescribed formality.

The Short Report

The majority of reports a manager receives and on which she or he bases decisions are relatively short. To help any manager make an effective decision, the report must possess accuracy, preciseness, and clarity; it must be logical and orderly. Likewise, it should be objective, verify all statements, utilize visuals when needed, explain unusual changes in statistical data, and present an attractive format.

As a general rule the short report deals with only one purpose—fact finding or inquiry, technical or nontechnical information, or recommendations. Similarly, it follows one of two presentation forms: for example, 1) introduction, discussion of details, findings, conclusions, and recommendations or 2) introduction, conclusions and recommendations, purpose, methodology, and findings. The writer's thought process may logically follow the first form (inductive) or the latter form (deductive).

A short report can be in memorandum or letter form.

The memorandum report is one of the most practical ways to transact business through writing. Concise, informal, and typewritten (usually, but not always), the memorandum can be used effectively to transmit information requiring a written document, to record and transmit data which might be confused if presented orally, to send identical information to several individuals, to record policies or decisions reached in meetings, to provide summaries of business meetings for committee members, and to pinpoint responsibility. The memo is a type of internal communication that handles routine business but may sometimes be mailed outside the firm.

The general pattern for a memorandum varies from one organization to the next, but its structure is basically the same (Exhibit 1-3). Every memorandum states *to whom* and *from whom* it is being sent. No salutation is used. Ordinarily a *subject* line is provided so the reader will know what is being discussed; however, many companies leave off the subject line if the report is fairly brief (one-half to one page). The *date* the memorandum is written and/or transmitted is also included. All in all, the memorandum is a flexible and convenient device for transmitting ideas, orders and policies that need attention.

EXHIBIT 1-3
Distinguishing Characteristics of a Memorandum

```
                          THIS COMPANY

     MEMORANDUM

          TO:   (The reader)              Date:   (Current)
        FROM:   (The writer)
     SUBJECT:   (Nature of report; similar to a title)
```

Memoranda usually are not signed although writers may add their initials at the close of the body of the memo or at the top of the memo next to their typed name. No complimentary close is used.

The letter report follows the same general format as that of any good business letter; however, its inner structure is somewhat more formal (Exhibit 1-4). A letter report may utilize graphs and tables and will be factual and objective. The singular "you-I" approach is sometimes discarded either for the third-person, impersonal point of view or for the corporate, plural "we-you." The right approach depends on the writer-reader relationship. The same essentials applicable to any writing should be adhered to: completeness, consistency, clarity, conciseness, and correctness. In many respects the letter report is organized as a long report.

Several different letter formats might be used (management newsletter, corporate annual, or periodic report), but the goal is the same: *providing information for the reader.* The choice between a memorandum report or a letter report may be one of convenience or preference or may depend on whether the report is sent internally or externally.

The Long Report

The long report is a detailed account of investigation and research; it is formal and makes maximum use of facts and figures. Objectives include persuasion, information, comparison, analysis, or argument. Whatever its purpose, the long report presents in a prescribed form an analysis of a

EXHIBIT 1-4
Suggested Format for Letter Report

AARDVARK, INC.

1. Date

2. The
   Inside
   Address

3. Salutation:

4. SUBJECT: (Identifying short title)

5. Authorization for writing report (one paragraph)*

6. Reasons for and nature of report (one or two paragraphs)

7. Summary of findings (one or two paragraphs)

8. Development of report—facts, theories, argruments, conclusions (as many paragraphs as necessary)

9. Concluding statements—proposal for action (one or two paragraphs)

10. Complimentary close

11. Typed signature and position of person signing letter

12. Reference initials

13. List of enclosures or attachments (as needed)

14. Carbon copy notations (as needed)

*In steps 6-9, the use of subheadings is permitted.

recommended solution to a problem (Exhibit 1-5). Most problems dealt with are complex and important; they must be carefully, concisely, and accurately analyzed to help management make sound decisions.

Long, formal reports can aid managerial decision making in at least four ways: First, they protect a manager from half-developed ideas, voluminous memoranda, and half-ready oral presentations. Second, long reports supply the manager with answers, not questions. Third, they permit the manager to

EXHIBIT 1-5
Organization for a Long Report

SUGGESTED FORMAT FOR A LONG REPORT

I. PRELIMINARY PARTS

   A. Cover

   B. Letter of Transmittal
      1. A letter usually is attached to the long report as a greeting and serves the same purpose as handing the report to the reader personally.
      2. A general plan for the transmittal letter is (a) authorization, (b) subject, (c) overall review of report, and (d) acknowledgements for assistance.

   C. Title Page
      1. Both the cover and title page should clearly state the subject of the report and the writer.
      2. The title page, in addition, should state the origin of the report, the organization for whom the report was prepared, the date, and any other names or codes necessary.

   D. Table of Contents
      1. Both major and minor sections of the report are listed with their page number.
      2. If several illustrations, charts, or graphs are used in the report you may wish to include a Table of Tables.

   E. Synopsis (summary of the entire report)
      1. The synopsis is the condensed report and shows the reader what is to follow in-depth.
      2. A general procedure for the synopsis is to include (a) the purpose of the report, (b) a concise statement of findings, and (c) the conclusions; if appropriate, the recommendations also may be included.

II. BODY OF THE REPORT (scope of your research)

   A. Purpose

   B. Methodology
      1. The body describes and discusses the overall picture.
      2. The problem is described, its history is analyzed, and facts are presented.
      3. All methods of research, equipment required, or coordination are described.

   C. Findings (statement of pertinent facts)

   D. Conclusions (statement of significance of findings)

   E. Recommendations (proposals for action)

III. ADDENDA

   A. Bibliography
      1. Books
      2. Periodicals
      3. Documents

   B. Appendix (exhibits not required in body)

   C. Index (usually nonessential; may be helpful if report is lengthy and detailed) indicate approval or disapproval of worker action. Fourth, they serve as an effective means of communication between departments, companies, or various groups of concerned people. (42)

The long report usually is ten pages or more and is arranged in the indirect, inductive plan. However, a more direct, deductive approach can be achieved with a synopsis at the beginning of the report. How to develop and construct reports will be amplified in Parts II and III of this text.

SUMMARY

This chapter presents a definition of the reporting process and a basic classification scheme for business reports based on direction, context, function, and format. *Directional reporting* deals with communication flows— upward, downward, horizontal, internal, and external. *Contextual reporting* looks at a specific subject matter or topic (accounting, sales, personnel, and so forth).

Functional reporting informs and analyzes; it offers one of the broadest categories for listing special types of reports—informative, interpretive, and analytical. These three classifications may find themselves housed in a formal long report, an informal short report, or any combination of formality and length. *Format reporting* considerations are concerned with presentation methods and have little to do with actual content.

Remember, reports are permanent records of research activity; they present information for someone about a specific theme. To be worthwhile this information must lead to intelligent decision making; if it does not, both reader and researcher have wasted their time.

In Part VI, Reading 1, "Improving the Effectiveness of Management Reports," will review some of the concepts and techniques of reporting that exist to improve the profitability of organizations.

DISCUSSION QUESTIONS AND EXERCISES

1. Why are clear and concise reports a major factor in the success of any enterprise?
2. One basic classification system for business reports is founded on direction, context, function, and format. Briefly describe each.
3. Why do you think a universally accepted report classification system is unavailable?
4. What are the basic differences between upward and downward communication? Cite advantages of each.
5. How do vertical reports keep an administrative finger on the pulse of an organization?
6. Why might communication be described radically rather than vertically or horizontally? Can you describe or diagram this concept?
7. What are three advantages of directional reporting?
8. What are the fundamental differences between internal and external reports?
9. Why might it be more difficult to write internal messages than external ones?
10. How have accounting reports changed in the last decade?
11. Illustrate how sales reports enable managers to make decisions about production, advertising, and marketing.

12. Explain why it is especially important to accurately, objectively, uniformly, and completely record data in personnel reports.
13. List and describe some of the types of functional reports.
14. Explain the report status hierarchy in decision making (Exhibit 1-1).
15. How might the form of a report determine whether the information conveyed receives acceptance or rejection?
16. What are the primary distinctions between formal/informal and long/short reports?
17. Illustrate the connotative and denotative differences between formal and informal reports.
18. What are the basic differences between a memorandum report and a letter report?
19. What are the criteria that dictates whether a writer should use a memo or a letter to transmit information?
20. List some advantages to transmitting ideas in written memo form rather than orally.
21. What are some objectives for the long report? Explain each.
22. Explain how long, formal reports aid managerial decision making.
23. Which report classification system seems most useful? Defend your selection.
24. How is report writing inseparable from advancement in management?
25. Procure a business report and share your comments on its format and classification with your teacher and fellow students.

2

The Importance of
Business Research

Each working day hundreds of thousands of pages of written communications circulate throughout the business world. The absolute cost cannot be figured, but a poor report costs more than a good one. The cost of damaging impressions that result from inaccuracies in reporting is appalling. At least 80 percent of the wrong decisions made by managers result from faulty communications—communications usually bound up in a report. Thus, immediate and future success depends on communication skills—the ability to issue, transmit, and fulfill messages, the ability to attain proficiency and profit through useful words that produce appropriate actions.

One of the purposes of this text is to present the necessary communication principles to accomplish the research and reporting functions. Since most reports are the result of some form of research (either formal or informal), it is necessary first to examine research methods.

RESEARCH METHODOLOGY

The primary purpose of research is to discover answers to questions. However, the questions must be answerable by observation or experimentation in the natural world. The research activity must grow out of an attitude of "why" and "how." Training in research techniques and the reporting processes must continue, since, if research processes are stopped, learning declines.

DEFINITIONS OF RESEARCH

Although some research techniques are unique to certain disciplines, the following definitions are generally accepted by all:

1. Studious inquiry or examination; critical, exhaustive investigation or experimentation whose aim is (a) discovering new facts and their correct interpretation, (b) revising accepted conclusions, theories, or laws in the light of newly discerned facts, or (c) making applications of new or revised conclusions, theories, or laws. (6)

2. The process of systematically obtaining accurate answers to significant and pertinent questions by the scientific method of gathering and interpreting information. (18)
3. Careful inquiring or examining to discover new information or relationships and expanding and verifying existing knowledge. (75)

From these three definitions we may infer that successful research is possible when the investigation is seeking to determine whether certain contentions are true. Some of the key words in the above definitions are "studious inquiry," "critical and exhaustive investigation," "correct interpretation," and "systematically." Research, viewed from these perspectives, then becomes dependent on the following:

1. There is the existence of certain beliefs about a proposition derived from vicarious or actual experience.
2. A diligent, comprehensive search for data must be conducted to test the validity of these beliefs.
3. The researcher must arrive at a conclusion with regard to the original hypothesis in the light of any newly-discovered facts. (22)

In this text, *research* will be defined as a *thorough examination of any area or question to discover new information or to confirm existing data.*

MAJOR CHARACTERISTICS OF RESEARCH

Research studies may be classified by very general characteristics (library, observation, generalizations) or very specific classifications (accounting, economics, finance, management, marketing). Kinds of research investigations come in all shapes and sizes—scientific, action, basic, and applied research; fact finding and critical interpretation; descriptive, historical, philosophical, prognostic, and sociological research; field study and case study; statistical, genetical, life and physical sciences, experimental and technological research; motivation and operations research; and curriculum development. In addition, chance, trial and error, and logic are often discussed in a study of research classifications. For simplification and application to business this book will be concerned primarily with *historical, descriptive, basic and applied, motivation,* and *operations research,* and secondarily with *the scientific method of research.* Keep in mind, however, that good researchers will use a number of methods and not limit themselves to one technique.

Historical Research

Historical research is concerned with how things have been in the past compared with how things are now. This style of research, a type of library research, seeks to explain the how and why of any changes that have occurred during a certain period of time. It is conducted primarily through the use of written material (government documents, professional journals, business records) and necessitates new generalizations and conclusions.

Descriptive Research

Descriptive research may be viewed as an inquiry into the status quo; it is concerned with the way things are now. Consequently, investigation centers around 1) conditions, relationships, practices, elements, values, and processes as they currently exist; 2) the *effects* of the elements of description; 3) current attitudes, philosophies, and beliefs; 4) trends that may be developing; 5) any associations among the elements of description; and 6) what might be desirable and how to get there. (22)

Basic and Applied Research

Basic (pure) and applied research are not mutually exclusive terms, although it is possible to speak of them as separate entities. The first is concerned with knowledge for its own sake while the second is concerned with knowledge for what it can contribute to practical situations. Basic research embraces original or unique investigation for the advancement of scientific knowledge. Applied research is usually pragmatic and implies problem-solving applications of data. Both basic and applied research add to the understanding of our environment, the climate of organizations, and ourselves.

Numerous possibilities for this kind of research should be evident to the manager who asks, "Is my business accomplishing what it is expected to?" or "How can we operate more efficiently?" These questions suggest legitimate research in which a manager learns objective approaches to the solution of important problems. Thus, research may be concerned with testing theories of business practice or with making administrative management decisions about a particular business.

Motivation Research

Motivation research studies the basic attitudes, habits, and emotions which cause people to make decisions. Its value lies in furnishing estimates of market potential, market saturation, and product acceptance and in suggesting effective sales promotion and advertising appeals. Likewise, motivation research attempts to relate human behavior—desires, emotions, reactions, or intentions. It determines why people behave as they do toward a particular marketing problem. The researcher must ask the right questions and interpret the answers properly.

Operations Research

Operations research (OR) is concerned with the investigation and analysis of the operational problems of organizations. It relies on whatever techniques and expert personnel are most appropriate to the research, investigates all aspects of the organization being studied, and emphasizes the reduction of data to mathematical formulas and equations. (18) Of all CR techniques, linear programming has probably been most widely adopted by business establishments.

The distinguishing characteristics of OR have been set forth as follows:

1. The primary focus of OR is decision making. The principal results of an analysis leading to a decision must have direct and unambiguous implications for executive action.
2. An appraisal which rests on economic effectiveness criteria is basic to OR. Measurable quantities typically include variable costs, revenues, cash flow, and rate of return on incremental investment.
3. OR relies on a formal mathematical model because of its broad applications and the definitive results obtained from its applications.
4. OR is dependent on an electronic computer because of the complexity of the mathematical model, the volume of data to be manipulated, and the magnitude of computations needed for implementation. (93)

Some writers include the term "action research" to describe OR, although action research (research done by those wishing to improve their own practices) is not usually as technical. This style of research is not antithetical to OR since both cases deal with the investigation and analysis of organizational and operational problems.

The Scientific Method of Research

The scientific method of research evolves from a genuine desire to know, stresses a quantitative approach, seeks to know not only *what* but also *how much,* and requires measurement. (74) Although it is sometimes limited to "pure science," scientific research may be conducted according to certain established procedures which require close control and objectivity.

The research process begins with a problem. Facts are then collected and critically analyzed and decisions based on actual evidence are reached. The thinking process analogous to these procedures includes a felt need, a problem, a hypothesis, the collection of data as evidence, and a concluding brief. After a solution has been found and the report written, there is some justification for appraising the general value of the conclusion. Inherent in all good research is the quality of good thinking. However, scientific research (even if it is excellent research) can tell only what has been believed or how people have behaved in certain situations or with regard to social issues; it cannot tell us what we should believe or how to behave.

BUSINESS AND ECONOMIC RESEARCH

Business and economic research employ several techniques, some of which are unique to the discipline. Both types of research seek knowledge for solving immediate problems. Any study of research in business and economics can be approached through one of several perspectives (functional, institutional, and industrial). (8)

Functional Approach

The functional approach to research is based on activities common to a wide variety of organizations and products. These activities (or functions) include buying, selling, advertising, credit management, warehousing, transportation, plant location, pricing, packaging, short and long-range planning, personnel management, legal supervision, accounting, quality control, and training.

Institutional Approach

The institutional approach depends on a study of the nation's business activities or classifications. These categories would be based on manufacturing enterprises, wholesalers, retail enterprises, raw-materials suppliers, credit-creating agencies, and credit-regulating agencies.

Industrial Approach

The industrial (or commodity) approach focuses on all characteristics, needs, opportunities, and environments related to a particular business establishment or product.

In addition to knowing the different techniques of economic research, it is equally important to know something about the reasoning procedures.

REASONING PROCEDURES

The importance of good thinking has been mentioned several times and it is extremely vital that sound reasoning procedures be used in the various stages of research and reporting. If managers write well, it is usually because they think well. Writing and thinking go hand-in-hand—if one is good, the other is likely to be good.

Several logical methods of thinking could be discussed, but two procedures which apply to both reasoning and writing are *induction* and *deduction*. Both are necessary to effective research and reporting. Induction establishes dependable rules; deduction puts those principles to work.

INDUCTIVE REASONING

Inductive reasoning may be considered the normal procedure in research or experimentation because it leads from particular facts to generalizations about those facts. To illustrate, the researcher begins with observations of facts or events; then on the basis of the observations he or she uses generalizations of similar facts or events. Four conditions are essential to satisfactory induction:

1. Observations must be correctly performed and recorded. Any data studied must be accurate and collected from the universe in which the researcher is interested.
2. Observations must cover representative cases. They must occur at various times and places and include all possible types of conditions and cases.
3. Observations must cover a sufficient number of cases.
4. Conclusions must be confined to statements which can be substantiated by the findings. They should not be too general or too inclusive. (18)

DEDUCTIVE REASONING

Deductive reasoning is the converse of inductive reasoning. Deduction moves from the general to the particular. With this method, what is true for all instances of a class must also be true for any single instance that is part of the class. Thus, one deduces a specific fact or conclusion from the relationship of two or more general facts or principles. There are at least two conditions essential to deduction:

1. The general fact, rule, or principle must be correct.
2. The general rule or principle must be applied only to those cases which properly fall under the general fact. (18)

For reasons which will become evident later on, many managers prefer a deductive reasoning approach to report writing.

SUMMARY

Few things are as important to a future in management as research and reporting skills. The complexity of business and industry requires sound and clear communications; thus you are inextricably bound to the processes of researching and reporting as you advance in business. The ability to issue, transmit, and fulfill messages based on research, as well as ability to attain proficiency through words which produce appropriate action, can become a passport to success. As a member of any organization, you are a part of a communication system—a system which demands involvement as a researcher and reporter. Any deterioration of responsibilities can produce a serious problem for the whole organization.

Reading 2, "Research in Business and Economics," discusses the importance of business and economic research in American business.

DISCUSSION QUESTIONS AND EXERCISES

1. Define research. What are its major characteristics?
2. How does historical research differ from descriptive research?
3. Describe basic and applied research and tell why these two terms are not mutually exclusive.
4. What are the components of operations research that makes it compatible with action research and vice versa?
5. Would motivation research qualify as scientific research? If not, why? If so, how?
6. What would make business and economic research different from research in other disciplines?
7. How and why do writing and thinking go hand-in-hand?
8. Explain the basic components of two important reasoning procedures.
9. Why might a manager prefer the deductive method of writing reports instead of an inductive approach to writing?
10. Prepare a short report (two pages) on how communication and/or report writing is important to you and your career. Be specific in the reasons you provide.

11. Familiarize yourself with the areas of your library where you would most likely find research materials for future projects in this course.
12. Obtain an organizational report and inform other members of your class of its purpose, central problem, and the kind of research necessary before the report was written.

3

The Value of Reports
for Management

Communication is considered *the* major source of information for business and industry. Accurate information can materially assist managers in their decision-making activities and is vital to business success. Some of the information received is acted on immediately, some is stored, and some is relayed back to other members of the organization. Only if managers receive information (usually within a report) can they weigh results, make decisions, and initiate appropriate action.

The oral or written report can be a major tool of management if the writer provides reliable information. Ironically, the larger and more complex the business, the greater is the need for communication. Its efficiency depends on the quantity and quality of information flowing through the personnel. Unfortunately, however, while the division of labor, delegation of authority, and elaboration of rules and regulations have helped to minimize environmental complexity, effective communication has been stifled.

The report should be a part of the total communication network of the organization. So let's pause at this point in our discussion of reports and research and consider briefly the communication process.

THE COMMUNICATION PROCESS

Since the end result of nearly all research is a report of some sort, you need to view communications as the life blood of any firm. Remember, in no situation is communication used under so many various forms and conditions as it is used on the job. But what is it?

Communication denotes the imparting or conveying of thoughts, opinions, desires, and data to someone else; but, it is more than just an exchange of evidence. To be effective, what you say or write must be understood by the receiver. Thus, communicators must be concerned with the *successful transfer of an idea* from one person to someone else. In this text, communication is defined as *the exchange of information between a writer (speaker) and reader (listener) which results in a common understanding.* Diagrammatically, the process of communication as it relates to report writing is depicted in Exhibit 3-1.

24

EXHIBIT 3-1
The Process of Communication via Reports

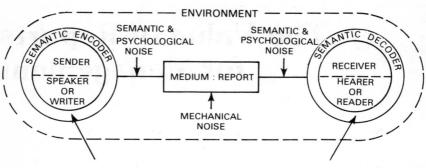

Source: Adopted from Robert R. Rathbone. "A New Approach to Effective Writing," *Journal of Technical Writing and Communication*, 2:181-88, July, 1972.

The process of communication by reports begins when the speaker or writer (sender) encodes a message into a report format and transmits it to a listener or reader (receiver). The writer 1) selects a message based on some form of research leading to the need for communication or a decision; 2) determines the thesis, intent, and content of the report; and 3) writes the message. The *semantic encoder* selects the medium (formal or informal report) and aids the sending of a message. The *semantic decoder* allows the receiver to translate the symbols used in the report, interpret the message, and respond as intended.

Noise (some form of disturbance), unfortuantely, may interfere with transmission and reception: *Semantic noise* may occur because of ambiguity, wordiness, vagueness, improper sentence or paragraph structure, writing or speaking on a different level than the receiver is capable of handling, and poor organization. *Mechanical noise* occurs because of spelling errors, sloppy layout, and other physical or format distractions. *Psychological noise* includes emotional reactions to a message by a receiver (doubt, boredom, disagreement, anger, indifference). (72) Noise may occur at any point in the transmission and reception of information, and everything possible must be done to alleviate interference.

There are many ways for communication to occur within organizations— interviews, written and oral reports, handbooks, meetings, bulletin boards, posters, films, inservice training, newsletters, or loudspeaker systems. Everyone communicates on the job, and it is impossible not to be influenced by someone. The average American spends anywhere from 60 to 90 percent of a working day engaged in some communicative activity. You may be giving or taking orders, planning with others, or reporting progress, and not be achieving understanding. Just because you are reading, writing, speaking, or listening does not mean your communications are successful. You need to insure that your reports not only effect understanding but also provide effective data for future action. The final criteria for all your reports should be the achievement of results. That is why you must provide information that aids successful decisions.

REPORTS AND THE DECISION PROCESS

The job of any researcher is to collect, organize, and report information necessary for making decisions. The quality of reports determines the quality of an organization's operation and output. Managers at all levels are basically information processors and reports provide their main sources of reliable information.

Reports for decision making are concerned with influencing the behavior of the recipients of information. Several factors that influence the effectiveness with which a message produces the desired response in the receiver are:

1. The communication *skills* of the sender determine whether the receiver is able to interpret the message. For example, a report composed of too much business jargon will not be understood. The sender's skills also will determine if the reader's needs and desires are considered. The skilled writer will be more flexible to the reader's level of understanding the problem.

2. The *attitudes* of the sender or receiver affects communication effectiveness. The more favorable the attitude, the more effective will be the communication. If the sender perceives the receiver as lazy, incompetent, and unskilled, the report will reflect this negative attitude and the receiver's actions will be negative as well. If the writer designs the report with the attitude of finding fault in someone else, it will not achieve positive results. The report should be written with a positive attitude.

3. Message construction is another important factor in effective communication. There are three important factors in each message: message code, message content, and message treatment. *Message code* refers to the vocabulary used to construct the message. Included as part of the code is the set of rules and procedures which must be followed. *Message content* refers to the material selected by the sender to express his or her purpose. Unnecessary mechanical roadblocks occur when the writer neglects to provide all the information needed for understanding. *Message treatment* concerns the amount of detail in the report, the arrangement of the data on the page, and the sequence of data on the report. The language chosen, the amount of detail, and the channel (medium) used to carry the message must be chosen with the receiver in mind.

4. The *skill level of the receiver* has an impact on the message constructed by the sender. The greater the receiver's familiarity with the subject, the message code, and the source, the more sophisticated the message can be. Throughout the reporting process the sender chooses a code that is comprehensible by the receiver and arranges the elements in a manner which permits understanding with minimal effort.

5. *Two-way communication* must be developed through reports. Any organization which hopes to function effectively must make it possible for information to flow upward *and* downward. Upper management and middle management must get much of their information from lower levels if they are to be soundly and accurately informed. When

management is accurately informed, it is in a position to make sound decisions and to communicate with line and staff. (79)

INFORMATION OF VALUE IN REPORTS

One of the important roadblocks to making correct decisions is the difficulty of obtaining accurate, significant, and pertinent information. In general, the information of value to managers is that which is limited to relevant data, which indicates comparisons or relationships, and which indicates where improvements or changes should be made, such as:

1. Internal and external information
2. Formal and informal information
3. Historical and projected information
4. Financial and nonfinancial information (69)

Although the pattern of reporting will vary with the company and with individual concerns, the fact remains that the reporting of all types of information is vital to the ongoing activities of an organization. Good reports are a service to management, an effective tool, an aid to decision making. That is why you need to be familiar with reporting requirements.

GENERAL REQUIREMENTS OF REPORTS

Managers need, day by day, much information to enable them to make decisions and to evaluate progress. Much of that needed information is available through research, so all that is required is the ability to place it in usable form. The general requirements for reporting data to management are:

1. Reports must be current and up to date.
2. Reports should be timely.
3. Reports must contain sufficient detail.
4. Reports should provide a complete coverage of the problem areas without being a burden.

Reports should be prepared and submitted to meet the needs of the person(s) receiving them. They should meet difficulties as they arise, before they get out of control, and take advantage of opportunities as they occur. Accordingly, reports must be presented with sufficient analytical detail so management can know precisely what factors contributed to or have a bearing on the problem.

HOW INFORMATION AFFECTS DECISION MAKING

As information in the form of reports moves from lower management to middle management to top management, different types of information are required for the various types of decisions to be made. Top management requires information of a broad, general nature which can be projected over a long range of time. Middle management decisions deal with the intermediate future involving an intermediate range of objectives. Information must be somewhat specific and needs to be projected over an intermediate time period included within the scope of long-run objectives.

Specific information relating to specific matters, instructions, and orders is the report design required by lower management. Their decisions relate to specific objectives to be secured in the short run. Generally, middle and lower level managers direct people in accordance with the information that has been handed them by their supervisors. The exchange of information among the levels of management must be a reciprocal agreement. Top management can build their decisions only on the information passed up from lower sources. Conversely, line supervisors and middle managers base their decisions on information passed down from top levels.

Decision making for all levels of management is based on information processed by the manager. This information is gained through experience, education, training, business meetings, and recreation; this information has a significant bearing on the interpretation of any particular report. The skill of the manager as a decision maker has a direct influence on the effectiveness of his or her decision. However, the business report is particularly vulnerable to criticism when the decision is defective in some manner. You must be involved in each step of the decision-making process to present sufficient and accurate information necessary for a constructive decision.

The decision-making process involves four major steps:

1. Framing the hypothesis of the problem and its possible solution
2. Testing the hypothesis by research
3. Establishing alternatives
4. Communicating the decision to others

Regarding the first step, framing the hypothesis, the challenge of recognizing and defining the problem may be the writer's assignment. This would be the case if you worked on the total decision-making process alone. Perhaps your contribution will be limited to providing reports which help to construct the model of the hypothesis, as is the situation in working on part of the process or in a group. In either case, the report should present data on the problem as well as examine reasons which cause its occurrence.

Testing the hypothesis is the objective exploration of all possible outcomes of certain alternatives. You are concerned with presenting in understandable form the various outcomes that resulted from testing the hypothesis. The difficulty of research is obtaining accurate, significant, and pertinent information. Rarely is all collected research data included in the report. Often much of the data has been of little or no significance in solving a particular problem. For the researcher/report writer, much of the work cannot be reflected in the report. Trying to do so would reduce the effectiveness of the report with unnecessary information. Thus you should focus on collecting, organizing, and reporting the information necessary for decision making. The base of your analysis and discussion of alternatives should be the significant objective research findings.

Establishing the alternatives and then selecting one is sometimes considered *the* decision-making step. You may either select the most plausible alternative and recommend its adoption or develop the alternatives only and leave the selection to management. Selection and recommendation will involve reporting all determinable advantages and disadvantages and presenting as objective a discussion as possible.

The decision-making process can (and frequently does) terminate with the selection of an alternative. The important step of communicating that selection is often overlooked, however. The need is not only to communicate the decision but also to communicate it in such a way as to secure acceptance of the decision. Timing of the release is a major factor to consider for acceptance of this decision. You must place the report in the right hands for its communication to be passed on. A major barrier is that of giving the report to the wrong person, bypassing the one who would communicate the decision.

These major components of the report as intricate parts of decision making outline several ways in which reports serve management. Remember, by developing a hypothesis, you give management time to study and analyze a proposal. Throughout the process the report makes information available to management in keeping with management's convenience and needs. It continuously serves as a basic device for internal communication. Finally, the report is the basis for planning and policy formation, for control, and for evaluation.

HOW REPORTS FACILITATE CONTROL

Reports can be the basis for control, but reports by themselves do not provide control; people effect control. To fully understand the nature of reports for management, you must understand the fundamentals of management control:

1. *Planning* is the process of allocating available resources and determining the direction and goals to be pursued.
2. *Organizing* is the process of structuring the framework within which managers operate.
3. *Executing* is the process of operating and accomplishing plans and programs.
4. *Evaluating* is the process of quantitatively and qualitatively measuring results and performance.
5. *Correcting* is the process of implementing changes in plans, programs, organizations, or operations to effect more efficient management control.

Obviously, these functions must be viable and operative if an organization's communication system is to be effective. Questions fundamental to control based on management reports are: "How are we doing? What are the results? Who is responsible for the results? Are the results in keeping with planned performance? What is the effect of the results on financial conditions? How can we improve?" The correct answer to these questions should lead toward effective communication through written reports for management.

SUMMARY

Reports permit managers, regardless of their distance from direct operations, to obtain a first hand account of activities. Reports enable managers to review all operations of a business in a condensed form. Most importantly, reports furnish information that serves as the basis for top-level decision making and action.

Readings 3 and 4 discuss the importance of "Reports that Communicate" and how reports relate to "The Business Decision Maker."

DISCUSSION QUESTIONS AND EXERCISES

1. Why is communication considered the major source of information for business and industry?
2. How can accurate information assist managers in their decision-making activities?
3. How is an organization dependent on the quantity and quality of information flowing through its personnel?
4. Define communication.
5. What are the basic components of the communication process? Diagram them.
6. What are some of the ways that communication occurs within organizations?
7. How much time does the average American spend communicating on a given working day?
8. What does the quality of a report determine?
9. With what are reports for decision making concerned?
10. Explain the five factors that influence the effectiveness with which a message produces the desired response in a receiver.
11. How does the attitude of the sender affect communication effectiveness?
12. Explain the three important factors in a message.
13. Explain the three concerns of message treatment.
14. How does the skill level of the receiver have an impact on the message constructed by the sender?
15. Why must two-way communication be developed through reports?
16. What four types of information are generally of value in a report for management?
17. What is one of the important roadblocks to making correct decisions?
18. Explain the five general requirements for reporting data to management.
19. What are the types of information needed by the various levels of management?
20. Why would a business report be particularly vulnerable to criticism when a decision is defective in some manner?
21. Explain the four major steps involved in the decision process.
22. What is one of the major barriers to overcome in communicating a decision?
23. How can a report be the basis for control?
24. What are the fundamentals of management control?
25. What are some of the questions, fundamental to control, that need answers?
26. What have you learned from this chapter that you feel is most important to your future role as a researcher and reporter? Share your ideas with a fellow student, colleague, or your instructor.

_____ Part II

Business Research Methodology

Analyzing, Clarifying, and Defining the Problem

Persons who succeed in business are those who can identify and solve problems. These people get results, and achieving results is what business is all about. You, too, can become an effective problem solver if you learn a few fundamental principles. These principles are important not only in solving problems but in making business decisions and writing business reports.

WHAT IS A PROBLEM?

Just what is a business problem, or any other problem for that matter? At the outset, let us suggest that problems exist only in people's minds

Based on this premise, let us define a problem as a mental imbalance that occurs when conditions in a given situation are not what a person thinks they ought to be (Exhibit 4-1). A problem may exist in the mind of only one person, or a number of persons may have similar perceptions of a problem. Keeping these ideas in mind, you must ask yourself when approaching a problem situation, "Am I the only one who thinks this is a problem? How do others view the situation?" If you find yourself alone, you might have some difficulty in mustering support to solve what you think is a problem. If others share your perception of the problem, however, support will be more easily obtained.

SOURCES OF PROBLEMS

Problems will come to you in two basic ways: You may discover the problem yourself. Because of the attitudes, assumptions, and expectations you hold, you can usually look around in almost any situation and see things that you think ought to be different. In a business setting, for example, you might see so-and-so who is not performing up to standard, you might see that materials coming from a certain supplier are consistently late, or you might see that sales of a particular product have been declining. These and

34

EXHIBIT 4-1
Hypothetical Illustration of a Problem

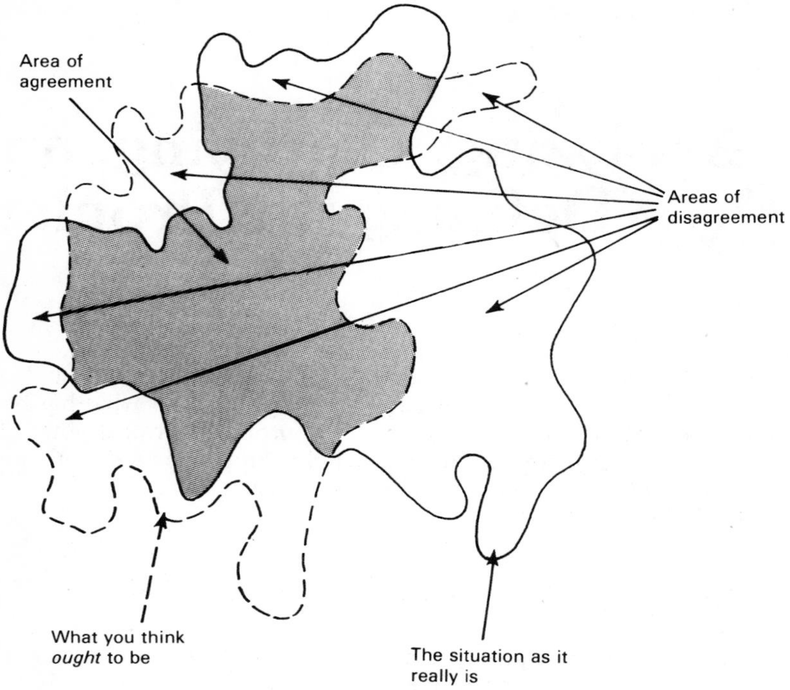

Area of agreement

Areas of disagreement

What you think *ought* to be

The situation as it really is

other similar conditions signal to you that something is not as it should be. Thus, you have a problem.

Problems may also come to you from other people who have perceived conditions they consider inappropriate. Superiors might assign you to solve a problem, or peers or subordinates might discuss a problem with you to either make you aware or to solicit your support in solving the problem.

ANALYZING AND DEFINING THE PROBLEM

Before problems can be solved they must be thoroughly analyzed and understood. It has been suggested that for every one hundred people trying to solve problems only one is really getting at the root of the matter. All the others are just hacking away at the leaves and branches. Business problems, even the most simple, usually have numerous roots being fed by the most unlikely sources. The effective problem solver will investigate and analyze these roots before trying to remedy the problem situation.

Read the following situation and see if you can determine the problem:

Kerry Bentley was a line supervisor in a medium-size plant that manufactured tents and sleeping bags. Kerry supervised the work of thirteen employees who worked on several phases of the sleeping bag production line. Six weeks earlier Aaron, a new person, had been hired to work on the filling machine, a machine that filled the sleeping bag ticks with insulating material. Two people were required to run the filling machine, and both had to work at the same speed since it was a two-man operation.

Aaron worked with Joe Ashton who had worked on the filling machine for about seven months. Aaron was slow at first, but during his first two weeks his work speed increased rapidly. By the end of the second week, Aaron's work had reached about 80 percent of standard. After the second week, however, Aaron and Joe's work leveled off, and after four additional weeks no appreciable increase was noticed. Kerry became concerned about the situation and decided it was time to take some action on the matter.

Based on the information you have, what do you think is the problem? Is it Aaron, the new worker? You would probably come to that conclusion first, wouldn't you?

The truth is that Joe, the seasoned worker, is really at fault. Joe is a rather slow-moving, inefficient worker. Before Aaron came, Joe worked on the easier, less complicated side of the machine where he could achieve his standard quota. When Aaron was hired, Joe was considered the "senior" of the two men, so Joe assumed the task of operating the more complex machine controls. On this assignment he was good up to about 80 percent of standard, but he just didn't have the physical agility to move any faster.

This situation illustrates the difference between a symptom and the real cause of a problem. A person with a cold has symptoms of fever, coughing, and a runny nose. These phenomena are not the *cause* of the person's problem, however. They are merely indicators or symptoms of a more deeply rooted problem. And in business such phenomena as decreased production, increased turnover, and increased absenteeism, are symptoms of something more deeply rooted.

CATEGORIES OF PROBLEMS

Business people work with primarily five major categories of resources: manpower, machines, materials, money, and methods. The effective manager creates an efficient mix of these five resources to accomplish the organization's objectives. These resource categories are not only the source of managerial success, but they are also the source of managerial problems. In identifying, analyzing, and solving problems the wise manager will examine all five areas to make sure the problem is completely understood and identified, thoroughiy analyzed, and carefully solved and implemented.

Methods

Essentially the methods analysis process involves breaking down and analyzing individual work methods, processes, and systems. The analysis focuses on unnecessary delays, unnecessary movement, and inefficiency that can be eliminated. In analyzing methods you have the option of calling on the services of a systems analyst or of trying to determine the problem and solve it by yourself or through your workers.

When analyzing systems and methods, first ask the well-known "who, what, how, when, where, and why" questions. Then after an examination of these details, decide which steps in the procedures and methods can be improved or eliminated.

Materials and Machinery

Since materials and machinery have so many characteristics in common, they are considered together. Materials and machinery used in the achievement of organizational objectives should be analyzed on a cost effectiveness basis. Basically you can ask, "Are the machines and materials we are using as good as other machines and materials we *could* be using?" Technological advancements, age, wear and tear, neglect, and a host of other factors can cause equipment to become obsolete. As in methods and systems analysis, materials and machines analysis should focus on problem areas—areas where the materials or machines are not necessarily up to the demands being placed upon them.

Money

Since businesses are established to make a financial profit, you must always be concerned about efficient and effective use of financial resources. Money problems take two different forms: 1) not having enough money, and 2) not using what you have in a wise manner. When sufficient operating capital is not available, you must investigate the financing resources available. When the money you have is not being used wisely, you need to investigate spending and investment practices. Numerous accounting ratios that serve as measuring sticks are available to you. Accountants and financial consultants can provide excellent advice when financial problems are encountered.

Manpower

Problems in any of the four resource categories just discussed have direct or indirect roots in the manpower category. Hence, business problems are always people problems, either directly or indirectly, and people problems are the most serious of all organizational difficulties. When a person is not measuring up to what you think he or she should, you have one of three problems: 1) the person is physically or mentally incapable of performing properly, 2) the person could do the work but does not know how or does not know the work that should be done, or 3) the person could do it and knows how but is not doing it for some psychological reason.

If the first condition exists, you must replace the person. No amount of training or motivation can solve a physiological or mental disability problem. If the second condition exists, you need to train the person. Training can take place in a number of settings: the person can be trained on the job, within the company but off the job, or outside the company. Several frequently used training methods are on the job training, vestibule training, role playing, correspondence instruction, formal educational instruction, programmed individualized instruction, and so forth. If the third condition exists, you have a motivational problem; and you must focus on changing the employee's attitude through some motivational process. Most motivational approaches involve increased responsibility and recognition, opportunity for advancement and achievement, and a sincere effort by management to focus on individual employees' well-being and to help employees achieve personal goals through employment.

OTHER BUSINESS PROBLEMS

Up to this point our discussion has centered mainly on problems resulting from what is versus what should be. Although many reports result from investigation of these types of problems, many reports also arise from simple information-seeking types of concerns. Someone in an organization feels a need to know the state of affairs of some aspect of the organization. Examples of these types of investigations are:

- How does our product X compare with our competitor's product Y?
- What marketing potential does City X have for our product?
- How does the public perceive our products, prices, and services?
- Do our hiring practices comply with federal government regulations?
- What does our safety and accident record look like?
- How does our turnover ratio compare with that of our industrial competitors?

Many times the findings of these studies will prompt other studies, however. For example, a study of the safety and accident records of a company might indicate serious problems. As a result of these findings, management might commission another special study to determine ways of solving the safety problem.

BASIC STEPS IN ANALYZING, CLARIFYING, AND DEFINING A PROBLEM

The process of analyzing, clarifying, and defining these business problems is basically the same as that used in working with the types of business problems discussed previously in the chapter.

1. Collect data related to the perceived problem area. After first determining that there might be a problem, accumulate information relating to your hypothesis. Information can be gathered by reading, observing, studying, and asking. As the data are being accumulated, ponder the problem in your mind in an attempt to understand the causes, consequences, and implications of the problem.
2. After the problem is clearly in mind, write it down. The process of writing forces you to organize your thoughts. You have probably heard it said that you don't really understand something unless you can explain it to someone else. In your writing you should include the following categories of information:
   a. Introduction to the problem. Explain the various historical and situational factors that are closely related to the problem. A good

aid in explaining this category fully is the list of the five *"M"* resources: manpower, money, methods, machines, and materials. Simply describe how factors in each of these areas have interacted to cause a problem situation.

b. Statement of the problem or purpose. Each part of a study should focus on one major problem. Each major part can then be broken down into smaller parts typically called factors. For example, a study that focuses on safety in a business could be subdivided into the following factor areas:

- Comparison with safety records of similar businesses
- Increase or decrease of accidents during a certain period of time in the company
- Most frequent causes of accidents in the company
- Accident records of individual departments
- Individuals who have suffered from more than one accident

c. Standards or criteria for evaluation. You should identify the objectives you plan to achieve as a result of your study and the criteria by which you will measure your research. The establishment of criteria is especially important in a problem-solving report, for the criteria will indicate whether you have really solved your problem or achieved your purpose. The criteria are simply well-articulated statements of your perceived "ought."

3. After you have written your explanation of the problem, subject it to the examination of others knowledgeable about the situation surrounding the problem and who have a direct interest in the problem investigation. Although this peer evaluation of your problem statement will usually elicit a variety of responses, some negative, this abrasive experience will usually produce positive results in the long run. The old adage "two heads are better than one" still holds true in most situations.

When others disagree with your point of view, the natural tendency is to defend your position and to try to convince others of the validity of your feelings. By avoiding this temptation and by carefully listening, however, you will glean some very helpful information that would otherwise not be made known to you.

4. After the evaluation of your problem explanation is completed, refine your problem definition and description. Implement the worthwhile suggestions of those who read and critiqued your first writing.

5. Take the steps necessary to undertake your proposed research study. In other situations, however, you will have to obtain authorization and resources to pursue the study. If you must obtain permission and resources from someone else, you will usually have to submit your problem statement as a proposal. The purpose of the proposal is to convince the authorizing person or group that your study is warranted.

An outline of a hypothetical business problem follows to give you an idea of the information that might be considered in analyzing, clarifying, and defining a problem.

I. Introduction of Background Factors and Problem Setting
    A. Inconvenience to contract out all reprographic (printing) work

    B. Expense is excessive
    C. Excessive time lag between ordering and supply
    D. Limited control over documents during printing process
II. Statement of problem (purpose or objective)
    A. Purpose of study to determine the feasibility of establishing an in-house reprographics center
    B. Factors important to the objective
        1. Equipment
            a. Cost of reprographic equipment
            b. Capabilities of reprographic equipment
            c. Warranty of reprographic equipment
        2. Vendor
            a. Reputation of vendor
            b. Delivery time
            c. Maintenance agreement
            d. Training program for equipment operators

In connection with the various factors, you would probably want to identify criteria, or standards, by which you can evaluate the alternatives from which you make your decision. For example, you might say that the new equipment should not exceed $5,500, should have an output rate of at least 8,000 impressions per hour, and should have at least a 90-day parts and labor warranty.

After you decide on the factors and criteria, you should rank them in order of the importance you place on each. This process forces you to decide just which features you "must" have and which ones you would "like" to have but which you could get along without. This ranking process is very important because most alternatives in a decision-making situation do not totally meet *all* the criteria the decision maker desires. Armed with ranked or weighted criteria, however, you can easily decide between two alternatives, one of which offers an important feature but lacks a less important feature and the other which lacks an important feature but offers a less important feature.

SUMMARY

To succeed in business you must be able to solve problems and achieve objectives. But before problems can be solved or objectives can be met, you must thoroughly understand them. You must understand the difference between problems and symptoms; otherwise your proposed solutions will treat the "effect" rather than the "cause."

Problems can arise in money, materials, methods, or machine areas, but nearly all business problems have at least some of their roots in the "manpower" or people area. People problems are caused by mental or physical limitations, by a lack of training, or by insufficient motivation. Because of the ability people have to work against organizational policies and objectives, people problems are the most serious of all business problems.

To do a good job of analyzing, clarifying, and defining a business problem you should 1) collect all data that are pertinent to the problem situation, 2) explain the problem in writing (including factors, criteria, and ratings), 3) subject your problem description to the examination of others qualified to evaluate it critically, 4) refine your problem description, and 5) take the steps necessary to undertake your proposed research study.

DISCUSSION QUESTIONS AND EXERCISES

1. Explain your definition of a problem.
2. What is the difference between a symptom and a cause? Give an example of each.
3. Why are people problems more serious than other kinds of problems?
4. If an employee's production suddenly falls below acceptable standards, what type of people problem is most likely to be the cause?
5. What is the major difference between information-seeking studies and problem-solving studies?
6. List and discuss five basic steps useful in analyzing, clarifying, and defining problems?
7. Follow the five steps you discussed in the preceding question in analyzing, clarifying, and defining a problem that you have noticed in your school, home, or working situation.
8. Discuss the difference between factors and criteria.
9. Why is the process of ranking so important in problem clarification?
10. Is absenteeism a symptom or a cause? Justify your answer.

5

Planning Methods to Be Used in Collecting Information

Business organizations operate on information. Generally, the organization with the greatest amount of available information used wisely is the one that will succeed. Conversely, the organization that has limited access to information will be either hampered or culled out because of inefficiency.

A business manager needs adequate information to make appropriate decisions, plan wisely, organize resources skillfully, and control and lead effectively. Because information is so vital to the organization, the person who knows how and where to find that information is always in demand.

Information to be used in research and decision making comes from primary and secondary sources. Primary research is original and seeks information that no one else has researched. Secondary research examines the findings of others, information that has already been researched and reported by someone else.

SECONDARY RESEARCH

As you assume an active role in business, you will find that using secondary research is usually easier and quicker than conducting primary research to answer your questions. Primary research is usually expensive and time consuming and should be used only when information cannot be procured any other way. Today a vast amount of business information is available. In fact, this massive quantity can make the process of finding the exact information needed a lengthy process of sifting and sorting.

SOURCES OF SECONDARY INFORMATION

Public libraries have traditionally been the memory of the nation with accumulated information of all kinds stored for public use. Joined with the public libraries are the educational libraries across the nation. While both public and college libraries contain general information on a full range of topics, the college libraries tend to have more technical and in-depth information. To meet the needs of students and professors, these libraries are expected to maintain current material in all areas of concern to the educational institution.

In addition to these general libraries, there are special and private libraries developed and maintained by private and governmental organizations. The information procured for these libraries usually fills the specialized needs of the sponsoring organization. Many of these organizations are willing to share their findings for worthwhile projects.

In all libraries there are accumulations of specialized bibliographies that will speed secondary research. These bibliographies are presented in trade directories, government publications, business periodicals, formal research reports, and special indexes. The Business Periodicals Index and the Reader's Guide to Periodical Literature should be familiar to all business students.

A type of library that has appeared within the last few years is a computerized data bank which uses a large computer facility to store information about selected topics. Information is categorized under a number of terms called "descriptors." When a person seeks information about a certain topic, he or she uses the special descriptors to tell the computer exactly what types of information are wanted. For example, a marketing manager interested in reading marketing articles and research reports about teenage buying behavior might use such descriptors as consumer behavior, buyer behavior, purchasing behavior, consumption patterns, or product selection. In addition, the manager would tell the computer the topics not wanted in that general area. For example, the researcher might want to exclude articles or reports that deal with adult buying patterns, children buying patterns, or organizational purchasing. Following the input of explanation, the computer would search its memory and print out a bibliography or an annotated bibliography of available information pertaining to teenage buying behavior.

These computerized data banks are available across the country via computer terminals housed in libraries and other institutions. Business information in such areas as production, management, finance, labor, marketing, business law, economics, accounting, personnel, office management, and computers is available.

Secondary information can be used to solve a problem or achieve an objective, or it can be a tool in conducting primary research. Many reports are based on both secondary and primary research.

PRIMARY RESEARCH

Survey research is widely used in business to gather information from employees, clients, and the general public. Survey research seeks such information as what current business practices are or how people feel about certain issues or products. This type of research involves interrogation conducted in one of three ways: 1) personal interviews, 2) telephone interviews, or 3) mail interviews.

Personal interviews. Personal interviewing is most effective when all the people to be interviewed are located in a relatively small geographical area. Otherwise, the time and expense spent in traveling from one person to another makes this type of interviewing economically impractical. Personal interviewing is usually used when the information needed is too complex to be gathered by another technique. For example, a problem being studied may require the interviewer to probe beyond the more superficial answers that might be obtained with another method.

It is sometimes assumed that personal interviewing is the most accurate of all survey research techniques. Although personal interviewing may be accurate in many cases, human errors may prevent a researcher from obtaining valid results. Questions perceived by the interviewee as an invasion of privacy or threatening in any way will probably produce false or partially true answers. Also, since the interviewer must interpret the respondent's statements, a certain amount of information loss results even though the respondent may be answering truthfully.

In spite of the problems, at least two major advantages are provided by this research technique. First, the alert interviewer can generally tell if the respondent is being truthful or if he or she is giving superficial or untrue responses. Second, the interviewer can rephrase questions, give more explanation, or probe more deeply if the initial questions do not produce the information desired. As a result, the information gleaned should be more accurate than that provided by interviews where no one is present to clarify questions or to interpret answers.

Telephone interviews. Telephone interviewing is most useful when interviewees are widely dispersed since the interviewer can communicate orally by telephone with people located many miles from each other. Although long distance calls are expensive, they are still more economical than personal travel.

In recent years a special telephone service called WATS (Wide Area Telecommunications Service) has been introduced to make long-distance calling more economical for businesses and other organizations that engage in frequent long-distance calling. For a set monthly fee, a company can make an unlimited number of long-distance calls. As a result, WATS can make long-distance calling even more advantageous than personal travel.

Although telephone interviewing does not offer face-to-face communication, it does retain many of the advantages of personal interviewing. The major advantage, of course, is that the interviewer can clarify, rephrase, and probe if necessary.

One of the major disadvantages of telephone interviewing arises from people's dislike for telephone soliciting. In recent years the telephone has been used heavily by sales representatives, and many people are resistant to anyone who intrudes via the telephone. Also, not everyone has a telephone; therefore, the interviewer cannot obtain a truly representative sample with telephone interviewing. Households with no telephone or an unlisted number are not represented if telephone surveying is used. Only a small percentage of people do not have telephone service, but the interviewer needs to be aware of this limitation.

Mail interviews. When interviews are widely dispersed or when a large number of questionnaires must be used, interviewing by mail should be considered. The mail questionnaire is a self-enumeration device in which the respondent must mark his or her own responses to the questions asked. An advantage of the mail interview is that the questionnaire may be filled out at the respondent's convenience. Also, mail questionnaires may enter doors that might be closed to personal or telephone interviewing.

Several serious disadvantages accompany the mail interview technique. Many selected participants will not return the questionnaires. Other problems occur when the wrong person completes a questionnaire, when only partial answers are given, when questions are improperly answered, and when a person intentionally gives incorrect information. With mail interviewing the researcher does not have the advantage of being able to clarify, rephrase, or probe to obtain the desired information.

Some success in increasing the rate of questionnaire return has been achieved by enclosing with the questionnaire a small sum of money—ten or twenty-five cents—as a financial incentive. A statement such as "Here's a quarter for a cup of coffee while you're completing this questionnaire" may make the person receiving the questionnaire feel more obligated to comply with the researcher's requests. Success has also been achieved by preceding the questionnaire with a telephone call or a letter asking that the participant complete the questionnaire when it arrives. A combination of two or more approaches may be better than a single technique.

The mail questionnaire is usually accompanied by a cover letter which explains the purpose of the research, explains what action is desired, and expresses appreciation for whatever the respondent can do to assist the research efforts.

The questionnaire itself may ask for certain demographic data, such as age, sex, marital status, occupation, and income in addition to questions related to the research problem. Questions may be open or closed; in other words, they may ask the respondent to answer in his or her own words, or they may specify several responses from which the person may choose. The closed responses may take several forms: Dichotomies such as agree/disagree or yes/no; multiple choice such as A, B, C, D or 1, 2, 3, 4; rankings such as 1st, 2nd, 3rd, 4th, and 5th choice; and ratings such as 1 = strongly agree, 2 = generally agree, 3 = neutral feelings, 4 = generally disagree, and 5 = strongly disagree.

SAMPLING TECHNIQUES

Survey research usually involves such large populations that interviews are conducted with only a sample of the total population. The underlying assumption of this sampling process is that the persons sampled will yield information consistent with that obtained if the entire population were questioned. If the sample does yield information consistent with what would come from the total population, it is "representative."

Whenever sampling is used in business studies, the researchers must determine the size of sample needed to produce representative results, although size alone does not ensure representativeness. Selecting too large a sample results in waste of time and money, and too small a sample produces inconclusive results. Statistical approaches have been suggested for determining a sample that is sufficient without being too large. These approaches use a statistical table containing calculated sampling errors that can be expected in a given sample size. The researcher makes such determinations as how much error can be tolerated, the estimated response rate, and the estimated number of usable responses. The researcher is then able to determine how many individuals must be contacted to achieve a representative sample.[1]

A clear distinction needs to be drawn between representativeness and validity, however. Validity is the property of the survey instrument, the survey technique, and the sampling method to yield the information that is really being sought. A larger sample may tend to yield more representative data, but unless the survey instrument and survey technique are properly designed and executed, the survey data may not be valid.

Random Sampling

Statisticians stress the importance of being random in selecting research participants. If participants are not chosen by random, personal bias in the selection process is likely to creep in and contaminate the research. True random selection gives every person in the total population an equal chance of being selected. To achieve this, every person in the population has to be identified for inclusion in the selection process. The actual selection can be accomplished by putting the names of all the population in a container and by drawing a sample without looking to see what names are being drawn.

Another process involves the use of a table of random numbers, generally produced by a computer. All members of the population are given a number, 1, 2, 3, 4, 5, and so forth. The numbers listed on the table of random numbers are then used to select the study participants. For example, if the table of random numbers has numbers 03, 46, 27, 61, 26, and 43 listed, the researcher chooses the members of the population who have been assigned these random numbers as study participants.

Quota Sampling

In most survey studies the researcher has several characteristics or factors in mind that he or she feels exert an important influence on the problem being studied. For example, if marketing researchers are trying to determine factors that influence purchase of a given product, they may assume that income, age, marital status, and family size are important predicting variables. To make sure that sufficient data are gathered to provide information from each of the factor areas, the researchers may decide to use quota sampling. Quota sampling will ensure that they get sufficient interviews from each income, age, marital status, and family size category to perform valid analyses. As individual interviewers conduct their interviews they are given quotas which they must fill for each factor area, and they contact enough people to reach their quotas.

It is apparent that quota sampling is not a random sampling process, but it does offer the advantage of increasing representativeness. Whereas a random sample might not yield sufficient numbers of interviewees in the $30,000-per-year-income bracket for meaningful analysis, quota sampling would produce enough samples in this category. Occasionally when sufficient numbers in a given subgroup are difficult to obtain, researchers use a weighting process to give the findings of the subgroup a representative impact on the total analysis.

Stratified Random Sampling

In an effort to increase the random quality of a quota sample, researchers sometimes use a process called stratified random sampling. As in quota sampling, certain subgroups are identified as important to the research. But instead of interviewing people in these subgroups just on a convenience basis, the researchers use a random selection process within each subgroup. A truly random selection process may be used, or a systematic sampling process that selects every kth person or unit may be employed. The systematic sampling process approaches random selection if the first selection is drawn at random because each person or unit in the total population has a nonzero chance of being chosen. The stratified random sampling process has the advantage of quota sampling in that it ensures that the important subgroups of the population will be represented fairly. It is also random to a large degree.

Point Sampling

Much business research involves sampling something other than people or groups of people. For example, researchers might want to know such information as percentage of faulty units produced on an assembly line, percentage of sales representatives' time spent in actual selling, percentage of time a particular telecommunications system is in use, or amount of inventory on hand. Rather than keeping a running total of this information, a chore that might be time consuming and that might produce personnel dissatisfaction, the researcher can sample at intermittent points of time or other units of measure. As sufficient samples are taken to ensure representativeness, the researcher can analyze the situation.

Reliability

Sample reliability refers to consistency of results. Reliability is generally a function of sample size although the survey instrument also affects reliability. Small samples are likely to contain chance errors. For example, if researchers wanted to determine the average spending of students in a particular college, they would likely get an unreliable sample if they surveyed only ten individuals from the entire population. As they increased the size of their sample, however, their findings would tend to stabilize; that is, there would be less fluctuation in the findings as increased data were gathered.

To determine when enough surveys have been accumulated to ensure reliability, the researchers first obtain a sample size they feel will achieve reliability. They divide the surveys into equal groups (for example, fifty or a hundred per group) and select one or more questions they want to make sure are reliable. Generally these questions will be the most important questions in the survey. The average responses are then determined for the first group, the second group, the third group, and so on. The percentage of each new group is cumulated with those of the preceding groups. As each new group is cumulated, the overall average tends to stabilize until any additional group's input does not affect the cumulative average to any significant degree. This cumulating process can be performed by a computer either with or without the grouping step.

An example of the cumulative frequency test to determine reliability is illustrated for one question in Exhibit 5-1. There you see a rather erratic pattern in the "Cumulative Percentage of Responses" columns during the first few calculations. Then as each new group of responses is added, the total outcome is affected less significantly. When a point of total stabilization is achieved, no additional surveys are necessary for the analysis.

EXHIBIT 5-1
Cumulative Frequency Test to Determine Reliability

	Product Choice			Cumulative Responses			Cumulative Percentages of Responses		
Group	A	B	C	A	B	C	A	B	C
1	18	12	20	18	12	20	36	24	40
2	9	24	17	27	36	37	27	36	37
3	9	18	23	36	54	60	24	36	40
4	20	16	14	56	70	74	28	35	37
5	16	17	17	72	87	91	29	35	36
6	14	20	16	86	107	107	29	37	37
7	12	17	21	98	124	128	28	35	37
8	11	19	20	109	143	148	27	36	37
9	16	20	14	125	163	162	28	36	36
10	17	18	15	142	181	177	28	36	35
11	14	16	20	156	197	197	28	36	36
12	14	17	19	170	214	216	28	36	36
13	15	20	15	185	234	231	28	36	36

OBSERVATION RESEARCH

When observation is used as a data-gathering technique, the researcher uses his eyes and ears as sensing devices to determine what happens in a given setting. No attempt is made to manipulate the setting; the researcher simply observes and records what is observed. A major factor of observation research is that it is limited to what can be seen or heard; it is not useful for determining feelings, attitudes, plans, or anything else that cannot be directly observed.

If proper procedures are followed, observation research will usually yield valid research results. The researcher must first have the problem or the purpose of the investigation well in mind. Usually the purpose will be to determine present conditions; otherwise another technique would be used. Next, the specific behavior or phenomena to be observed should be identified, and a form for keeping a record of all observations developed. This form should be trial tested to ensure that it meets the needs of the observer and of the research project. Finally, effective training and orientation should be given to all who serve as observers so the data will be accurate and complete.

Observation research is generally more costly than is the survey technique and is generally considered a slower method of gathering data. In addition, just as with survey research, careful controls must be maintained to make sure the data gathered are representative, reliable, and valid.

Observation research can be used effectively in such areas as time-and-motion studies and marketing studies, although it is somewhat limited in its application in other areas of business. Offices and production operations use observation to determine what procedures are presently used. An analysis of the procedures is then conducted to reveal areas in which significant improvement is needed. Marketing researchers use observation to determine current consumer patterns. This helps them design marketing strategies.

EXPERIMENTAL RESEARCH

Experimental research is generally thought of as the purest form of research since it involves more rigid experimental controls. Although the chances for research contamination in interrogation and observation are very great, the chance of contamination in experimental research is more limited. Essentially, this research method involves controlling and manipulating the research setting according to the desires of the researchers.

Generally an experimental research study will involve at least two groups of individuals—a control group and an experimental group—although more than one experimental group can be used. Both groups are measured according to some predetermined criteria at the beginning of the experiment. During the experiment the researcher subjects the experimental group to treatment that is different from that experienced by the control group. After the experimental group has received the treatment, both the experimental and the control groups are measured to determine the change that has occurred since the first criteria measurement was taken. Any significant difference between the two groups is then attributed to the effect of the special treatment given to the experimental group.

Assume that a company wanted to measure the impact of a special training program on the output of its sales representatives. The researcher assigned to the project would likely proceed as follows:

1. Randomly assign all sales representatives to either the experimental group or to the control group.
2. Measure the present production of the two groups.
3. Subject the experimental group to the special training.
4. Measure the production of the two groups after the training is completed.
5. Analyze the results.

Exhibit 5-2 suggests the hypothetical outcome of the research study just mentioned. When the first measurement was taken during week 1, the two groups were relatively equal, although this is not always the case. (When the two groups prove to be different, special statistics are used to equate the groups.) After the treatment a change occurs; this continues for a period of two months, at which time it tends to stabilize. The difference between the

EXHIBIT 5-2
Results of Experimental Research Conducted with
Two Groups of Sales Representatives

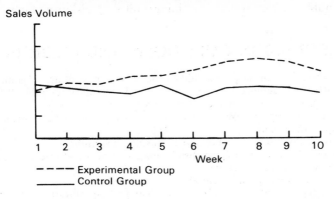

- - - - Experimental Group
_____ Control Group

volume rates of the two groups is attributed to the special training given the experimental group.

Experimental research is somewhat limited in its application in business, but it can be used whenever the researcher can control and manipulate the study variables in the manner just discussed. Because of the quality of research produced by this method, experimental research should be used whenever feasible. Experimental research could be used very effectively by organizational behavior specialists to determine the impact of training on an organization, by marketing personnel to determine the impact of a marketing change on consumption, or by most any manager to determine the impact of a policy change on employee behavior.

A modified form of the experimental method involves just one group subjected to the special treatment. As with the multiple group method, a measurement is taken before the treatment and again afterwards. The change noticed between the two measurements is attributed to the effect of the treatment. Although this form provides more flexibility, it opens the door for so much research contamination that the chance of getting quality research results is greatly decreased. Consequently, at least two groups should be used whenever possible.

Another form of experimental research involves the use of a computer that creates a simulated environment in which the study variables are manipulated and evaluated. This technique is quick and enables the researcher to test many more variables than would be economically feasible in real life. The disadvantage of this approach, however, is that the computer cannot truly represent people in the situations it creates. This method of research has exciting possibilities, however, and the future will probably see significant improvement in its usefulness.

SUMMARY

Information to be used in research and decision making comes from primary and secondary sources. Primary research is original and seeks information that no one else has researched. Secondary research examines the findings of others, information that has already been researched and reported by someone else. Because business organizations operate on information, both research sources are important to decision making.

DISCUSSION QUESTIONS AND EXERCISES

1. Why is timely information so vital to the effectiveness of any organization?
2. Describe the difference between primary and secondary research. When would you use primary research? Secondary research?
3. What are descriptors? What part do they play in securing information from computer data banks?
4. Why is survey research so popular in business research?
5. What are the advantages and disadvantages of personal interviews, telephone interviews, and mail interviews?
6. Why is proper sampling essential in survey research?
7. What is representativeness? Reliability? Validity? Stabilization?
8. What types of information can usually be determined by the use of observational research?
9. Why is experimental research considered the purest research method?
10. What is the main drawback of computerized experimental research?

ENDNOTE

1. For additional information concerning sample representativeness, consult Leslie Kish, *Survey Sampling* (John Wiley, New York, 1965).

6

Preparing the Working Plan

In earlier chapters you have learned to analyze, classify, and define the problem to be researched; you have determined the types of information needed to solve the problem, and you have planned the methods to collect information. Now you are ready to prepare a written *proposal* for solving the problem. This proposal, or tentative *work plan*, will set forth a logical approach to what you desire to accomplish.

A carefully written proposal will help in several ways. It will

1. Give you an opportunity to review the research steps to be taken.
2. Provide an opportunity to discover possible errors or faulty thinking.
3. Serve as a guide throughout the investigation.
4. Embody nearly everything needed to write the introduction to the report.

This chapter provides a guide for the initiation of research studies.

WRITING THE RESEARCH PROPOSAL

An investigator is accountable to those in authority; that is, you will report to a superior. Executives do not like to spend company money on a research project unless the result will ultimately justify the expenditure. Any proposed or assigned study must present the sources of information, the methods to be used for collecting and processing the data, the scope and limitations, and the approximate time and cost involved. Frequently, the person responsible for the final authorization may need background information about the origin of the problem and the research objective. Thus, the proposal should include four major sections: problem statement, objectives, related research and literature, and procedures to be used. A sample working plan which encompasses these areas is shown in Exhibit 6-1.

PROBLEM STATEMENT

The statement of the problem opening the proposal must convince the reader that the project is important. The reader needs to know how the

EXHIBIT 6-1
A Sample Working Plan for Research

ORGANIZATIONAL DEVELOPMENT SPECIALISTS

MEMORANDUM

DATE: March 27, 1977
TO: Francis Delacorte, Manager
FROM: Robin Dial
SUBJECT: Tentative Working Plan for Development and Application of a Management Information and Control Program

Here is the research report proposal you authorized March 1.

PROBLEM STATEMENT

The topic of this study is a marketing management, information, and control system for THE SHOE STORE. A model will be constructed after a study of several management and marketing information systems. An attempt will be made to adapt features of models studied to a system for THE SHOE STORE in Oklahoma City.

The proposed study is initially restricted as follows:

a. The system will not be constructed for EDP equipment because no such equipment is available for the store involved.

b. The formulation, application, and testing of the system will necessarily be limited by the time available for this study, a period of approximately two months duration.

c. The thoroughness of system implementation will be subject to the pressures of continuous business operation. It will be imperative to gradually introduce procedural changes into the existing business structure.

d. It will be necessary for business reasons to keep much sales, cost, and personnel information confidential. The report will express results in terms of percentage figures or hypothetically potential figures.

OBJECTIVES

The primary objectives of this study are:

a. To develop a model of a retail management information and control system.

b. To apply the system developed to THE SHOE STORE in Oklahoma City.

c. To analyze the effects of the application of the system.

RELATED RESEARCH

A tentative bibliography which will provide a foundation for the material on the previous page:

a. Alderson, Wroe and Stanley J. Shapiro. *Marketing and the Computer.* Englewood Cliffs, New Jersey: Prentice Hall, Inc., 1963.

b. American Management Association. *Control Through Information: A Report on Management Information Systems.* AMA Bulletin No. 24. American Management Association, Inc., 1963.

c. Anthony, Robert N., John Deardon, and Richard F. Vancil. *Management Control Systems: Cases and Readings.* Homewood, Illinois: Richard D. Irwin, Inc. 1965.

EXHIBIT 6-1 (continued)

<u>Robin Dial</u>
Page 2

   d. Berlo, David K. *The Process of Communication: An Introduction to Theory and Practice.* Holt, Rinehart, and Winston, Inc., 1960.

   e. Day, Ralph L. *Marketing Models: Quantitative and Behavioral.* Scranton Pennsylvania: The Haddon Craftsmen, Inc., 1964.

   f. Fisk, George and Donald F. Dixon. (ed.). *Theories for Marketing Systems Analysis: Selected Readings.* New York: Harper and Row, Publishers, Inc., 1967.

   g. Kotler, Philip. *Marketing Management.* Englewood Cliffs, New Jersey: Prentice Hall, Inc., 1967.

   h. Malcolm, Donald G., Alan J. Rowe, and Lorimer F. McConnell. *Management Control Systems.* New York: John Wiley and Sons, Inc., 1960.

   i. McDonough, Adrian M. and Leonard J. Garret. *Management Systems: Working Concepts and Practice.* Homewood, Illinois: Richard D. Irwin, Inc., 1965.

   j. Prince, Thomas R. *Information Systems for Management Planning and Control.* Homewood, Illinois: Richard D. Irwin, Inc., 1966.

   k. Young, Stanley. *Management: A Systems Analysis.* Glenview, Illinois: Scott, Foresman and Company, 1966.

Business records also will be used, although it is difficult at this time to know exactly how each reference will contribute to this study.

PROCEDURES

This project is of practical value to the management and personnel of THE SHOE STORE. It is anticipated that the system developed will be of general value to other shoe retailers, general retail managers, and business scholars.

The working hypotheses for this study are:

   a. A management information and control model can be developed for centralized area management of retail shoe stores.

   b. Application of that system will result in more effective management controls, generate a meaningful flow of information for decision making, and increase profits through cost reductions and more effective application of resources.

The time period alloted for the study, development, and application of the system is from April 1 to May 31. The final typewritten report will be submitted to you on or before June 15.

project would contribute either to theory or to knowledge of general or specific phenomena, how it builds on previous theory, or contributes to new theory. The value of specific applications of the knowledge to be gained and the potential importance of these applications should be described. One or two concrete consequences would be helpful.

The most common error made in preparing the problem section is stating the problem in either too grandiose or too narrow terms. A balance is required between "The organization will fall apart tomorrow if I don't solve this problem" and "I'd like to know this for my own personal edification." Too often a problem is so broad it could not be solved if all the company funds were appropriated. Do not be ashamed to reduce the scope of what is intended; a seasoned researcher knows she or he cannot solve all the world's ills.

If the problem section of the report contains a two or three-sentence sketch of the approach to be used, the reader can get a perspective on the proposal. It is especially important in a lengthy section to give the reviewer a succinct statement that summarizes the point being made.

The problem section provides the backbone of the report. If unusual definitions of terms are to be used throughout the proposal, define them early in the report.

OBJECTIVES

The purpose of the research should be clearly and briefly stated where it can be easily found. You may find it helpful to phrase objectives either as questions that research hopes to answer or as hypotheses that it hopes to test. The section on objectives follows the general statement of the problem by describing specific goals. It grows out of previous research by

1. Citing goals which go beyond what has already been accomplished.
2. Opening new territory.
3. Redoing a study in a new and better way.
4. Reproducing an important study to ascertain the validity of its findings.

The proposal reviewer needs to see specific, concrete, and achievable objectives. List each, therefore, in no more than a sentence or two in approximate order of importance or potential contribution. Or list broad objectives first, followed by specific objectives.

The importance of the "objectives" section cannot be overemphasized since it forms a basis for judging the remainder of the proposal. It sets the stage for showing how you intend to solve the problem presented in the first section. Because objectives come in the first part of the proposal and are written early, they frequently state more than will be possible to undertake when the project is outlined in concrete detail. When the proposal is completed, it should be reread. Make sure the objectives section really fits the problem statement and that the procedure section adequately encompasses all the objectives.

There are three possible errors in writing the objectives section:

1. To present a set of vague generalities rather than cleancut criteria against which the rest of the project can be judged.
2. To bury the objectives in a running description of the project.
3. To include objective statements which are not handled by the proposal procedures.

RELATED RESEARCH

No research project is completely new. The extent to which you build your project on what has already been done is an indication of your command of the current state of the field or condition in the company. It is also an indication of the extent to which the proposed project moves the field or company ahead in some significant manner. Some sections of the proposal, therefore, should deal with how the project will contribute to this forward movement. A section on "related research and literature" provides this opportunity.

In writing this section there are four steps to follow:

1. Select research studies or company records which provide a foundation for the proposed project.
2. Discuss these studies in detail sufficient to aid the nonspecialist to understand their relevance.
3. When applicable, describe how other research contributes to this study.
4. Indicate how your study moves beyond the others or will improve the company.

Your review usually should encompass the most recent literature in both content and method. An outdated review hardly adds to the impression of scholarliness; however, some research is "classic" and should be checked. Complete dependence on secondary sources such as other literature reviews may be most appropriate, and you will want to check some of the original literature firsthand. Be highly selective in your research and cite only those studies which indicate the base from which your study is beginning.

The related research section is an excellent place to indicate your scholarly competence and professional maturity. In discussing other studies, point out their technical flaws and indicate how you will avoid these pitfalls. Indicate whether the findings of the studies were correctly interpreted by their authors and how they should be viewed to fit the study you propose. What you do with the references, and the skill you show in selecting and evaluating their contributions, are the bases for judging this section.

Indicate the theoretical base for your study if there is one. Science is a systematically accumulated body of knowledge. Theories interrelate individual findings, making general implications that can be transferred to new situations. This section of the report indicates your grasp of the ways in which the current theory in the field is being built on or tested and how solidly this theory should be held. If this is more than just a library-oriented study, you can indicate your familiarity with the company's history, records, practices, and policies that have produced the problem.

Too often the "related research" section is written as an afterthought. For example, after a graduate student's "fresh new idea" has been developed into a study, she or he goes to the library to complete the remaining section on related research. Such a practice makes the reconciliation of past research activities with the "new" project difficult.

Being human, it would be natural for you to claim your idea as original and unrelated to what others have done. But research programs cannot keep "rediscovering America" to satisfy the ego of individual investigators. Few projects start from scratch. Hence, if a statement such as "no research is available" is used, cite the closest research which was found and show how it falls short. Indicate the sources and references you checked.

PROCEDURE

The "procedures" section is usually the most carefully read part of the proposal. Up to this point you have expressed what you hope to do. The section on procedure gets down to business in operational terms. Frequently, proposals which sound as though they will revolutionize a field are more mundane in the "procedures" because the techniques proposed for attacking the problem will produce less than what is promised.

In most formats, "procedures" will need adaptation to describe adequately approaches to problems other than experimental. For example, if the study involves sampling, elaborate on the sampling section. If it is a case study, combine the sections on sample, design, and data collection into a single description of how and where you will gather data. Be sure to provide as much objectivity as possible. If there is no previous literature relating directly to the study, make application from other closely related areas.

REVIEWING THE PROPOSAL

After stating the problem, reviewing the available research, formulating the objectives, and describing the procedures, ask yourself four major questions about the proposed project:

1. Does the proposal flow logically from section to section?
2. Does it accurately reflect your scholarly ability?
3. Is there enough detail?
4. Would a reader who is pressed for time be signaled to the critical parts of the proposal?

DOES THE PROPOSAL FLOW LOGICALLY FROM SECTION TO SECTION?

A helpful point to remember is that research is basically a chain of reasoning. A strong proposal reflects this by the structure and internal consistency. A report must hang together, be consistent among its parts, and have no weak links. Build the problem statement to assure that the objectives appear important and desirable.

The statement of objectives and method of solution should be based on and move beyond past research, showing what has already been done, how it was accomplished or how it failed, and the goal of the present study. The problem statement and objectives considered together will suggest the next step—which group to survey and the method to be used. The precision of the objectives will suggest how precise the measure must be and the nature of the analysis (statistical or other) to be employed. The analysis, in turn, will determine the conclusions and implications.

Flaws in structure and consistency are most easily seen either by those unfamiliar with the proposal or by the writer after the ardor of preparation has cooled. Even the most experienced proposal writer benefits from a critical review by others. Often a nonspecialist will give the most helpful review. Putting the proposal aside for several days and reading it again later will provide the perspective necessary to find flaws.

DOES THE PROPOSAL ACCURATELY REFLECT SCHOLARLY ABILITY?

The foreword (as well as the material which follows) is an indication of the scholarliness of the proposal. The foreword is particularly important if you have done no previous research work as evidence of your competence. A reviewer is more likely to overlook flaws in a proposal from a person who has demonstrated ability to carry out similar research successfully than from a person whose ability is untested.

IS THERE ENOUGH DETAIL?

Proposal writing has a fine balance. You should describe the study in sufficient detail that the reviewer is convinced that the problem is worth investigation and that you can handle it. But do not give so much detail that every single possibility is spelled out and all flexibility is eliminated. The scope of the proposal should be broad enough to allow some exploration.

Length of the proposal is debatable. Page limitations are usually set merely to prevent excesses and to keep the reading load within proper bounds. When deciding whether to run over the prescribed length, within reasonable limits, it is usually better to include information than to omit it.

Don't try to crowd all detail into the main body of the proposal. Use appendices to provide needed auxiliary information. This permits the reviewer to have on hand information needed to make a decision but does not force readers to read unnecessary information.

ARE THE CRITICAL PARTS OF THE PROPOSAL SIGNALED?

Ideally writers expect their proposals will be given the time necessary to adequately comprehend and evaluate them; for that matter, so do the reviewers. However, reading is often done under time restrictions. It is always safest to assume that the proposal might have to be reviewed under pressure.

Good writing, like good acting, uses nonverbal gestures. Use punctuation, underlining, spacing, paragraphing, diagrams, flow-charts, enumeration, tables, and other devices to command the reader's eye. Use topic sentences, subheadings, or paragraphs to signal content to come. Help the reader find the essential substance. For example, set forth a succinct statement of the purpose of the research in the problem statement section. Similarly, list the objectives in order of importance. Remember, research is essentially a scholarly activity.

EVALUATING THE PROPOSAL

The research proposal should state specifically, yet concisely, *what* will be done, *how* it will be done, *to whom* it will be done (all pertinent characteristics of the subjects should be specified), *why* it will be done (there should be a sound theoretical and/or experimental rationale for the proposed use of each major procedural step, independent variable, and dependent variable), and what the *analyses* of each category of data will be. The written proposal is actually the first section or chapter of the report.

To know how most reviewers in a research department evaluate proposals, consider each of the following elements before submitting a research work plan to your instructor.

Statement of the Problem

This section defines, limits the project, and indicates the significance of the effort. The statement of the problem explains the need and why something should be done to meet that need.

1. Does the statement convince the reviewer that the project is important?
2. Does the statement indicate how the study builds on previous theory or contributes to new theory?

Related Research and Literature

Reference to related research will support the need for the research.

1. Does the related research section select studies that provide a foundation for the proposed study?
2. Does the related research section indicate the proposed study will move beyond previous studies?
3. Does the related research section indicate the researcher's scholarly competence? (Does it point out the technical flaws in the studies cited and indicate how these pitfalls will be avoided in the proposed study?)

Objectives

The objectives suggest the selection of procedures and evaluations. Objectives should be measurable. There may be an objective for each need identified in the statement of the problem.

1. Are the objectives specific and concrete? Are they achievable?
2. Does the objectives section fit the problem statement?
3. Are the hypotheses and objectives testable?

Procedures

The procedures section describes how the objectives will be met. The reader should be walked through the study as the methodology is spelled out. Procedures may include a description of the population to be served and the technical approaches to be used.

1. Does the procedures section "bring the study down to business" in operational terms?
2. Is the outline of this section adapted to the purposes of the study so that important aspects are properly viewed?

SUMMARY

This chapter has dealt with the ingredients of a research proposal, an important communication tool. In nearly all instances reports are suggested or assigned to you, and when they are assigned you need to be familiar with a standard work plan. The plan described here may suggest more detail than you actually need, so modify it to your individual needs or to the needs of the one assigning the report topic.

Reading 5, "Planning for Effective Researching and Reporting," sets forth one example of a work plan that has proved effective toward producing a research proposal.

DISCUSSION QUESTIONS AND EXERCISES

1. What is a "proposal"? How can it use your research techniques?
2. What are the primary components of a proposal to be identified to the person who authorizes the study?
3. Explain the four major sections of a research proposal.
4. Why is the statement of the problem so important?
5. Discuss the most common error in preparing the problem section.
6. Why should the problem be limited?
7. What opportunity does the section on related research provide?
8. What four steps should be followed in writing the related research section?
9. How can you demonstrate scholarly competence and professional maturity in the writing of the related research section?
10. How will researching other studies contribute to a stronger research project?
11. What are the bases of an objectives section?
12. How or why should the objectives section be related to the problem statements?
13. What are three possible errors that can be made in writing the objectives section?
14. Discuss four ways objectives may grow out of previous research.
15. Why is the procedures section the most carefully read part of a proposal?
16. Why is objectivity important in writing the procedures section?
17. What are the four major questions that should be answered when you review the proposal?
18. How is research a chain of reasoning?
19. Proposal writing has a fine balance in what way?
20. Discuss some of the nonverbal gestures of good writing?
21. Discuss four questions the research proposal should specifically answer.
22. Prepare a research proposal on a topic of your own choosing or on an assigned topic, and submit it to your instructor. If approval is granted, begin a thorough research process for completion of your project. The text and your instructor will provide other details as you progress.

7

Constructing and Using a Questionnaire

An obvious and direct way to get an answer from people is to ask them questions. This is a fundamental research technique used by the report writer to learn what a person knows, believes, feels, desires, intends to do, or has done. The written *questionnaire* is a way of asking questions according to a definite plan of inquiry; its purpose is to obtain information for the research proposal and the final study. The questionnaire seeks specific information which can be studied and from which conclusions can be derived. The asking of questions to obtain this information, however, is a complex undertaking. Also, it is impossible for any researcher to develop an unbiased, perfectly worded question. The goal, therefore, must be to obtain usable data.

You, as a researcher, must make several decisions. You must consider the physical appearance of the questionnaire to help insure that the respondent will answer and return it. How long should the questionnaire be? Is paper color an important factor? What spacing of questions is advisable? The tiniest detail may mean the difference between a carefully answered and returned questionnaire and a discarded one.

Question format is also important. You may ask questions which require lengthy written answers. Multiple-choice, true-false, one-word answer, and other brief-reply questions require less of the respondent's time, however, and so may be more appealing to him or her. You must decide the best question format.

The following sections discuss in detail these problems—question wording, question format, and physical appearance—so you may better understand how to construct a questionnaire. Misuses of the questionnaire technique and ways to facilitate usable returns will also be discussed. The emphasis in this chapter is in preparing the questionnaire for handout or for mailing.

QUESTION WORDING

In designing a questionnaire you need to consider four basic points before writing a question. First, what is the purpose of the questionnaire? To ascertain facts, test knowledge of respondents, or discover beliefs, opinions, and attitudes?

Second, who is the respondent? If low educational-level people answer the questionnaire, terminology should be used that will be easily understood. If children are asked, questions should be kept simple. There will be considerable loss of information when identical wording is used for both middle-class and extremely poor or minority-group respondents. The biases of the group questioned should be considered.

Third, what processing is required after the data have been collected? You must consider the whole study. Will the results eventually be computerized? Should the questionnaire respondent be identified?

Fourth, will the questionnaire be used in future surveys? If the questionnaire will be used again, questions should be designed with a view to uniformity of results.

When designing the questionnaire, ask only pertinent questions. Secure comparable data when possible and be tactful with personal questions. Avoid questions likely to give inaccurate responses or those which require much work (mathematical). No matter how careful you are, however, some problems will arise. If respondents do not understand one choice of a multiple-choice question, for example, they will undoubtedly eliminate it and pick another. If none of the choices is understandable, they may pick one anyway. If respondents have no strong opinion on a question, they are more influenced by wording, just as a shopper who has no particular shampoo in mind may pick the one in the prettiest bottle. Consequently, you must construct the questionnaire according to certain fundamental rules. The suggestions listed in Exhibit 7-1 will help you improve the wording of your questions.

Respondents generally will not put a great deal of effort into answering a questionnaire. Word each question to require a minimum amount of writing. Many answers can be indicated by a simple "yes," "no," number, underline, X, or circle. In this way there is no problem with unreadable handwriting.

QUESTION FORMAT

There are six basic question formats or ways to present a question. Usually more than one form is used in a questionnaire. The possibilities are open-end or free-answer questions, two-way or dichotomous questions, multiple-choice questions, checklists, free story or case questions, ranking items (listing), and intensity scales. The first three are most commonly used in questionnaires.

The Open-End or Free-Answer Question

The open-end or free-answer question allows a variety of responses but is difficult to handle statistically. The respondents are free to offer any ideas they may think of. This type of question may require only a few words or a lengthy answer ("In general, what do you think is the cause of bankruptcy?"). No possible answers are listed; respondents must write their own opinion. A respondent may be more willing to answer "What is your wife's name?" than "Are you married?" Or you may wish to personalize some questions ("Would *you* vote to . . . ? Why?"). Also, you probably will want to

EXHIBIT 7-1
Fundamental Rules for Questionnaire Construction

1. Use simple words. Make your questions easy to understand.
2. Make your questions concise; avoid unnecessary phrases.
3. Phrase questions so they obtain the exact information desired. The more specific a question is, the better the answer will be.
4. Avoid multiple meaning questions; cover only one point per question.
5. Avoid ambiguous questions which may mean different things to different people.
6. Avoid leading questions; questions suggesting an answer produce bias.
7. Link prestige names, when possible, to the questionnaire. (Be aware, however, that the use of a personality's name in a questionnaire may lead to biased answers because the respondent is relating to the name rather than strictly answering the question.)
8. Avoid words with emotional connotations (e.g., communist, alien, patroit, hawk, dove, rich, etc.).
9. Avoid personal questions (e.g., questions regarding age, income status, morals, and personal habits).
10. Check questions to evaluate internal consistency.

Source: Adapted from Mildred Bernice Parten, *Surveys, Polls, Samples: Practical Procedures* (N.Y.: Cooper Square Publishers, Inc., 1966) pp. 200-213.

allow for all possible responses; "no opinion" or "other, please specify" answers should be included. A respondent does not always have an opinion or cannot always answer a question. Obviously, these types of questions could not be used when answers are to be recorded on a computer card. Being nondirective, however, an open-end question can allow a broad range of responses, provide quotable individual responses, and eliminate bias.

Dichotomous or Two-Way Questions

Dichotomous or two-way questions present opposing alternatives from which the respondent may choose. Often they also include a third "no opinion" choice so respondents are not required to choose from the two opposing answers if they have no opinion. Official voting ballots use the dichotomous question. This type of question is easy to statistically manipulate ("Do you approve or disapprove of House Bill 389?" Approve—Disapprove—No Opinion). The respondent's choice could be circled, underlined or checked. Remember, however, that "yes/no" "right/wrong," "agree/disagree" replies may seem definite when in fact they possess many degrees between the extremes. Forcing a dichotomous choice from your respondent will provide inaccurate information.

Multiple-Choice Question

Multiple-choice questions include several answers from which respondents pick the one closest to their own opinion. All possible answers or degrees of opinion must be present, and each alternative must be mutually exclusive and realistic. This style of question requires careful preparation, but it also provides helpful information about a person's probable beliefs or actions.

No more than five choices in each multiple-choice question should be allowed, and each choice should be reasonable for the group surveyed. In a long checklist, rotate the order of possible answers for different groups. People are more likely to pick items at the head of the list.

An embarrassing question could be best asked in multiple choice form. If respondents see their answer as one of the choices, they may select it since obviously someone else has thought of it too. The choice would not identify the respondent as "abnormal"; whereas in an open-end question respondents might not wish to disclose their true feelings. However, respondents might pick a multiple-choice answer just because it sounds better than the others or because they understand one choice and not the others. An alternative labeled "none of the above" might be included to avoid the forced-answer situation. Of course, anonymity (being unidentified) relieves most respondents and helps them feel more at ease in answering each question honestly.

Checklists

Checklists include a question and usually from three to fifteen possible answers. Format-wise they are similar to multiple-choice questions. For example, "Which line of clothing do you like best? Brand A—, Brand B—, Brand C—, Brand D—, Other—, No preference—." This type of question is popular in mail questionnaires. Respondents can quickly mark their choice, and the researcher can easily tabulate results.

Free-Story-and-Case Method

The free-story-and-case method involves an interviewer who fills in a questionnaire or writes a summary after a "free" conversation with the respondent. The interviewer may have psychiatric or social work training. No specific questions are asked.

Ranking and Listing

Respondents may be asked to rank items in a list in the order of their preference. The list should be short, but, if many possibilities must be included, the respondent may be asked to rank only the four or five most important and to leave all others blank. This format does not allow for different intervals between items. This disadvantage may be vital when the respondent feels there is a wide gap between items 3 and 4 and a very close relationship between 4 and 5.

Omitting any important possible alternative can lead to bias. Even including an "other" answer may not help because respondents tend to limit their answer to only the alternatives listed.

Intensity Scales

Intensity scales may be used to ascertain the degree of opinion. A question or statement is posed and respondents circle the response closest to their feelings on the matter. A three-point rating scale might read: "very important—fairly important—not important." A four-point rating scale might be: "many—some—very few—none" and a five-point scale: "strongly approve—approve—undecided—disapprove—strongly disapprove." There are also seven and ten-point scales. A "no-reaction" response typically lies in the center of the scale with extreme reactions at the ends.

PHYSICAL APPEARANCE

The physical appearance of a questionnaire is important because it creates a first impression. Before respondents ever read a question they notice the size, paper quality, color, printing, spacing, and length of the questionnaire. If it is not attractive, no matter what the subject matter, they may discard it.

What size should a questionnaire be? There are several choices. The standard 8½ by 11 size fits easily into most file cabinets, and people are accustomed to handling this size paper. Postal cards are easy to sort and file and would obviously be quick for the respondent to fill out.

A short, easily filled-out and returned questionnaire will probably yield a higher response than a long, tedious one. Respondents may disregard a questionnaire if it looks too long or complicated. The Bureau of the Census uses cumbersome 16 by 23 sheets which require specially made bindings for storage. Of course, you may need information that can be obtained only through a longer type of question. But, psychologically, respondents accept smaller sizes better.

You should be concerned also with the quality of paper. If the questionnaire will be handled several times or by several people, the paper must be durable (20 pound). Obviously, the paper should take ink without blotting. If the questionnaire will be sorted and counted by hand, strong, flexible cards or paper with smooth surfaces are best.

Some color other than white might produce better returns. White, however, is often the best choice because black printing shows up well. Conspicuousness may be desirable in a mail questionnaire or to a questionnaire handed out with a minimum of instruction, however. Marketing studies show yellow to result in the greatest percentage of returned questionnaires; pink is second. If the researcher is using several different types of questionnaires each one could be a different color to avoid confusion. Or if one respondent will receive several questionnaires, alternating light colors would be better than using only one color.

A neat printing job improves the questionnaire's appearance. No respondent wants to fill out a sloppy questionnaire. You may even wish to vary print type within the questionnaire (a script type could emphasize important words in a sentence or in a heading). One-third more copies should be printed than you think will be needed, since some will be wasted or lost and a few messy ones will have to be recopied. Several copies should be sent if the questionnaire is going to a group of people (department) instead of to just one individual. Also, there may need to be a follow-up mailing.

Interestingly, studies show the color of the stamp used on a mail questionnaire affects a response. A purple stamp or printing permit brings highest returns, then blue, red, brown, and green, with black bringing poorest returns. (6) If the stamp is very new or commemorative, response may improve while the stamp is a novelty. Also, if a stamped, preaddressed return envelope is included with the questionnaire, returns are higher than if a business reply envelope is used. This method is more costly however.

Thoughtful spacing of questions in a questionnaire can lead to better answers and more returned questionnaires. Questions must be spaced so they can be read easily. A questionnaire that has small margins and is full of print discourages a respondent. The questionnaire should have an appealing layout. Dashes, bold type lines, or dotted lines can separate sections of the questionnaire. Blank space before a section or question will draw attention to that area of the questionnaire. For a question that requires a written answer, generally the more space allowed for the answer, the longer the answer that will be obtained.

Questionnaires should not be printed on both sides of a page, because it is easier to fill out a questionnaire with printing on only one side. Also, you can better tabulate results and work with the questionnaire. Blank back pages are available for research notations.

Careful consideration of a questionnaire's appearance can help bring an effective response. To insure the success of your questionnaire, you also should know something about misuses of the questionnaire techniques.

MISUSES OF THE QUESTIONNAIRE TECHNIQUE

The questionnaire technique is a popular research tool; however, researchers frequently misuse it. Ten common mistakes with questionnaires are listed in Exhibit 7-2. While the arrangement and appearance of a questionnaire are extremely important, so is the inclusion of proper, pertinent questions. For example, "requesting information readily available from other sources" is disgusting to a respondent. Therefore, make sure you have thoroughly gathered the secondary research material before going after primary research data.

EXHIBIT 7-2
Common Misuses of Questionnaires

1. Requesting information readily available from other sources.
2. Failing to create an incentive to respond.
3. Including trivial questions a respondent might consider ridiculous or unimportant.
4. Including questions which could result in misleading answers.
5. Including ambiguous questions.
6. Failing to include all qualifications needed to provide a reasonable basis for response selection.
7. Failing to phrase questions to avoid the academically or socially accepted response.
8. Asking questions which require too much complex thinking by the respondents.
9. Failing to fulfill commitments made to respondents.
10. Using a questionnaire whose form and length is discouraging to respondents.

Source: Adapted from J. Francis Rummel and Wesley C. Ballaine. *Research Methodology in Business* (New York: Harper and Row, Publishers, 1963), pp. 108-127.

How do you "create an incentive to respond"? A questionnaire should be presented so that it will attract attention and induce a response. Some of the frequently used techniques for facilitating usable returns are:

1. Sending a cover letter with the questionnaire to explain the importance and purpose of the study.
2. Guaranteeing anonymity.
3. Enclosing preaddressed and stamped return envelopes or reply cards.
4. Using various follow-up procedures.
5. Selecting an appropriate time to mail the questionnaire.
6. Making sure the questionnaire and accompanying materials have a professional appearance.
7. Offering a financial reward.
8. Promising to send a copy of the results of the study.

Certainly you will always be concerned with the wording of questions. If questions are ambiguous, misleading, and careless you will not receive valid information. Likewise, asking trivial or too complex questions will probably result in very few returns. Plus, if the questionnaire is long and cumbersome, the respondent may be psychologically adverse to using it.

Finally, if you make a commitment to a respondent (promising to send him or her a copy of the results of your study), be sure to follow through. Most respondents enjoy knowing the outcome of a study in which they participated.

Many of these errors occur because of failing to test the instrument before administering it. Even when you think you have the questionnaire just the way you want it, a pretest can help eliminate some problems you may have overlooked. This pilot test can involve giving the questionnaire to several selected individuals representative of the target group and studying the results—possibly even talking with the respondents about the questionnaire. Undoubtedly the questionnaire will need to be revised at least once and probably several more times before it is ready for the final survey group. Question wording, physical appearance, and question format can all be pilot tested. Several individuals in the pretest group may be offended by certain words, the color, or a lengthy checklist. In a discussion, pilot respondents can voice their views and clear up problems that could arise with the actual survey group.

SUMMARY

To construct an effective questionnaire, give consideration to question wording, physical appearance, question format, and the common misuses. No questionnaire or question can be perfect and bias-free, but the suggestions provided in this chapter can help you develop a questionnaire which will best suit your needs in a particular survey. By carefully wording the questions, providing an attractive physical appearance, and selecting the correct question format, you can expect to receive a good response.

DISCUSSION QUESTIONS AND EXERCISES

1. Discuss the easiest way to obtain information from people. What type of information might be revealed?
2. Explain the four basic questions a researcher needs to consider before attempting to write a question.
3. What are the fundamental rules for questionnaire construction? How will each aid responses?
4. Why might you wish to personalize certain questions?
5. Why would rotating the order of answers in a long checklist be a valid idea?
6. Why is the physical appearance of a questionnaire so important?
7. Discuss the effect color might have on a respondent's willingness to complete a questionnaire.
8. What paper size ordinarily should be used for a questionnaire? Why?
9. Are there any general guidelines as to the length of a questionnaire? Explain your answer.
10. Discuss the psychological effect of long versus short questionnaires.
11. How will thoughtful spacing of questions lead to better answers and more returned questionnaires?
12. Why should questionnaires be printed on only one side?
13. What are the seven basic question formats or ways to present a question? Illustrate all seven indicating the major three types.
14. What are the common misuses of questionnaires? How will they hinder responses?
15. Discuss some of the frequently used techniques for facilitating returns?
16. Why do many errors occur in a questionnaire? How might these be overcome?
17. Why is it impossible for all questions to be perfect and bias-free?
18. Which questionnaire format do you think would be most beneficial to the research you normally do? Why?
19. Develop three questions for each questionnaire format and try them out on your friends. Revamp each question after your pilot study and submit to your teacher. Which style is easiest for you to handle?
20. Devise a questionnaire for gathering information in a research project approved by your teacher. Be sure to test it before using it on your sample group.

Utilizing Interview Techniques in Data Collection

The knowledge gained from the preceding chapter about questionnaires is foundational for interviewing. Before you can effectively interview someone, you need questions to ask and an order in which to ask them. Interviews allow you to observe individuals or groups in action and learn facts, opinions, and beliefs about a particular subject. To gather that information you will need an interview schedule (a questionnaire or interview form). Interviews can be used to put together certain data already obtained or to check discrepancies or contradictions in material. They also may serve as an evaluator of other sources of data or as a check on the reliability of other data.

THE INTERVIEW AS A COMMUNICATION PROCESS

Interviewing is communicating with a purpose. If one person is to interview another person or group of people, communication must be effective. The ultimate success of the interview depends on the interviewer. He or she must be aware of the communication process to be able to modify the interviewee's behavior and to open the lines of communication. Interviewees also must be alert to their own prejudices so they can be objective about any questions asked.

There are many advantages and disadvantages in interviewing. The disadvantages, in particular, relate to verbal and nonverbal communication.

ADVANTAGES OF THE INTERVIEW METHOD

There are several reasons why interviews are preferred over other forms of data collection. Interviews usually bring higher response rates than other data collection techniques. An interview allows clarification of confusing questions and observation and oral question-asking by the interviewer. The interview may produce more accurate information and greater depth of response than other methods because an interview can be adapted on the spot to the understanding level of the interviewee.

The interview also can provide more control over the sequence of answers because later questions may not be affected by earlier replies, since the interviewee may not remember exactly what he or she said. Also, the interviewee is prevented from asking anyone else about the answers to the questions. A main advantage of the interview is that the interviewer can observe the environment and the personal characteristics of the interviewee. This observation will help the interviewer gain more insight into factors related to the research problem.

DISADVANTAGES OF THE INTERVIEW METHOD

Although the advantages of interviewing far outweigh the disadvantages and although the interview method is superior to the questionnaire for information gathering, there are problems. Interviewing is time consuming, energy sapping and may be too expensive. The interviewer may have trouble limiting the responses of some individuals, or both interviewer and interviewee may be influenced by extraneous factors (stress, physical ailments, environment). Too, the interviewee may report information inaccurately. Because of these problems, researchers may use too small a sample.

VERBAL COMMUNICATION PROBLEMS

In communicating with others, interviewers must be aware of the problems that can be caused by semantics (variations in word meaning). Interviewers should not take for granted that what they say means the same to them as to an interviewee. Because of semantics, interviewers should become familiar with any colloquialisms used by a particular social class, age level, ethnic group, geographic region, or religious group to be interviewed.

Another barrier occurs when an interviewer is not thoroughly familiar with the topic of the interview. The need for an appropriate vocabulary can be important when dealing with individuals representing special fields of interest. When an interviewer goes into an interview he or she should be familiar enough with the subject to ask intelligent, meaningful questions.

NONVERBAL COMMUNICATION PROBLEMS

Nonverbal communication might be defined as messages (or communications) not coded in words. Nonverbal communications include the tone and speed of voice, gestures, facial expressions, postures, and all messages which accompany the spoken word. To prevent nonverbal communication problems the interviewer must observe auditory clues (changes in pace, pitch, and intensity) and visual clues (gestures, facial expressions, and body positions) that contribute to breakdowns in communications. A calm face but a nervous twisting of the hands could reveal that the respondent is not relaxed.

Interviewers can achieve an effective interview by being sensitive to verbal and nonverbal communication problems. Strive for good rapport with the interviewee to maximize information gathering and to maintain good rapport in your interviews. These attributes will help accomplish the purpose of the interview.

GUIDELINES FOR THE INTERVIEWER

Three objectives should be accomplished during an interview: 1) explain to the interviewee the reasons for the interview and the need for cooperation; 2) motivate the interviewee so that he or she will be interested and cooperative; and 3) obtain the information desired.

Interviewers should realize that to be effective they must create an atmosphere that will put the interviewee at ease and keep communication flowing freely. The interviewer should communicate positive attitudes toward the interviewee. To be successful the interviewer must be selected to fit the task. The interviewer should be aware of any negative feelings he or she has on the topic being discussed. Feelings must be controlled so they will not influence the direction of the interview or the interviewee's response.

There are eight specific steps for conducting an interview, keeping it flexible, and fitting the situation to the interviewer's personality:

1. Structure the interview climate to make the interviewee comfortable.
2. Provide the interviewee with a clear understanding of the reasons for the interview.
3. Listen to the interviewee's message.
4. Relate ideas presented to concepts previously stated.
5. Evaluate each statement as it is made.
6. Guide the interviewee from point to point and probe with pertinent questions when necessary.
7. Develop a program of action if the situation demands it.
8. Summarize and close the interview. (54)

Many of these points will be amplified in the following sections as we talk about facilitators and inhibitors of effective interviewing.

INHIBITORS OF EFFECTIVE INTERVIEWING

Inhibitors to communication are factors that prevent a free flow of communication. Some of the factors that inhibit an interviewee from talking freely and endanger the success of the interview are: *competing demands, ego threat, etiquette, trauma, forgetting, chronological confusion,* and *inferential confusion.* (34)

Competing demands. Competing demands occur when the interviewee would rather be doing something else with his or her time. To avoid this, sell the fact that the interview is important.

Ego threat. Ego threat exists when the interviewee is afraid that the information requested may threaten self-esteem. He or she may be afraid the interviewer will disagree or disapprove of the answers given. Fear of embarrassment inhibits the respondent. Reassure the interviewee that statements will not be condemned or that the respondent will not be shunned for anything said.

Etiquette. Etiquette barriers operate when the interviewee feels that answers to certain questions should not be discussed with the interviewer or that the particular interviewing situation is inappropriate. Selecting an appropriate interviewee and place for the interview could prevent the etiquette barrier.

Trauma. Trauma is caused when the interviewee experiences unpleasant feelings when reporting certain incidents. Try to make the interviewee as comfortable as possible during the interview.

Forgetting. A respondent may forget certain types of information and the interviewer may need to probe to help him or her remember.

Chronological confusion. The interviewee may confuse the chronological order of certain experiences. Probing may help the respondent remember the correct chronological order, if exact sequence is important.

Inferential confusion. Inferential confusion occurs when the respondent becomes confused or gives inaccurate answers to questions because of misunderstanding what the interviewer said during the interview. To prevent this, provide clear, unbiased examples and definitions for the respondent to answer.

These inhibitors to communication can make the interviewee unwilling or unable to provide information during an interview. The interviewer should be aware that there are problems that can prevent a successful interview and learn to understand and to cope with these problems.

FACILITATORS OF EFFECTIVE INTERVIEWING

The facilitators of communication enhance the free flow of information between the persons involved in the interview. Facilitators should be recognized as the factors that encourage the interviewee to talk freely and openly. A few of the facilitators of communication are *recognition, sympathetic understanding, new experience, extrinsic rewards.* (34)

Recognition. Everyone wants recognition. Use every opportunity to give the interviewee sincere recognition for a positive effect on the interview.

Sympathetic understanding. All people want to share their joys, fears, and sorrows with others. Therefore, show a sympathetic attitude and use this technique to achieve the objective of the interview.

New experience. Sometimes an interview is a new and exciting experience for the interviewee. Keep him or her interested.

Extrinsic rewards. The respondent may see the interview as a means to an end (recognition, publicity). Use these extrinsic needs to keep the interviewee calm and interested.

Interviewers should use these facilitators to keep the interviewer motivated and willing to answer the questions with an open mind. Just as you conducted a pretest with your questionnaire you also should pretest your interview questions and technique.

METHODS OF RECORDING INFORMATION

Not only should an interviewer relate to the behavior expectations of the interviewee by establishing a favorable communicative atmosphere but also be aware that the method of recording information plays a crucial role in the reliability and validity of the interview. Therefore, a recording method (copious note taking, idea outlining, or tape recording) should be selected that will allow efficient and accurate analysis and interpretation of the data. Whatever method is chosen, listen attentively to the respondent and keep the interviewee's mind on the questions to be answered.

ORGANIZATIONAL CONSIDERATIONS OF AN INTERVIEW

In most public speeches there is a beginning, a middle, and an end. Interviews are similar. However, the interview is a constantly changing affair; the event involves interaction and/or transaction between people.

INTERVIEW SEGMENTS

The interview has three identifiable segments: the opening, the body, and the closing. As in a public speech, there are no specific time allotments for each segment. Time depends on the interview situation and the relationship of the two parties.

The *opening* can vary from a brief introduction to a lengthy explanation of the purpose and background leading up to the interview. The opening is generally when rapport is established, purposes are made clear, and/or orienting material is expressed. Some aspects of the interview opening may be presented prior to the actual interview as an introductory letter or when the appointment is made for the interview. First impressions may facilitate or inhibit the interview.

The *body* of the interview can be very flexible with no specific plan or sequence, or it can be very specific with little flexibility. An interview can be highly structured or have no structure at all.

The *closing* will be determined by the opening and body. It also will be determined in part by the style of interviewing used, the type of questions asked, and the responses gathered. Pay special attention to the following information and you will be able to close the interview successfully, having received the information desired.

PATTERNS OF INTERVIEWS

Within two general limitations of *purpose* and *situation,* interviewing methods or styles may vary widely. The variations in style and format become apparent when we view the organizational procedures used by different interviewers or by the same interviewer in different situations. Some circumstances call for structured patterns and others call for flexibility.

Interview patterns can differ according to the detail, questions, the sequence of topics, and the answers needed. The patterns also can differ in the freedom the interviewer allows the interviewee in determining the topics, the sequencing of topics, and the amount of detail he or she can contribute to the objective of the interview.

A *scheduled interview* calls for specific questions (with specific wording) asked in a fixed order. The interviewee is restricted by a predetermined choice of answers for each question. Thus, the schedule can limit the techniques of the interviewer and the information which the interviewee can provide. A *nonscheduled* interview, on the other hand, is one in which the interviewer is led by only a central objective, and the method of reaching the objective must be decided during the interview.

Topic control is the extent to which the interviewer controls the discussion topic. The interviewer makes decisions on the central focus and the scope of what is and what is not to be discussed. The interviewer has to take the initiative of shifting the objective of the discussion or changing the scope or direction of the topic.

Even if the interviewer has a clear understanding of the dimensions and patterns of the interview—that is, if he or she has chosen the most appropriate interview form, selected the interviewee, determined the objective, and has obtained a high degree of interaction—a successful interview cannot be assured. Success can be determined only by the communication that takes place between the interviewer and the respondent during the interview—that is, if he or she gets valid, reliable, and complete information. The questioning process must not only elicit information but must communicate enough cues about the information desired to allow the interviewee to respond.

One of the first considerations in organizing an interview is the method of questioning to be used. Asking a good, stimulating, effective question is difficult. The success of the interview method requires preparation.

TYPES OF QUESTIONS

With the fundamental dimensions of style defined, we can now examine the types of questions that may be used in an interview. An understanding of the question/answer process is essential to discovery and measurement. There are many ways of classifying types of questions. Regardless of the system used, the first step in developing skills in the question/answer process calls for an ability to identify types and uses.

Open Questions

Every question carries an indication of length of response necessary for adequate coverage. The open question calls for a response of more than a few words. One type of open question is referred to as the *open-end* question, which is a vague, general question that does no more than specify a topic or ask the respondent to talk ("Why don't you tell me something about yourself?").

Another type of open question is the *direct question*. It identifies or limits the topic area as well as asking for a more specific reply. This kind of question is sometimes classified separately from the open question ("What did you do on your last research project?").

Closed Questions

In contrast, the closed question calls for a specific and often limited response. Some examples of closed questions are: "Tell me what two subjects you liked best and what two subjects you liked least in school." "Did you feel that the tape recorder hindered the outcome of the interview?" As you can see, closed questions can vary in the amount of information required to answer, but generally they are answered in only a few words.

Yes/no or *bipolar* questions are an extreme type of closed questions that do not allow any freedom of expression except "yes," "no," or "I don't know."

The important principle in the use of open and closed questions is that they affect the length of response. Some guidelines to consider in the use of open and closed questions are:

1. Open questions, generally speaking, are used in the beginning or early stages of an interview or when a new topic has been introduced.
2. Closed questions are often used as follow-ups to the open question; hence, the closed question may produce responses that are more valid, relevant, and specific. The closed question may obtain the desired information more directly than the open.
3. The amount of participation may be altered by the proportion of open and closed questions asked in an interview. For example, if you select someone because of his or her special knowledge on a subject, you might gain more information by using open questions.

Open questions sometimes indicate a respect for the judgment of the respondent. If you then follow up with closed questions related to what already has been said, this will indicate that you have been attentive to what the interviewee has said. The use of mostly closed questions could have an opposite effect, however, indicating that you are not interested in the respondent's full expression. It is important to realize that the use of open and closed questions depends on the purpose of the interview and the individual differences of interviewees.

Mirror Questions

Generally speaking, mirror questions are used to help encourage the interviewee to expand on an incomplete response. The mirror question is often a restatement of what the interviewee has just said. For example, if the interviewee has said: "I don't approve of management's explanation on the new policy," a mirror question might be: "You don't think management went far enough, then, in its explanation, and that's why you don't approve?"

Probing Questions

Closely related to the mirror question is the probe. The probing question is asked to direct the thinking of the respondent to further explanation of what has been said. In a sense it is a follow-up question to a superficial or incomplete response. It allows a deeper investigation into the reasons for an attitude or belief or for encouraging the interviewee to offer more specific information. The probe is not always just a "why" or "how," although these are common. Generally, the probe serves two functions: to motivate further communication and to control the interaction by directing the respondent to the objective of the interview.

Probes can be brief vocal sounds or short phrases such as "I see," "Please continue," "Uh-huh," "Go on," or "Why do you feel that way?" This secondary type of question can be introduced at any time in the interaction. It can also indicate that the interviewer is attentive and interested, serving as encouragement for the respondent to continue speaking. One caution in using the probe is that it can bias the responses of the interviewee by implying that certain responses are more acceptable than others.

The probe does not have to be vocal. It could be nonverbal—silence. Timing is of utmost importance, and experienced interviewers know the importance of silence for a respondent to formulate a response. Sometimes respondents are slow and must be given time.

Leading Questions

A leading question directs the respondent or at least makes it more tempting to give one answer than another. The leading question suggests the answer the interviewer expects. The interviewer obviously should avoid leading questions.

The leading question, if used incorrectly or for the wrong reason, can produce responses that are not valid or reliable. For example, an open question designed to elicit attitudes toward wage and price controls might be: "How do you feel about wage and price controls?" A leading form of this question might be, "You wouldn't say you were in favor of wage and price controls, would you?" This form of leading question is obvious and is easily avoided. However, many leading questions are not so obvious because of the interviewer's biases. Usually these questions cannot be recognized without careful question analysis. For example, a more subtle form of the same question might be: 'Would you say you are in favor of wage and price controls?" The question calls for the respondent to answer with a "yes" or "no."

Expectation is a component of the leading question; this occurs when the interviewer anticipates a certain response. For example, if the interviewer asks, "Are you voting in this year's election?" the question is a direct, closed question with no specified direction or response. If the question is phrased, "Of course, you are going to vote in this year's election, aren't you?" he or she is expecting a "yes" response. The leading question is slanted; it suggests the response.

Another type of leading question is the *loaded question,* which uses loaded words and may trigger high emotional responses because of the implied connotations. The question can be emotionally loaded favorably or unfa-vorably. In our culture there are many words that carry high emotional loadings, and when used without thought they may create unpredictable and tangential responses. They may even create a dilemma for the respondent. Thus, questions that are not stated objectively are considered loaded. When used in a planned way, however, they can encourage immediate participa-tion, highly motivated interaction, and/or may provide a cathartic experi-ence for the respondent. It is apparent that the loaded question should be used with caution and probably not at all by the inexperienced interviewer.

To be an effective and efficient interviewer, you must become familiar with and be able to recognize the kinds of questions that may be used. With practice, you can develop the appropriate skills of questioning.

TYPES OF INADEQUATE RESPONSES

While developing the necessary skills of asking effective questions, you also must develop skill in recognizing inadequate answers to your questions. If the primary question produces an inadequate response, probing is neces-sary. If, on the other hand, the primary question produces an adequate response, the probing question is unnecessary.

The kind of probe to be used depends on the kind of inadequacy and the reason for the inadequacy. The following are some of the types of inadequate responses.

Irrelevant Answer

This response skirts or has no relation to the question asked. The problem is not one of too little or too much information but of irrelevant infor-mation. There are several factors to consider before you attempt to direct the interviewee to the desired objective. Was the response a result of misunder-standing or lack of comprehension? Or, was the response an attempt to avoid a direct response?

Partial Answer

The partial response is generally easy to detect and easy to deal with, if you are alert and know exactly what and how much information is needed. The partial response is relevant to the question but doesn't provide enough information to answer the question completely. Beginning interviewers are often so concerned with the next question that they don't evaluate the answer they are receiving, or they are unwilling to seek further information for fear of offending the respondent.

Inaccurate Response

An inaccurate response is both common and difficult to detect for the inexperienced interviewer. The answer may be inaccurate because the re-spondent wishes it to be or because he or she doesn't have the correct information. In either case the information is not acceptable and can be detrimental to the results of the interview. If the inaccuracy of the response is detected or suspected, related questions can be asked immediately or later in the interview to check for certainty or consistency in the response. The interviewer should watch for what may not necessarily be an incomplete or irrelevant response, but one that may be slanted or distorted because of prejudices of the respondent.

Nonresponse

The reasons for the interviewee remaining silent are varied—anything from not understanding the question to refusing to answer the question. If the interviewee makes no response, you will have to decide whether to ask a probing question or drop the matter completely.

Oververbalized Response

This type of response is the opposite of the nonresponse but can also be considered inappropriate because the interviewee goes beyond the objective or range of the subject. The interviewee is offering more information than is needed. This often occurs in the courtroom when the lawyer asks for a specific answer and is given a rebuttal or more information than is asked for.

CAUSES OF INADEQUATE RESPONSES

The causes of inadequate responses are numerous and complex. To handle inadequate responses successfully, you must be able to determine and identify the inadequacy. Once this is done, you must formulate a probe or series of probes to eliminate the inadequacy.

Sometimes the interviewee doesn't understand the question, may not be motivated, or may have a conflict of motives. In addition, problems such as a lack of information or background, an inability to verbalize or recall information, or an embarrassing disclosure might cause an inadequate response.

The most common weakness related to the art of asking questions is that interviewers may take too much for granted (assume questions will produce adequate responses and therefore don't evaluate the responses received). The inexperienced interviewer often jumps to conclusions with little or no evaluation of the responses received. The biggest problem is that the interviewer assumes the interviewee has the same understanding and frame of reference as the interviewer. Such assumptions are not only unrealistic but unwarranted. The interviewer must be critical of the questions he or she asks and the answers received. The successful outcome of an interview is based on efficient and effective questions and the ability to recognize inadequate responses.

SUMMARY

A successful interview involves communication between two people; therefore, special problems confront both the interviewer and the interviewee.

These problems are considered inhibitors to communication. The interviewer should be familiar with these inhibitors and try to overcome them during the interview.

Facilitators to communication can be used to help the interviewer conduct a smooth interview. For an interview to be successful, the interviewer and interviewee must reduce fears and desires. Rapport must be established to enable the interviewee to respond without bias or prejudices.

DISCUSSION QUESTIONS AND EXERCISES

1. What is the purpose of the interview?
2. When is the interview preferred over other forms of data collection?
3. Discuss the advantages and disadvantages of the interview.
4. How is an interview a communication process?
5. Discuss the verbal communication problems of interviewing.
6. Discuss the nonverbal communication problems of interviewing.
7. List three objectives of an interview.
8. Why is creating an atmosphere important to obtaining information?
9. List eight specific steps for conducting an interview.
10. What is an inhibitor and a facilitator of effective interviewing?
11. What are the seven factors that inhibit an interview? Discuss each.
12. How does fear of embarrassment inhibit a respondent?
13. How can an interviewer prevent "inferential confusion"?
14. Discuss the four facilitators of effective interviewing.
15. Discuss the basic methods of recording information.
16. How is "clarity" a help or hindrance to successful interviewing?
17. Why is "feedback" important to communicating and interviewing?
18. How are the three parts of public speaking similar to interviewing?
19. Define "scheduling" and "topic control." What are the differences?
20. Why is "asking a good, stimulating, effective question" a difficult task?
21. What are five types of questions that may be used in an interview? Discuss.
22. Explain the basic differences between open and closed questions.
23. How can the probe be nonverbal in nature?
24. How is expectation a component of the leading question?
25. What are five types of inadequate responses? Discuss.
26. What is the most common weakness related to the art of asking questions? Why?
27. On what is the successful interview based?
28. If your instructor requires you to participate in interviews for the research you are conducting, choose your respondents at this time and begin your interviewing. It will be especially beneficial to you to prepare your schedule of questions first and practice on your peers before gathering the actual data from interviewees.

9

Interpreting the Information Gathered

Once you have collected all the data in its rough form ("raw data"), your next step is to put it into a form which permits analysis and interpretation. Raw data by itself is useless; it must be summarized, counted, tabulated, or grouped according to the uses to be made of it. Any operations performed on the raw data will depend on the kind of information to be presented. The purpose of this chapter is to provide guidelines for manipulating raw data into a polished, meaningful research report.

ANALYSIS AND INTERPRETATION AS THE BASIS OF EVERY ACTIVITY

From the time you first became aware of your research problem, you have used the process of analysis and interpretation. Any activity associated with a problem and its solution is part of this process—in other words, *everything* you have done.

When you construct the outline, you will divide some items into smaller parts and group others into broader categories. Preparing recording forms will require you to synthesize the data. You put the data back together, to a degree, when you construct illustrative tables. Analysis and interpretation, then, is the process of dividing, grouping, and studying information in terms of how it will be used.

PROCESSING THE DATA

When you have completed your research and gathered your data, there are some general points to keep in mind when working with raw data. Exhibit 9-1 provides a skeletal outline of points to keep in mind when molding raw data into meaningful work.

After you have completed the research and gathered the necessary facts and ideas, you face the problem of organizing and interpreting the information so it has significance. Then the material must be outlined for effective presentation to the reader to achieve the purpose of the investigation.

EXHIBIT 9-1

A Skeletal Idea of Points to Keep in Mind When
Molding Raw Data into a Meaningful Work

GUIDELINES FOR HANDLING DATA GATHERED IN A RESEARCH STUDY

1. Study data carefully to determine the proper method of handling.
   a. Present them logically.
   b. Be resourceful.
2. Be objective and open-minded.
   a. Do not base your reasoning on lack of facts, faulty analogy, or silence.
   b. Do not bias the results of the study by omitting some of the returns, subjects, or data gathered.
3. Set up specific standards of tabulating and analyzing.
4. Keep a record of the decisions made while classifying or analyzing so your interpretation of data may be consistent.
5. Use machine tabulating and scoring whenever available, not only to save time and hassle but also to insure greater accuracy.
6. Use imagination as well as reasoning in interpreting the meaning of the data.
7. Be sure you know statistical procedures and how to use them in research before attempting to analyze the data statistically.
   a. Be sure that the mathematical model used fits the data you have collected. Check with a statistician.
   b. Use tables of reciprocals and square roots to save time and to reduce the chance of inaccuracies in computation, if mechanical means of handling the data are not available.
   c. Translate the findings into standard statistical terms.
   d. Do not use complicated statistical techniques on relatively simple data.
   e. Do not expect complicated statistical techniques to improve faulty raw data.
8. Use a uniform basis for comparison. Do not describe some in terms of fractions, some in terms of percentages, and some in terms of ratios. Percentages are the most accurate; fractions and ratios are very effective in showing relationships.
9. Use tables and figures only to clarify the findings or to point out relationships and similarities.
   a. Keep tables and figures as concise and simple as possible.
   b. Show no more than two or three kinds of closely related facts in a single table or figure.
   c. Make tables and figures sufficiently informative that they can be correctly interpreted without reference to the text.
10. Collect, organize, and interpret significant past facts and trends of attitudes or events if conducting historical research.
    a. Select and reject facts carefully.
    b. Show relationships and contributions to present-day practices and understanding.
11. Do not generalize on the basis of too few cases, especially in case studies and similar types of research.
12. Do not assume that present practices are correct—evaluate them. Time changes most things.

Source: Adapted from Dugdale, Kathleen. *A Manual on Writing Research* (Bloomington, IN: Kathleen Dugdale, 1962).

The first step in organizing data is sorting and arranging similar data into groups (classifying). Classification of data may take place during or after the gathering process. There are four general classifications of data: qualitative, quantitative, chronological, and geographical.

1. Facts and ideas about a subject are *qualitative*. They may be recorded on notes and may be secured from bibliographical research, interviews, letters, experience, observation, or experimentation.
2. Data expressed in terms of figures adaptable to statistical treatment are *quantitative*. This type of information is usually the result of questionnaires, although information can come from other sources. Interviews, observations, and the like sometimes consist of responses which can be counted.
3. Data classified according to areas or regions are *geographical*.
4. Data arranged according to time sequence are *chronological*.

One purpose of classifying is to organize similar data into groups. By doing so relationships between groups can be discovered. The type of data being processed will determine the procedure to be followed.

The first step in organizing *qualitative data* is to examine them as a whole, considering them for completeness and for significance to the problem at hand. Then the data should be broken down into component parts and arranged to show relationships. This procedure may necessitate forming new groups, perhaps combining some.

In organizing and interpreting *quantitative data* you must check for accuracy and pertinence. Each piece of data should help accomplish the purpose of the study.

The next step is to prepare the data for tabulation. The best way to tabulate data is to use a work sheet. For example, if you used a questionnaire to gather data, you can use a blank one to compile and tabulate answers to each question. Tabulation enables you to compare, analyze, and evaluate responses. The type of responses called for in answers on a questionnaire naturally determines how to set up the work sheet for tabulating results. For example, all questions demanding a "yes" or "no" answer may be checked together on one sheet, and questions requiring an "always," "frequently," "seldom," or "never" response may be tabulated on another.

After the data have been edited and work sheets set up, tabulation is possible. Data may be counted and the responses recorded in the proper places on the work sheets. It may be necessary to divide questionnaires into groups according to categories derived from the corollary information and check each group. Then totals for each group may be reached. When the work sheets are completed, a single master or recapitulation sheet can be made up from them, showing the number and type of responses for every question. Sometimes this summary sheet is arranged with the same headings as the work sheets. However, sometimes it is necessary to work out different combinations and headings. After the recapitulation sheet is filled in, the data can be examined for significance and relationship to the problem.

Quantitative data should be examined and tested for reliability by statistical procedures. The data may be checked for proportionality to determine whether they are representative or the standard error of deviation may be used. The purpose in examining the data is to discover their degree of validity. Unreliable and nonpertinent data must be discarded.

A chief difference between handling qualitative and quantitative data is that you should present quantitative data in tables or graphs to make the data meaningful and comprehensible. Pragmatically, the process of organizing and interpreting data are the same.

TABLES AND STATISTICAL MEASURES

An analysis of the data will probably determine how they can be arranged in tables. You can compare figures, think through relationships of one fact to another, evaluate the importance of the material, and decide on the significance of the figures. These like figures can be grouped together for presentation in tables.

When tables are set up they must be interpreted (more about tables as a graphic display in a later chapter). Usually percentages must be determined to show the relationship of one figure to another. For example, "50 responses out of 139 replies" does not express the relationship as effectively as "35.97 percent of the responses." The 35.97 percent could also be expressed in simpler terms: "about three in ten." Using small, round numbers (36 percent instead of 35.97 percent) makes the data even less complicated and easier to understand.

Use of statistical measures in evaluating data and interpreting tables helps to spot trends. Three statistical averages used to find the central tendency or trends indicated by the data are the mean, median, and mode. The *mean* is the arithmetical average and is obtained by totaling figures and dividing the number of cases. The *median* is the midpoint between the upper and lower halves. It represents the midpoint of a list of figures arranged in rank order. The *mode* indicates the pattern followed most often. It is the point of highest frequency, where more cases occur.

These three averages refer to different ideas. The mean is the true average and shows what the situation would be if all things were equal. It provides only information about the general magnitude of the scores; it does not provide information about the size of differences among scores (variability). The median does not indicate a true picture; there are as many cases above as below it. It is the "middle of the road." The mode is the score with the largest frequency; that is, its pattern is established by the occurrence of the highest number of cases.

Interpreting data in a table calls for considering the totals first and looking at the table as a whole. Then an examination of the appropriate statistical measures—the range, the extremes, and the exceptions—should be made. All this is a basis for drawing statistical conclusions. Before final conclusions can be drawn, however, quantitative and qualitative data must be considered in their proper relationship.

CONCLUSIONS AND RECOMMENDATIONS

As a result of an interpretation of data and reasoned judgment, you can now draw conclusions and formulate recommendations. This is done by carefully examining the results of the investigation point by point to find a general pattern or a solution to the research problem. Restudy your data and ask: "Does the information I have obtained fulfill my objective?" The purposes are the aims or long-range goals of the report, and the objectives are the obstacles that must be overcome or the short goals that must be reached to accomplish this aim. The conclusions you make at this point should start with the purpose and then move from the objective to the data.

Conclusions reached through statistical measures and deductive and inductive reasoning disclose whether the conclusion is true or false. Conclusions reached statistically can be tested by rechecking the statistical processes and techniques used and by considering their validity in relation to other evidence and data secured. A final conclusion must be practical and workable.

Recommendations are the logical outgrowth of conclusions supported by data. Just as conclusions fulfill the objectives of a report, so recommendations achieve the purpose of the report. More will be said about conclusions and recommendations in a later chapter.

SUMMARY

After you have gathered raw data, you need to organize and interpret it by examining, editing, tabulating, and statistically measuring the information. Then with the data at the heart of the study, look for a common thread on which to draw tentative conclusions. Tentative conclusions must be tested for validity and reliability before they can become final conclusions. Once final conclusions are made, practical, definite recommendations can be formed and the report-writing stage of the study can begin.

DISCUSSION QUESTIONS AND EXERCISES

1. What is "raw data" and why is it useless by itself?
2. How is analysis and interpretation the basis of every research activity?
3. How are analysis and interpretation associated with everything a report writer does?
4. What are four guidelines for starting the analyzing-interpreting process for the final written report?
5. Look at Table 9-1 and select those points of processing that seem most critical to you. Discuss.
6. Discuss the steps in organizing quantitative and qualitative data.
7. What are the four general classifications of data? Discuss each.
8. Explain the basic difference between qualitative and quantitative data.
9. Compare the processes of interpretation and organization.
10. How is a table beneficial to interpretation and organization?
11. How does the use of statistical measures help to spot trends?
12. Define the three basic statistical averages used by report writers.
13. Define conclusions and recommendations.
14. If you have not already begun processing the information you have gathered, begin now. Get all your information together, review it, prepare any forms necessary, and start recording for interpretation. Be objective about all information gathered; do not allow bias to influence interpretation. As soon as all information is organized, processed, analyzed, and interpreted, see what tentative conclusions and recommendations seem to be shaping up.

_____ Part III

The Process of
Report Writing

10

Basic Composition of Research Reports

The objective of any piece of writing is to communicate ideas to another person. Consequently, as a writer you have not accomplished your writing mission if the reader does not react the way you expect. Like it or not, the reader, not the writer, is the final judge of the writing, and it doesn't help to say "but that's not the way I intended it!" You must approach each business writing task from the *reader's* point of view.

To empathize with your readers, ask a few basic questions as you approach the writing task:

- *Who* will read this report?
- *Who* will be affected by this report?
- *What* will the reader look for in the report?
- *What* will the report be used for?
- *Why* do the readers need the report?
- *When* will the report be used?
- *Where* will the report be used and stored?
- *How* can the report be made most useful for all the readers?

With the answers in mind, the writer can attack the writing task.

READABILITY

Writing authorities have determined that reading difficulty is affected most by two factors—sentence length and word difficulty. The sentence, stripped to its bare essentials, is a subject and a verb, and the more we add to that basic structure, the more complex the sentence becomes. Additional words and phrases help to fine-tune expressions and to show relationships between ideas. But there seems to be a point of diminishing returns, a point at which extra words and phrases make a sentence more difficult rather than easier to grasp.

The effective business writer is able to sense when enough meat has been put on the skeleton of the sentence, when enough modification and amplification have been given to the basic sentence structure. On the one hand the writer must avoid excessive short, choppy sentences that have a mechanical sound to them. On the other hand, he or she must avoid the tendency to flaunt adjectives, adverbs, and phrases which many people overuse to impress others. Some sentences need to be long while others can be relatively short, but writing authorities have suggested that the average sentence length for business writing should be approximately sixteen words.

Word difficulty, another major factor that affects readability, must be a constant concern of the business writer. Since words are the basic symbols used to represent thoughts, words that mean the same to both writer and reader should be used. Whenever a writer uses a word that may have a different meaning to the reader, miscommunication is possible. The terms "liquidity," "cognitive dissonance," "core," and "acid test ratio" are familiar to finance, marketing, computer, and accounting people, but to the general public, these terms are relatively meaningless.

While it is simple to compute the average sentence length in a piece of writing, it is considerably harder to measure word difficulty because it is an individual matter. A word that is difficult to one will be common language to another. Nevertheless, the writer must be aware that difficult words are a major roadblock to understanding. Most authorities use a syllable count to objectively determine difficult words in a passage of writing.

GUNNING FOG INDEX

One of the most popular and easiest readability formulas to use as a measurement of writing is the Gunning Fog Index developed by Robert Gunning.[1] To compute the fog index of a passage of writing, select a writing sample of a hundred or more words and follow three basic steps:

1. Determine the average sentence length. Count the number of sentences in the passage. If two independent clauses are found in a single sentence, count each clause as a sentence. Then divide the total number of words in the passage by the number of sentences you found in the passage. The result is the average sentence length.
2. Determine the percentage of difficult words. To do this, count the number of difficult words in the passage. Consider words having three or more syllables difficult. Do not count words that are normally capitalized, that are made into three syllables by the addition of "es" or "ed," or that are a combination of short, easy words such as "nevertheless" and "bookkeeper." Difficult words that occur more than once should be counted each time they occur. Divide the total number of difficult words by the total number of words in the passage to obtain the percentage of difficult words.
3. Compute the fog index by adding the results obtained in steps 1 and 2 and multiplying the sum by 0.4 (Exhibit 10-1).

The fog index corresponds to grade levels common to U.S. school systems. For example, a high school senior (grade twelve) should be able to comprehend writing with a fog index of 12; a high school freshman should be able to comprehend writing with a fog index of 9. To make certain that your writing can be properly understood by your audience, you should generally aim your

EXHIBIT 10-1
Gunning Fog Index Exercise

"My comments are related to a *persistent preoccupation* with the need for placing an increased demand on *priorities* when planning our *various* forms of *communications.* The *acceleration* of *communications evidenced* by a *proliferation* of means and *material* devoted thereto, is stretching to a *critical* point the intended *audiences' capabilities* to *assimilate* masses of *information,* even when confined to that *considered* to be *absolutely essential.* Therefore, it seems, it has become *increasingly important* that a *concentrated* effort be made to filter down the contents of our *communications* to only the most *pertinent.*" (90 words)

Number of sentences	3	
Average length		30
Number of long words	23	
Percentage of total		25.5
Sum		55.5
Multiply sum by		0.4
Fog Index		22.20

writing at slightly below the reading (education) level of your audience. If you are writing to a general audience, rather than to a specific group, aim your writing at the tenth or eleventh grade level.

SENTENCE CONSTRUCTION

Sentences are composed of phrases and clauses; therefore, you should have a basic understanding of these important building blocks. A phrase can be defined simply as a group of related words without a subject and verb and can serve as noun, adjective, adverb, or verb. The underlined parts of the following sentences are phrases:

- Writing a report requires a high degree of skill.
- The woman giving the report is chairperson of the group.
- Her report, while very detailed, was irrelevant to the main issue.
- The assistant was hurriedly writing the report.

A clause is a group of related words containing a subject and a verb. A clause which communicates a complete thought and can stand alone is an independent clause; it is a simple sentence. A clause which cannot stand alone as a complete sentence is a dependent clause; it depends on an independent clause to give it meaning. The following sentence is an independent clause:

The personnel problem is our major concern.

The following sentence contains a dependent clause, underlined once, and an independent clause, underlined twice.

Because he was the best qualified accountant, he was given the job.

   With an understanding of phrases and clauses, you can comprehend the different types of sentences available to you as a business writer. Four basic sentence types, their definition, and examples are given below:

1. A *simple sentence* contains only one independent clause although it may contain several phrases. Example: The questionnaires were sent to 1800 business organizations.
2. A *compound sentence* contains two or more independent clauses, may contain several phrases, but no dependent clauses. Each independent clause could stand alone as a simple sentence. Example: Joseph conducted the interview, and Maria analyzed the results.
3. A *complex sentence* contains one independent clause and at least one dependent clause. Example: When the research assignment was given, the date for completion was firmly established.
4. A *compound-complex sentence* contains at least two independent clauses and at least one dependent clause. Example: Before you joined the staff, errors were very frequent; consequently, we were very inefficient.

   Words and sentences are the writer's main building blocks, and you must learn how to use these resources to communicate your ideas clearly and forcefully. By manipulating words and sentence structure you can either emphasize or deemphasize ideas, and you can, to a very great degree, control the thinking and the perception of your report readers.

EMPHASIS

   To persuade others to act and think as you want them to, you must control their perception to a certain extent. To do this you omit some ideas, you hide some ideas, and you emphasis some ideas. Many sales writers use capitalization, underlining, color, illustrations, handwriting, and dozens of other gimmicks to catch the attention of the reader. But most readers soon tire of these mechanistic emphasis techniques, and their use may be detrimental to the communication. Effective business writers do not rely on such mechanical devices to achieve emphasis. Instead they use more subtle techniques, many of which are explained in the following sections.

Emphasis by Sentence Type

   The different types of sentences convey information about the relationships of thoughts expressed in the sentences. The simple sentence, for example, suggests that the main idea stands alone. The compound sentence suggests that the two ideas it contains are relatively equal in importance and have an important relationship. In the complex sentence, the independent clause receives the greater emphasis and attention. The two independent clauses in the compound-complex sentence are said to be equal and related, but the dependent clause takes a secondary position. Consequently, you should remember that emphatic ideas can be skillfully expressed in a simple sentence and in the independent clause of a complex sentence. Sentences can be deemphasized in compound sentences and in the dependent clauses of complex and compound-complex sentences.

Emphasis by Voice

Writing can be expressed in two types of voice—active and passive. When cast in active voice a sentence shows the doer of the action as the sentence subject. In passive voice the receiver of the action is the subject. (It is important to remember that only sentences involving *action* have an active or passive voice; therefore, others cannot rely on voice as an emphasis aid.) The following two sentences show the difference between active and passive construction:

Active: The production manager ordered 500 rolls of new material.
Passive: Five hundred rolls of new material were ordered.

You can see that in the active-voice sentence, the production manager was emphasized; in the passive-voice sentence, the 500-roll order received the greatest emphasis and the manager was not even mentioned. Unless there is reason to use passive voice, you should generally favor active-voice construction in your business writing. When you want to deemphasize the doer of some action, however, passive voice is an excellent technique to use. For example, the following sentence shows effective use of the passive voice:

The decision was made to terminate the employee after two weeks.

This sentence gives the result of the decision but protects those who made the decision from publicity or criticism.

Emphasis by Position

Writing authorities have generally agreed that the first and last positions in writing are more emphatic than middle positions. The first and last words in sentences, the first and last sentences in paragraphs, and the first and last paragraphs in entire compositions, therefore, should be used to convey information important to the reader. Conversely, middle words, sentences, and paragraphs should be used whenever something needs to be mentioned but does not merit much attention. In the following examples you will notice how position is used to emphasis or deemphasize.

1. Words
   - Errors by the dozens were noticed in his report.
   - In his report dozens of errors were noticed.
2. Sentences
   - Ellen has been a problem employee since she was hired in the accounting department. For example, she has been late to work on numerous occasions, she has made numerous errors in her work, she has had a number of problems with her fellow workers, and she has required an unusual amount of supervision. I am unable to give her a positive recommendation.

- Ellen has required an unusual amount of supervision because of problems she has had with her fellow workers. I am unable to give her a positive recommendation as she has been a problem employee ever since she came into this department. She has made numerous errors in her work and has been late to work on numerous occasions.

Emphasis can also be achieved by using one-sentence paragraphs, and deemphasis is achieved by writing long paragraphs. Whereas the entire contents of a single-sentence paragraph can be read in a single sweep of the eyes, the contents of a long paragraph must be digested bit by bit. During the reading of long paragraphs the mind has a tendency to become tired and to stray from the paragraph content. More will be said of optimal paragraph length later in this chapter.

Emphasis by Tone

Writing is generally said to be expressed in positive, neutral, or negative tone. Positive and negative tone are more emphatic, and neutral tone is generally less emphatic. Negative information, however, can be best de-emphasized when expressed in positive tone. For example, if you had to mention that your company's product sales had declined by 7 percent during the last year, you might write: In spite of the 7 percent decrease in sales, Brand X still ranks third in national sales. Or you might write: In the depression period of 19—, Brand X sales fell by only 7 percent.

In report writing you should be cautious about writing in overly positive or negative terms, since the reader may be suspicious of emotional writing. Unless there is reason to do otherwise, business report writing should generally fall between neutral and slightly positive.

PARAGRAPH DEVELOPMENT

As words grow into sentences, so do sentences grow into paragraphs. As much care needs to be given to paragraph development as is given to sentence construction. The factors of length, unity, and coherence are important in understanding paragraph development.

Length

Business writing authorities suggest that report paragraphs should rarely exceed ten to twelve lines. One of the reasons shorter paragraphs are preferred is that long paragraphs look difficult to read. Look at the two sample pages on page 95 and see if you agree that the one on the left looks easier to read.

Another advantage of shorter paragraphs is that they provide less chance for misreading and distraction. Like long sentences, long paragraphs become so complex that they have a diverse effect on readability. Although paragraphs should be broken when the main concept of the paragraph has been adequately communicated, you may need to make more frequent breaks to avoid paragraphs longer than twelve lines. In such cases begin new paragraphs where you find the most logical breaking points.

 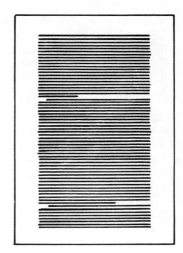

Unity

Unity in paragraphs refers to oneness of thought. Unity relates closely to paragraph length, because when a complete concept or thought has been developed you should begin a new paragraph. As you prepare to write your business report, you should plan your writing by jotting down the major concept to be developed in each paragraph you write. Then as you follow your plan, you will be assured of paragraph unity.

Coherence

Coherence refers to the logical organization of the words and ideas of writing. A coherent report takes the reader on an organized step-by-step journey from the beginning to the end. An incoherent report, on the other hand, tends to meander and leave logic gaps along the way.

Overall report coherence can be achieved from following a well-organized plan. In addition, coherence aids, such as introductory paragraphs, summary paragraphs, headings, and subheadings, can be used to aid total report coherence. More attention is given to overall report coherence in the next section.

Coherence within individual paragraphs is achieved by using logical thinking so that one sentence naturally follows the one before. The two following paragraphs are written to illustrate the difference between coherent and incoherent writing. Notice how the first paragraph wanders and jumps from thought to thought; then see how easy the second paragraph is to follow.

1. How effectively do you use your time? Everybody has the same amount of time; the important thing is how they use it. Business people are as guilty as most anyone. Major time wasters are telephone calls that are unnecessarily long, nonbusiness conversations, and personal inefficiency. Do you control your time or does your time control you? Every day should follow a plan.

2. When it comes to wasting time, business people are as guilty as anyone. Major time wasters in business are telephone calls that are unnecessarily long, nonbusiness conversations, and personal inefficiency. The secret to effective time use is not in getting more time—you have all the time there is. Instead, following a daily plan will enable you to control your time and will make you more efficient and effective.

Along with using common sense and logic in achieving coherence, you should be aware of a number of words and phrases that act as direction signals to a reader. The following list provides a good source of coherence aids that help to show the relationships among ideas to be communicated.

and	therefore	accordingly	instead
but	nevertheless	furthermore	on the other hand
or	consequently	although	in addition
also	otherwise	not only	because
so	hence	moreover	whereas
nor	besides	still	conversely

A coherence test that you may want to apply to your writing is to have an associate read your writing aloud. As he or she reads, notice any pauses, puzzled expressions, rereading, or questions that occur. Mark these trouble spots and rewrite them until your critic agrees that they are clear and coherent.

ORGANIZATION OF THE REPORT

To assist the reader in comprehending the full impact and message of your report, you must follow an appropriate order. At least seven different classifications of order can be used. They are: direct, indirect, geographical, important to least important, chronological, topical, and alphabetic.

Direct Order

When the direct method is used, the main conclusions or recommendations of the report are given at the beginning of the report. The rest of the report then contains detail supporting the conclusions and recommendations. The direct order has not traditionally been popular in formal writing, but it is increasing in popularity among those who must read numerous business reports—especially in short, informal reports. The direct order saves time for the reader since he or she can get the gist of the message without reading the entire report.

The table of contents for a direct-order report might look something like this:

Conclusions and Recommendations
Background and Statement of the Problem
Methods for Solving the Problem
Findings of the Research
Analysis of the Findings
Conclusions and Recommendations (Summary or other appropriate ending for the report)

Indirect Order

Basically the indirect order is opposite from the direct order. The indirect order has traditionally been recommended for business writing. Even today it is used in most long or formal business reports. Following the indirect order, the report first gives the supporting detail and follows with the conclusions and recommendations. Unless the reader skips to the end of the report, he or she must read through the entire report to get to the essence. The indirect order is recommended if the reader needs to be educated or persuaded before being given the gist of the message.

The table of contents for an indirect-order report might look like this:

Background and Statement of the Problem
Methods for Solving the Problem
Findings of the Research
Analysis of the Findings
Conclusions and Recommendations

Geographical Order

The geographical order is used when the content of the report pertains to various locations. For example, a report might be dealing with production quotas of various branches of a company. The report would logically group sections of the report under such headings as: San Francisco Operations, Denver Operations, Dallas Operations, and Chicago Operations.

Important-to-Least-Important Order

If a report must discuss several related items which differ in importance, the writer might want to arrange these sections in an important-to-least-important order. When such an arrangement is used it is usually wise to precede the sections with a statement like "The following sections, listed in order of importance, . . . "

Chronological Order

Many reports have sections that give a historical accounting of several events. In such cases a chronological order is probably the most logical. Financial growth of a company, for example, could be given in one-year segments beginning with the organization of the company and continuing until the present time.

Topical Order

Topical order simply refers to the grouping of related topics and subtopics together. In many cases there will be no real reason for one topic to precede another, so the sections can be grouped as logically as possible according to their relationships. An annual report, for example, might deal with the marketing, financing, production, research and development, personnel, and general management of an organization. The information to be included in the report would, therefore, be grouped under the various topics listed.

Alphabetic Order

The alphabetic ordering of several sections of a report is self-explanatory. The alphabetic order should be used only if there is no other order that seems appropriate because the alphabetic order has no logic in itself. Notice the illogical order that might result if sections were arranged alphabetically instead of chronologically: April, August, February, January, June, July, and so forth.

In most reports a combination of these approaches will be appropriate. For example, a report might have an overall direct order; a chronological order in the introductory section; an important-to-least-important order in the problem statement section; a topical order in the findings section, and an alphabetical order in a special definition section. As a report writer you must first learn what tools are available to you and how and when to use these tools.

SUMMARY

A comparison can be made between the business report writer and a carpenter. To build a house the carpenter follows a plan. To accomplish the various phases of the plan, he or she uses materials and tools that are available. The carpenter knows what all the tools will do and uses them wisely to build a sound structure. Like the carpenter, the business writer also follows a plan. The writer uses his or her writing techniques to build the words and sentences into a well-organized and structurally sound report.

Because good writing is so important, you will want to digest Reading 6, "Ten Commandments for Effective Written Communications," and Reading number 7, "Gamesmanship in Written Communication."

DISCUSSION QUESTIONS AND EXERCISES

1. Why is the ability to empathize so important to the business writer?
2. Considering the effect of word difficulty and sentence length on readability, what guidelines will you follow in your own report writing?
3. Write a short essay on some phase of business with which you are familiar. Then compute the Gunning Fog Index for that writing. If you feel the index is too high or too low, rewrite the essay and change the level of readability.
4. What is the difference between a phrase and a clause?
5. Under what conditions would you use the following types of sentences: simple, compound, complex, compound-complex?
6. Why is excessive use of underlining, capitalization, coloring, and other mechanical emphasis techniques discouraged in business writing?
7. Under what conditions would you use passive-voice sentences?
8. How can positive tone be used to deemphasize negative information?
9. Why should short paragraphs be used in most business writing?
10. How do paragraph length and unity relate to each other?
11. What guidelines would you recommend to a person to make sure that his or her writing was coherent?

12. Using the essay you prepared for Exercise 3, subject your essay to a coherence test. Have another person read your essay aloud, and notice any pauses, puzzled expressions, rereading, or questions that occur during the reading.
13. Give an example of a situation in which you would use each of the seven different orders mentioned in the chapter.

ENDNOTE

1. Reprinted from "The Technique of Clear Writing" (McGraw-Hill, 1968) by written permission of the author and copyright owner, Robert Gunning.

11

Organizing Your Report for Presentation

Business people are constantly challenged to produce more and better reports. Emphasis is often placed on analytical and interpretive report preparation. Thus, to be able to transfer meaning is a very important skill in a report writer. What to say is not the only problem you will encounter. There are also the problems of deciding on the *why*, the *how*, and the *how much*. If you are to write well, you must communicate to someone else what you know—an idea, a fact, or a relationship. The statement, "I know what I want to say but just can't say it" cannot stand in report writing.

Executives value their time highly; they usually insist that reports which they are expected to read should give them the information they need quickly and directly. Generally, they will judge whether a report merits any more time than it takes to read the title. Of course, other members of the firm may be interested in reading parts or all of your report. Keeping your objective in mind, you should design and organize the report to take no more of any reader's time than is necessary.

PREPARING AN OUTLINE

Before you start writing the report, you have planning to do. How do you start? You decide first *what* you want to tell the reader; that is, you *outline*. The outline is the blueprint of the report, the skeleton of the finished presentation. A good outline sets forth the structure of the report and the support for that structure. The finished outline can serve as a table of contents.

There are at least three reasons for using an outline.

1. The outline will help plan and organize factual information needed in the report.
2. An outline will help present facts in a logical and convincing series or pattern.
3. An outline will help determine what to eliminate, add, or develop.

CONSTRUCTING THE OUTLINE

Generally, the findings and conclusions are the most important components of any report and should receive emphasis in the presentation. The amount of detail included will depend on the subject, but if you develop the report through a step-by-step process, the writing should follow a logical sequence (Exhibit 11-1).

EXHIBIT 11-1
Steps Which Should Be Included in Your Report Outline

STAGES IN PREPARING AN OUTLINE

I. Select and Limit the Subject of Your Report
  A. Phrase your specific purpose
  B. Consider your purpose in light of any limiting factors (i.e., time, audience, occasion, etc.)
  C. Restate purpose
II. Develop A Rough Draft of Your Outline
  A. List the main points you expect to cover
  B. Arrange main points into a systematic sequence
  C. Insert subordinate ideas under appropriate main points
  D. Note supporting materials to be used under each main point
  E. Check your rough draft to make certain it covers your subject and fulfills your purpose
III. Put Your Outline Into Its Final Form
  A. State your main points as complete sentences
  B. State your subordinate ideas as complete sentences
  C. Fill in supporting materials in detail
IV. Recheck Your Entire Outline To Make Sure It Accomplishes Your Purpose

Source: Adapted from Alan H. Monroe and Douglas Ehninger, *Principles of Speech Communication* (Glenview, IL: Scott, Foresman & Co., 1975), pp. 149-150.

Good Outline Form

As much detail as possible should be included in the outline to help the reporting process. Also, the outline should meet certain basic requirements. For example, each unit should contain only one idea; important ideas should stand out and less important points should be subordinate. Also, a logical relationship among the divisions of the outline should be established, and a consistent set of symbols (Roman numeral, decimal, or alphanumeric) should be used throughout.

Outline Symbols

There are several styles to help systematize, classify, and organize your material. The most common is the Roman numeral style, but the decimal and alphanumeric can also be used (Exhibit 11-2).

EXHIBIT 11-2
Report Outline Symbols

Roman Numeral	Decimal	Alphanumeric
I.	1.0	A.
A.	1.1	1.
1.	1.11	*a.*
2.	1.12	*b.*
B.	1.2	2.
II.	2.0	B.
A.	2.1	1.
B.	2.2	2.
1.	2.21	*a.*
a.	2.211	(1)
b.	2.212	(2)
2.	2.22	*b.*

Each of the three outline styles is similar; the choice of which to use is a matter of preference. All provide a logical approach to writing and speaking.

USING OUTLINE CAPTIONS THAT TALK

Although you are concerned principally with the topic outline at this stage, you might be interested later in the "talking" outline. In this type you use captions that not only name the criterion or topic but also indicate briefly the outcome of the section. This caption is popular with business writers because, like the newspaper headline, it emphasizes the main point, the main finding, and even a conclusion. By reading the captions, the reader can get the gist of the entire report. The following segments of an outline are examples of captions that talk:

    A. Diamond Ring Sales Are Up
    B. Silverware Sales Remain Unchanged
    C. Costume Jewelry Sales Are Down
    D. Watch Sales Make Rapid Advance

Obviously this style cannot be used until data findings are made and conclusions are drawn. If you are writing a report to be read by top management executives, you may want to use talking captions unless your subject is controversial or you feel that management would not be receptive to your findings without evidence of their validity.

WRITING THE MAJOR DIVISIONS

Once you have completed the outline in detail and have collected the research data, you are ready to write the report. Most of the thinking behind the writing has been done. You have defined the problem, determined the sources of information necessary and the means of collecting it, gathered and analyzed the data, and outlined the report. Now is the time to put the information in rough draft form. (A short report is included at the end of this chapter to illustrate an attempt at report organization and writing.)

WRITING THE DATA SECTIONS

There are three parts in the data-gathering and interpretation section—introduction, presentation of data with explanation, and conclusions. The *introduction* will prepare the reader to receive the data. After the introduction, you will present and *interpret the data;* then you will present *conclusions* regarding the contribution of the data to the solution of the problem. If you are writing a long, detailed report, it will be more effective if you include all three parts in *each division* of your report.

Introduction

The function of any introduction is to prepare the audience. Good speakers begin with what the listener is to get from the speech. They indicate points to be brought out and an indication of the organization of the speech before getting into the subject matter. Good report writers will do the same when they present data.

The introduction to each data section tells

1. The significance of the data
2. The part of the problem-solving procedure applicable to that particular section
3. The plan and order of data presentation

Significance of the Data

Why are you presenting the specific data in the report? What is the significance of the data? If the significance is obvious, do not state it and risk insulting the intelligence of your reader. Do bear in mind, however, that what is obvious to you may not be obvious to someone else.

Problem-Solving Procedure

The written report of your procedure for solving a problem should include information about the nature and sources of data and steps in collecting and processing the data. That part of procedure applying *only* to this subsection should be stated here. If none of the procedure applies *only* to this subsection say nothing about procedure in this subsection.

Plan of Presentation of Data

Readers should be told what they are going to read and the order in which they will read it. Although only one item of coverage may be involved, you will usually have more than one step in your analysis of the item. Explaining these steps helps you, the writer, as well as the reader. It insures that you have analyzed sufficiently and that the account of the analysis is logical and coherent.

Presentation of Data, with Interpretation

There are a number of guidelines to follow in the presentation of data. For example, the narrative should be written so it can be read and understood without any tables or graphic devices. If, however, the basis of the narrative is a table or graph, the report should be "keyed" so readers can refer quickly to the illustration if they desire. You can key illustrations to the narrative by inserting the illustration number in parenthesis immediately following the first statement about the data; for example (Table XX). Unless the presentation is very lengthy, no further mention of the illustration is necessary. If the discussion illustrated by the table or graph is very long the illustration can be inserted at the end of the discussion. In this case, the page number on which the illustration appears should be included and keyed to the text (Table XX, page 00).

Conclusion

After you have presented the data, you must use your judgment regarding the contribution of the data to solving the problem or to answering the question asked in that segment of data. Your final statement about a specific criterion is a value judgment, a *personal opinion*. In drawing conclusions you can sometimes say "yes," "no," "maybe," "to a degree," "probably," "probably not." What does the data contribute?

WRITING THE CONCLUDING SECTION

The concluding section of a report is the "ending." This section synthesizes the meaning of all data that have been presented, analyzed, and interpreted. It is the answer to the problem stated in the introduction.

Content of the Concluding Section

The ending section usually includes conclusions. (An information report may only have summaries.) The concluding section may include recommendations. The relationship between a conclusion and a recommendation can be illustrated in this way: a conclusion, normally, gives the cause of the difficulty; a recommendation suggests a course of action to remedy the problem.

Conclusions

Be selective in deciding what to put in the concluding section. Certainly you would not include in one list all fifty conclusions (if there happened to be that many) that appear throughout the data sections of the report. The greater the amount of data covered by the conclusion the more useful, generally, the conclusions are to the solution of the problem. As a general rule, include in the ending section any conclusions drawn from a consideration of *all* the data.

Recommendations

While all problem-solving analytical reports will have a conclusion, a recommendation is not necessarily required. Whether you include suggestions depends on this purpose of the report.

Arrangement of the Contents of the Concluding Section

There is, of course, no one plan for the arrangement of the elements of the concluding section. *Psychological* arrangement would be recommendations, general conclusions, and intermediate and specific conclusions. *Logical* arrangement of the elements would be the exact reverse—intermediate and specific conclusions, general conclusions, and recommendations. The arrangement in any particular report must be the one that will make the section most comprehensible and coherent for the reader. Whatever arrangement is chosen, an introductory statement telling the reader how the section is arranged is advisable unless the arrangement is obvious.

When your readers are aware of the problem and the attempts to solve it, they will want to know "how it turned out." Tell them immediately after the report introduction. In other words, arrange the overall report psychologically by following the statement of the problem with the answer.

Busy executives do not have time to read completely the dozens of reports that cross their desks. They must read selectively. The concluding section may be all they need to read to make a decision. They may read further to see how you arrived at your conclusions. They will not read the report in its entirety unless they are particularly interested in the subject matter or how the conclusion was reached. For that reason, the conclusions *within* the report must follow logically the presentation of data on which they are based and from which they emerged.

If you will observe the following suggestions, the concluding section—and, the entire report—will be more functional for your reader.

1. *The conclusions and recommendations should be numbered.* When the report is being discussed, the recommendations and conclusions can then be referred to conveniently.

2. *The conclusions and recommendations should be as brief and to the point as possible.* In general, the basic data on which specific conclusions are based should not be included in the ending section.

3. *All conclusions, except strictly general ones, should be keyed to the data sections from which they are derived.* If readers want to see the data behind the specific or intermediate conclusions, they should be able to turn quickly to the point where the discussion begins. If the conclusions are grouped in the ending section under headings identical to the headings of the data sections and subsections, they are automatically keyed. However, if they are not grouped in this way, you can key each conclusion to the place in the report where the discussion begins by inserting the appropriate page number in parenthesis at the end of each conclusion. Should you use this method, explain to the reader in an introduction to the concluding section.

4. *Conclusions should be kept to the minimum necessary to the solution of the problem.* Executives frequently complain that reports contain too many conclusions, many of which are irrelevant or are really not conclusions at all.

5. *The ending section must be coherent.* Reading a hodgepodge of conclusions, some general and some specific, in no planned sequence, is a frustrating experience for any reader.

WRITING THE INTRODUCTORY SECTION

Although the introduction of the report appears first, it probably should be written *last*. Since many introductions appear throughout a report and have relationships with each other, they should be written at the same time—after all data subsections have been written. This is not to say, however, that they will not have been planned earlier.

Delayed Writing of Introduction

You will find it advisable to postpone writing the introductory section until all other sections are written for at least two reasons: First, the introductory section covers topics dealing with all other report sections; therefore, it seems logical to complete the other sections before you write the introduction. Second, you may make changes as you develop the report. You may decide that a certain data section is more important to the solution of your problem than you thought in the beginning. Writing the introduction last will insure its fit with the remaining sections.

The major introduction of a problem-solving analytical report usually includes origin of the problem, statement of the problem, scope and limitations, purpose, procedures for solving the problem, and report plan.

Origin of the Problem

Usually the reader will want to know how the problem originated. What circumstances brought about an awareness of the problem?

Statement of the Problem

The reader will naturally want to know what the problem is. The problem-statement probably should appear as an interrogative sentence because it is a question which you hope to answer, even though your answer need not be conclusive. For example: "What advertisement best suits the local independent retail shoe merchant?"

Occasionally, your problem statement will contain words used in a special or restricted sense, with a meaning different from the usually accepted definition. Therefore, you will need to define these words so your reader cannot misunderstand.

Words that appear elsewhere may need to be defined. If the words are used throughout the report, they should be defined in the introductory section. On the other hand, if they are used throughout one major data section but in no others, they can be defined only in the introduction to that section.

A hypothesis is sometimes given in connection with the problem statement; this is your informed guess at the probable outcome or solution to your study. Although hypotheses are not often found in business reports, an exception would be certain studies made in the research departments of large companies. Likewise, many research theses and dissertations contain a statement of hypothesis.

Scope and Limitations

The scope and limitations may be discussed under one heading or separately, depending somewhat on how the term "limitations" is defined. If by "limitations" you mean those criteria that are not a part of the problem (delimiting factors) and if by "scope" you mean those factors that are a part of the problem, then it would be logical to discuss them together. If, however, you define "limitations" as those things which have hindered or impeded your efforts in securing data, then you would likely devote a separate subsection to the item.

Purpose

The purpose (objective, goal, or aim) of a report is what you hope to achieve when the problem is solved. For example, "The basis of this study is to determine the sales effectiveness of sorority house representatives and to research new promotional techniques concerning representatives and their houses."

Procedures for Solving the Problem

Procedures are ways of collecting, recording, analyzing, and interpreting data. If they apply to all data in two or more major data sections, they must appear in the major introduction. However, procedures that apply to only one section should appear only in the introduction to that section. You have already discussed your procedures when you wrote your proposal (Chapter 6). Therefore, all you need to do here is to repeat in your introduction what you said in your proposal.

Report Plan

The report plan or preview is the last section of the report introduction. Here the reader is told the order in which the major report topics or sections will be discussed and, even more important, why a particular order is followed. The reader should know what to expect and why.

SUMMARY

Reporting principles are much the same, regardless of the subject area, as are the techniques that make reports easy to read or hear. This chapter was concerned with two major principles of report organization: *outlining* and *writing*. Using these aids, you should be able to organize the data you have gathered and analyzed into a systematic, logical unit and to write the rough draft. Keep in mind that the final report should communicate and motivate. Exhibit 11-3 is a brief, formal report using the concepts discussed in this chapter.

Reading 8," How to Develop a Presentation Objective," will assist you in making your reports functional. Although this reading was originally intended for oral technical reports, the steps in developing objectives are also applicable to business report writing.

EXHIBIT 11-3
Sample Short Report

AN ANALYTICAL SALES STUDY IN
CONJUNCTION WITH SORORITY
HOUSE REPRESENTATIVES FOR
THE SHOE STORE

An Analytical Research Study
Presented to Management Personnel of
THE SHOE STORE

---

by
Robin Dial
January 31, 1977

EXHIBIT 11-3 (continued)

TABLE OF CONTENTS

SYNOPSIS

This analytical study for THE SHOE STORE was undertaken *(a)* to determine the sales effectiveness of sorority house representatives and *(b)* to research new promotional techniques concerning representatives and their respective houses.

Research methods mainly consisted of direct comparisons of sales records which listed purchases made by sorority members. Also, research consisted of an analysis of questionnaires and informal interviews held at THE SHOE STORE.

This research study failed to establish its basic assumption that sales had steadily decreased over the past six years. The sales records for the last quarter of 1976 also failed to prove the tentative conclusion that sales would increase substantially because of a new advertising and promotional technique.

With no definite proof for the effectiveness of the advertising campaign, conclusions for this study are limited. Recommendations have been made based on this report's findings. The recommendations have proved this research study to be a worthy and contributing effort.

EXHIBIT 11-3 (continued)

CHAPTER I

INTRODUCTION

The need for effective advertisement and promotional campaigns is becoming greater and greater in the modern retail business. Advanced advertisement and promotional techniques are introduced to the public every day through national advertising agencies. National retail outlets benefit greatly from these national campaigns. But what advertisement best suits the local independent retail merchant?

This study will take an analytical view of one segment of advertisement and promotion for THE SHOE STORE. This segment will be sorority house representatives, with emphasis on recorded sales for each house.

A. PURPOSE:

The basis of this study is to determine the sales effectiveness of sorority house representatives and to research new promotional techniques concerning representatives and their houses.

B. SCOPE:

Five areas of study contribute to the scope of this study.

1. Recorded sales for each house (representative's sales book) recorded after each individual purchase.
2. Results of style shows as seen through sales records and questionnaires.
3. Results of house displays as seen through sales records and questionnaires.
4. Results of bulletin board advertising within sorority houses as seen through questionnaires and informal interviews with customers at THE SHOE STORE.
5. Conversation about THE SHOE STORE within the house as seen through questionnaires.

C. DESIGN:

This study will first make comparisons between past sales records and the sales record for this year. A new advertisement and promotion system was used to stimulate sales in the current year. Second, an analysis will be made on questionnaires completed by members living in the sorority houses.

D. LIMITATIONS:

This study will be limited in the scope that direct results of sales will only be determined by the registered sales in the representative's sales book for the period October 1- December 31 for the years 1970, 1971, 1972, 1973, 1974, 1975, and 1976. An additional limitation will be that direct sales comparisons will only be for the houses in which THE SHOE STORE has had a sales representative every year and those for which questionnaires were returned: i.e., Tri Delt, Theta, Alpha Chi, Pi Phi, and Kappa.

E. IMPORTANCE:

The completed study will serve as a review of past sales trends and advertising techniques. Changes for future advertising and promotion will be considered to stimulate future sales.

EXHIBIT 11-3 (continued)

CHAPTER II

REVIEW OF RESEARCH

A. SALES RECORDS

Three types of analysis have been made of the recorded sales for the five houses this study has been limited to. Table I presents each sorority house's sales for the seven year period. As the reader may note, this table shows relatively unstable sales for the seven year period.

Table II represents total sales for the individual houses. This table compares houses for the highest and lowest total sales. Again, total sales are unstable but seem to indicate a decreasing trend.

B. QUESTIONNAIRES

An analysis of the returned questionnaires was made on 402 completed questionnaires. The total includes questionnaires from the five houses on which this study is based: Tri Delt, Theta, Alpha Chi, Pi Phi, and Kappa.

In comparing shoe displays, style shows, announcements, and bulletin board advertising, the greatest attention getter was the style show with 65.5% compared with 11.2% for representative's announcements about THE SHOE STORE, 20.5% for shoe displays, and .02% for bulletin board advertising. Comparing purchase motivators, sorority women were more strongly motivated to purchase by style shows, with 46.9% compared with 21.3% for shoe displays (Tables I and II).

TABLE I

Total Sales Per House

	Tri Delt	Theta	Alpha Chi	Pi Phi	Kappa
1970	$ 1188	$ 891	$ 691	$ 1963	$ 1236
1971	1062	987	624	2715	810
1972	720	759	384	1050	780
1973	870	1308	561	993	942
1974	939	1569	804	729	525
1975	570	501	1494	1098	690
1976	726	990	261	1743	669
Total	$ 6075	$7005	$ 4719	$10311	$ 5652

TABLE II

Total Sales Per Year

	1970	1971	1972	1973	1974	1975	1976
Tri Delt	$1188	$1062	$ 720	$ 870	$ 939	$ 570	$ 726
Theta	891	987	759	1308	1569	501	990
Alpha Chi	591	624	384	561	804	1494	261
Pi Phi	1983	3715	1050	993	729	1098	1743
Kappa	1236	810	780	942	525	690	669
Total	$5889	$6198	$3593	$4674	$4566	$4353	$4389

EXHIBIT 11-3 (continued)

C. INFORMAL INTERVIEWS

Informal interviews given at THE SHOE STORE revealed that the representatives were doing an effective job, but they indicated that shoe prices were too expensive for their budgets.

CHAPTER III

FINDINGS

A. TOTAL SALES

The combined sales records for the years 1970 through 1976 (October 1- December 31) show Pi Phi with the largest total sales. Total sales vary from house to house; because from year to year there is a different representative for the houses, no trend can be established for total house sales.

B. INDIVIDUAL HOUSE SALES

Individual representatives vary from house to house and from year to year; therefore, it is difficult to establish a definite trend for total sales within one house. Three out of the five houses being analyzed show an increase for the last quarter of 1976 where additional advertising and promotion was used. Because of such unstable sales, this report cannot establish any definite trends.

C. QUESTIONNAIRES

A total of 900 questionnaires were distributed to the five houses, with 402 being completed and returned, yielding a 44.67 percent return. The objective of the questionnaires was to evaluate advertising techniques for THE SHOE STORE in conjunction with the house representatives. Questions varied very little from house to house. A total analysis of the 402 completed questionnaires reveals the style show as the greatest advertising technique used within the house. Suggestions were requested concerning the effectiveness of the sorority house representatives and how the representative could be more effective. Table III contains a summary of responses from the questionnaires.

Some of the suggestions are invalid to productive advertising, but several of the sugestions should be considered. These suggestions should be considered on an individual house basis in an attempt to stimulate sales by better advertisement for that house.

D. 1976 SALES SURVEY ON STYLE SHOWS AND DISPLAYS

In the last quarter of 1976 only, record was kept of purchases directly related to style shows and show displays. Whenever a purchase was made by a sorority member, she was asked if her purchase motive was because of the style show or the shoe display. Her response was recorded to give record to a limited portion of purchase motives. A combined total of the five houses reveals that 19.3 percent of sales were contributable to the shoe display and 16.5 percent were contributable to the style shows (Table III).

114

EXHIBIT 11-3 (continued)

TABLE III

List of Suggestions

Tri Delt:
1. THE SHOE STORE should be sure that the representative is fully aware of new shoe shipments and current prices.
2. Prices at THE SHOE STORE are too high.
3. The representative should "talk it up more" about THE SHOE STORE.
4. THE SHOE STORE should get a new representative.
5. THE SHOE STORE should not have style shows during dinner.
6. THE SHOE STORE should have more displays in the houses.

Theta:
1. The representative should make more conversation about THE SHOE STORE.
2. THE SHOE STORE should have more displays and style shows.
3. THE SHOE STORE should have more bulletin board advertising.
4. The representative should live in the house.

Alpha Chi:
1. THE SHOE STORE should have more style shows and displays.
2. THE SHOE STORE should have more representatives per house.
3. Shoes are too expensive.
4. Sell shoes after style shows.
5. The representative should offer rides to THE SHOE STORE at designated times.
6. Give shoes away. Free displays.

Pi Phi:
1. With a shoe purchase, give a free certificate toward another pair.

Kappa:
1. People aren't going to buy without money.
2. Have more announcements about new shoes.
3. Have more displays.
4. Give free samples.

CHAPTER IV

CONCLUSIONS AND RECOMMENDATIONS

This report began with the basic assumption that for the last six years, sorority house sales had steadily declined because of continuing lack of interest both on the part of the sorority sales representatives and THE SHOE STORE.

A. TENTATIVE CONCLUSION

The study had hoped to prove that new and additional promotional techniques in direct relation to the houses and more effective representation by the house representatives would show a definite increase in sales. An entirely new advertising form and two previously used promotional techniques were used in the attempt to increase sales.

EXHIBIT 11-3 (continued)

The new form of advertisement was a bulletin board advertisement that was placed in each individual house. Included on the advertisement was the representative's name, THE SHOE STORE's advertising sign, and a listing of all the shoe brands sold.

The style shows, the most effective form of advertising within the houses, were used with greater consistency between the houses and greater emphasis was placed on seasonal shoe styles.

Shoe displays have been used for advertising before but in no orderly pattern; during this study displays were set up in each house on selected weekends. The specific weekends were selected to correspond with home football games and weekends that attracted parents to the houses.

The combined techniques were closely observed and analyzed to gain whatever information might be produced toward their effectiveness.

B. CONCLUSIONS

Observation of recorded sales for the past six years has failed to correspond to this report's basic assumption. The recorded sales for this year, 1976 (October 1— December 31), have failed to correlate to the report's tentative conclusion. There are varied changing amounts of total sales and individual house sales; therefore, this report has no proof on which to base any definite conclusions.

C. RECOMMENDATIONS

This report has not established any definite trends in past sales for the sorority houses. The 1976 sales data did not prove that the new advertising and promotional techniques were effective in increasing sales. Therefore, my personal recommendations to THE SHOE STORE will be my own opinion. This opinion is based on three years work experience at THE SHOE STORE and my direct relations with the house representatives.

1. Consideration should be given to the fact that this is the first year for the new promotional techniques. They should be continued and given a longer period to prove their effectiveness.
2. The list of suggestions presented by the sorority women should be given serious consideration. The suggestions should be considered for each individual house and additional promotional techniques should be adopted in relation to those suggestions.
3. Each sorority representative should spend a minimum of two hours a week at THE SHOE STORE becoming familiar with the shoes and their prices.
4. THE SHOE STORE should be more selective in choosing their representatives. Whoever the representative may be, she should have a genuine interest in shoes and THE SHOE STORE.
5. The style shows should be given much greater consideration. Since they are the most effective advertisement method for THE SHOE STORE within the sorority house, they should be carefully planned. Models should be carefully selected for the shoes they are to model. A greater emphasis should be placed on seasonal shoes and correct accessories to be worn with those shoes.

An analysis and consideration of this report by THE SHOE STORE should lead to future advertisement and promotional judgment that will be effective toward increased sales.

DISCUSSION QUESTIONS AND EXERCISES

1. Why is the statement "I know what I want to say but just can't say it," invalid?
2. Why should an outline be used? When should it be constructed?
3. What is a good procedure to follow in preparing an outline?
4. What are the most commonly used report outline symbols?
5. What are the basic requirements an outline should meet?
6. Explain the difference between a topic outline and talking captions. Which type would you use in constructing an outline of a problem on which you have not yet collected data? Why?
7. Why may talking captions be preferred by readers of a report?
8. What is the main purpose of the concluding section of a report?
9. What do the terms "logical arrangement" and "psychological arrangement" mean, as they apply to the analytical report? Which arrangement is preferred for the data sections and subsections of a report? Why?
10. Why is the psychological arrangement so frequently used in business reports?
11. What are specific conclusions and their source? Intermediate conclusions? General conclusions? Which conclusions are the most important and why?
12. When does the concluding section include recommendations? When not?
13. Define a conclusion and a recommendation.
14. What is the purpose of an introductory statement to the concluding section of a report?
15. What is the purpose of numbering the conclusions and recommendations in the concluding section?
16. Explain the meaning of the term "keying" the conclusions. Should all conclusions be keyed? When are they automatically keyed? Show how to key a conclusion.
17. Why would a report writer delay the writing of the introductory section to a report?
18. Explain why the topics covered in an introduction will vary among reports.
19. What relation does the problem statement have to the origin of the problem?
20. Explain the relationship between the hypothesis and the statement of the problem.
21. Why is it sometimes necessary to define words in a problem statement?
22. Explain two possible meanings or interpretations that might be given to the term "limitations."
23. Is the purpose of a problem-solving analytical report always to make recommendations for management consideration? Explain your answer.
24. Why are explanations of procedures frequently found in some parts of a report but not in others?
25. Describe why you might explain a particular order for presenting the major topics or sections in a report.
26. Classify (group into divisions) the data you have been gathering for your research project.
27. Based on your classifications of criteria in exercise 26 prepare a detailed formal outline of your research project to submit to your instructor. Follow as many guidelines given in this chapter as possible for your outline.
28. Write the major sections of your investigation, based on (a) your outline and (b) the procedures studied in this chapter. Be concerned primarily with getting information on paper. You can polish the writer writing style later.

12

Visual Communication Techniques

Undoubtedly you have heard the statement that one picture is worth a thousand words. Business communication experts have long realized the impact that can be made by well-designed graphic illustrations to complement the basic business report. Because of the importance tables and graphs play in business reports, your report writing instruction would not be complete without a basic understanding of table and graph construction.

TABLES

Tables cannot truly be categorized as graphic aids or visual aids; but because, like graphs, they summarize a group of data, they are included in this chapter. Tables consist of rows and columns of statistical data or alphabetic information. Tables have traditionally been numbered with large Roman numerals, although many contemporary reports are using Arabic numerals instead, the table number and title centered in uppercase letters above the table. The first table to appear in a report should be number I (or 1), and all following tables should be numbered consecutively including those in appendixes. Exhibit 12-1 shows basic table format with the various parts identified.

EXHIBIT 12-1
Basic Table Format

TABLE NUMBER
TITLE

Stub Head	Column Head	Column Head	Column Head	Column Head
Stub	Data	Data	Data	Data
Stub	Data	Data	Data	Data
Stub	Data	Data	Data	Data
Total	Sum	Sum	Sum	Sum

More complex tables may have two levels of column headings as shown in Exhibit 12-4. In a few instances tables may require a "total" column rather than a "total" row; however, many tables do not need either. Footnotes and source notes should be placed immediately below the table in typical footnote format.

Tables may be constructed in three basic formats: open, ruled, and boxed. Exhibit 12-2, 12-3, and 12-4 illustrate these three styles.

EXHIBIT 12-2
Open Table with Alphabetic and Numeric Information

Recipients of Annual Service Award
19--
Mountain-Plains Manufacturing, Inc.

Name	Department	Years of Service
Joe Williams	Shipping	4
Sarah Poecker	Office	4
Charles Warenski	Administration	16
Rudolph Tolski	Customer Service	8
Sheila Mashika	Personnel	6
Jason Allen	Receiving	3

EXHIBIT 12-3
Ruled Table with Source Note

JKL Corporation
Statement of Combined Net Assets
(Figures in Thousands)

	1977	1976
Assets		
Current	$ 73,418	$ 45,802
Property, plant, and equipment	536,002	431,945
	609,420	477,747
Less Liabilities		
Current	73,109	39,360
Long-term debt	196,867	208,216
Other	67,309	29,331
	337,285	276,907
Combined net assets	$272,135	$200,840

Source: John J. Kempse, "Hypothetical Report," New York, 1977.

EXHIBIT 12-4
Boxed Table with Two Levels of Column Headings

Number of Patients Treated at
Meredith General Hospital
1968 to 1978

Type of Patient	Year					
	1968	1970	1972	1974	1976	1978
Adult:						
Surgical	2,926	2,981	3,104	3,241	3,429	3,672
Nonsurgical	5,626	5,722	5,906	6,281	6,499	6,745
Youth and Child:						
Surgical	2,804	2,875	2,929	3,018	3,126	3,374
Nonsurgical	733	748	826	931	1,061	1,220
Births	2,291	2,343	2,354	2,481	2,462	2,511
TOTAL	14,380	14,669	15,119	15,952	16,577	17,522

You can see that the difference between the open and ruled tables is the addition of full-width rulings between the table number and title and the column headings, between the column headings and the columns, between the columns and the total row, and after the total row. There should be one space above and below all horizontal rulings in the table. The difference between the ruled format and the boxed format is the addition of horizontal rulings between all columns in the table. In most cases the sides of tables need not be ruled; however, in some cases you will want to enclose the table completely by making a vertical ruling at both margins and a horizontal ruling above the table number and below the last item in the table, whether a total row or a source note.

GENERAL GUIDELINES FOR CONSTRUCTING TABLES

At least three spaces should be left above and below all tables to separate them from the text.(90) Tables should be placed as near their reference in the text as possible, although it is preferable to locate them after the paragraph in which they are first mentioned. If there is insufficient room for a table on the page where it is first mentioned, it should be placed at the first paragraph break on the following page. Reference to tables should be by table number rather than by writing "as the following table indicates."

Footnotes should be indicated by raised letters ([a], [b]) or by symbols (*,**) if the table consists of numbers; if the table consists of alphabetic information, the footnotes should be indicated by raised numbers ([1], [2]). These footnotes must not be numbered in sequence with the regular text footnotes, however; a new series should begin for each table.

When information is not available at a point in a column, indicate the unavailability with a dash (—), three or more periods (. . .), or by the abbreviation *n.a.* If all the figures in a column are in thousands or millions, for example, the last three or six zeros may be omitted if a note in the column heading indicates "figures in thousands" or "amounts in millions." When financial columns are included in a table, the first figure and the total figure in each column should be preceded by a dollar sign ($).

Many beginning report writers make the mistake of giving insufficient interpretation of tables they include in their reports. As a result, the reader must ferret out the important conclusions that arise from the table. Therefore, you should consider the table an aid, not a self-explanatory entity. Statements such as "Table XX indicates a close relationship between . . ." or "As Table XX illustrates, . . . " help the reader to understand quickly the important information that can be gained from your tables. Tables should be referred to by number, not by " the following table" or "the preceding table."

GRAPHS

Graphic aids replace quantities with lines, bars, and segments of circles. Because there is a more visible difference between bars of different lengths, for example, graphs can create a greater visual impact than the figures they represent. Three different types of graphs—line, bar, and circle—are used most frequently in business reports and are explained and illustrated in the following section. Throughout these sections the terms "charts" and "graphs" are used interchangeably and should be considered to be synonymous.

LINE GRAPHS

Line graphs are used to show change in one or more variables over a period of time. The Y axis (vertical) of a line chart is used to show the quantity of measurement being used in the graph, and the X axis (horizontal) shows the period of time included in the chart. Exhibit 12-5 illustrates a simple line chart.

When two or more lines are included in a line graph, they must be clearly distinguishable. Color or variations in the lines (solid lines, dots, dashes, dots and dashes) may be used to ensure that the reader can discriminate among different lines. As Exhibit 12-6 illustrates, a legend must be included to identify the different types of lines used. In most cases, no more than three lines should be used in a single chart, especially if the lines intersect at any point in the graph.

Another form of line graph is the component line graph which shows the several parts which make up 100 percent of the variable being illustrated in the graph. Exhibits 12-7 and 12-8 show two variations of the component line graph.

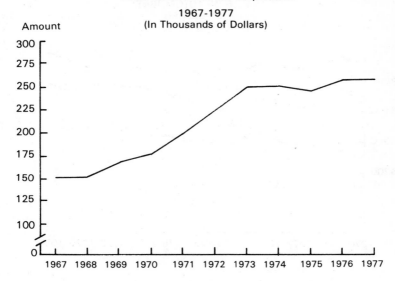

EXHIBIT 12-5
Single-line Graph with Straight-line Break

Gross Revenue of ABC Corporation

1967-1977
(In Thousands of Dollars)

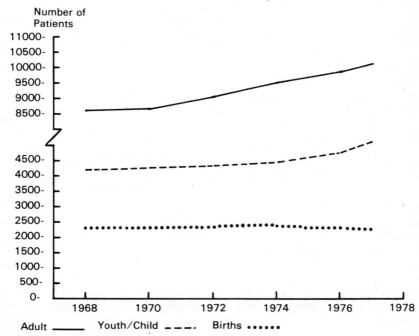

EXHIBIT 12-6
Multiple-line Graph with Z Break

Number of Patients Treated at
Meredith General Hospital

EXHIBIT 12-7
Component Line Graph with Raw-Value Y Axis

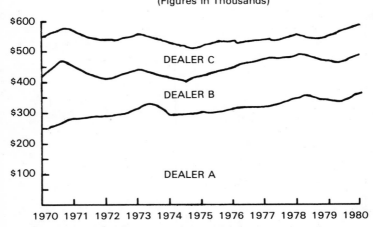

SALES OF AUTOMOBILES
BY DEALER
(Figures in Thousands)

EXHIBIT 12-8
Component Line Graph with 100 Percent Y Axis

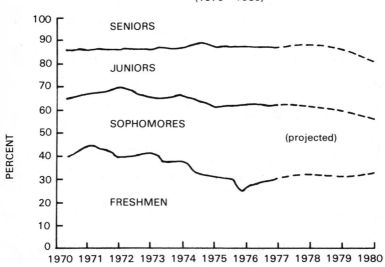

Enrollment at State University
by Class
(1970 - 1980)

Line Graph Guidelines

Several guidelines should be followed in designing line charts. Violation of these guidelines frequently results in misrepresentation of the data being displayed.

1. The Y axis should begin at zero. If the path of the data is far above zero, a break in the Y axis can be made. Exhibits 12-5 and 12-6 illustrate two acceptable ways to break the Y axis. The X axis begins at the point of time corresponding to the first data point.
2. Tick marks corresponding to the quantity points on the Y axis and the time points on the X axis should be clearly marked. Grid lines behind the lines on the chart should be marked very lightly, if they are used at all. Too many lines on a chart give a cluttered appearance.
3. The distance between the tick marks on the Y axis and those on the X axis should not be too disproportionate. You can see that expanding the distance between the tick marks on the Y axis would suggest to the reader much more radical change than is really true. Therefore, select the distance between the tick marks that will give the most accurate picture to the reader.
4. Make all values on the Y axis an equal distance apart arithmetically. For example, use values such as 25, 50, 75, and 100 rather than 21, 48, 72, and 100.

Care in constructing graphs will not only give them a neat appearance but will also make them easier to read and understand.

BAR GRAPHS

Closely associated with line graphs are bar graphs used primarily to show the values of one or more variables over a certain period of time or at a particular point in time. Bar graphs are usually more difficult to construct than line graphs, but a bit of care will enable you to produce attractive bar graphs. While line charts can be useful for analytical purposes, bar charts are usually used for simple comparison. Consequently, bar charts should be kept relatively simple and should communicate their intended message as forcefully and clearly as possible.

Bar graphs are constructed much the same as line graphs, including the X and Y axes. Instead of representing the variables with lines, however, bar charts show the quantity or value of the variables with vertical or horizontal bars. Exhibit 12-9 shows the basic parts of vertical and horizontal bar charts.

The charts shown in Exhibit 12-9 compare only one variable over a certain time period. In many cases, however, you will find it necessary to compare two or even three variables over a time period. Since each additional variable adds complexity to a bar graph, you should avoid comparing more than three variables on any one chart. Exhibit 12-10 shows a multiple-bar chart used to compare two variables.

Frequently a report writer wants to show various parts of each bar in a bar graph, in which case a component bar chart is useful. Each bar in a compo-

124

EXHIBIT 12-9
Vertical and Horizontal Bar Graphs

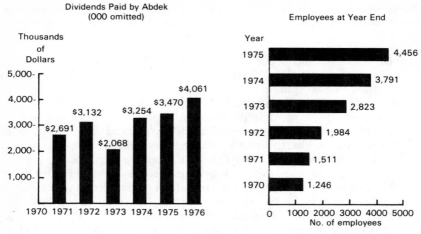

Dividends Paid by Abdek
(000 omitted)

Employees at Year End

EXHIBIT 12-10
Multiple-Bar Chart with Cross Hatching
Daytime and Evening Students
Attending Foothills Community College

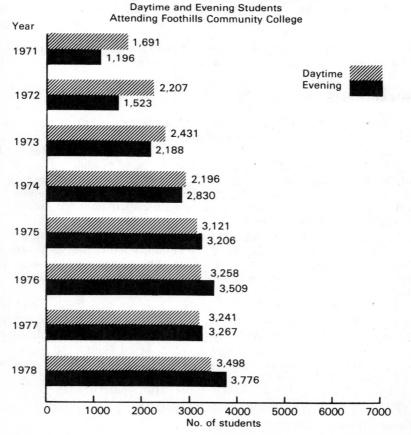

nent bar chart is assumed to be 100 percent, and the subdivisions of each bar equal 100 percent of the bar. Subdivisions may be expressed in raw figures or may be shown in percentages. The type of data shown in component bar graphs could also be illustrated in circle charts, although a single circle chart cannot show change over a period of time. A component bar graph is illustrated in Exhibit 12-11.

EXHIBIT 12-11
Component Bar Chart with Cross Hatching

Enrollment at Foothills Community College
1971-1978

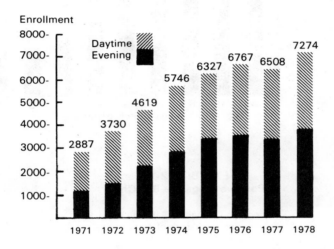

Bar charts are not always used to show change over a certain time period; they can be effectively used to show the status of several variables at a certain point in time. When such a comparison is wanted, it is frequently helpful to the reader to rank the bars in ascending or descending order. With such an arrangement the reader can tell at a glance the variables that fluctuate most from the average. You can readily see in Exhibit 12-12 that Sales Representative *A* is the most productive and that Sales Representatives *C, F,* and *G* are least productive.

The final bar graph to be discussed is the positive-negative bar graph. This type of graph is used when the data to be illustrated have both positive and negative values. With the positive-negative chart the zero line is not placed at the left of the horizontal bar chart or at the bottom of the vertical bar chart. Instead it is placed at or near the middle of the graph to provide ample space on either side for the positive and negative bars. As with most bar graphs, the positive-negative bar graph can be used to show the change of variables over a period of time or to show the value of several variables at a single point in time. Exhibit 12-13 illustrates the productivity of several products during a calendar year.

EXHIBIT 12-12
Single Bar Chart with Bars in Descending Order

Productivity of Sales Representatives
January - June, 1978

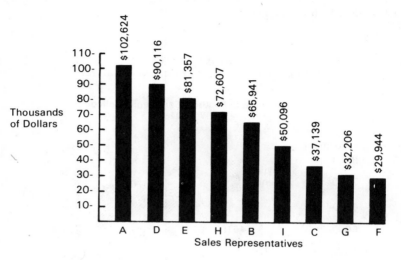

Thousands
of Dollars

Sales Representatives

EXHIBIT 12-13
Positive-Negative Bar Chart

Percentage Change in Sales by Product
for the Month of April

Percent Increase or
Decrease from Average

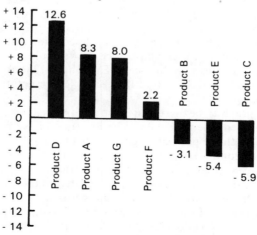

Guidelines for Constructing Bar Graphs

Several principles should be well understood as you construct bar charts for your business reports. These principles, presented here as guidelines, will enable you to get maximum impact from the bar charts you employ.

1. Keep the width of all bars equal. The width is not as critical as consistency. If a bar is both longer and wider than its counterpart, the difference between the two bars will be exaggerated.
2. Keep the same width of space between all bars. This width is usually one-half to one-third the width of the bars themselves. In multiple bar charts, there is no space between the bars shown at each time point. Between each time point, however, space is provided to help the reader differentiate between the several groups of bars.
3. Label the bars and the values of the bars clearly. When a multiple bar chart is used, provide a legend somewhere within the boundaries of the chart to identify the variable which each bar represents (Exhibit 12-10). The value of each bar can be identified by a numeric figure located within the bar itself or at the end of the bar as shown in Exhibit 12-12 and 12-13.
4. Use color or crosshatching to show contrast among several bars. Different colored bars provide ease of discrimination for the report reader. Colored adhesive strips can be purchased for the construction of bar charts, and these strips can be attractively applied with little difficulty. When color is not possible, however, the use of crosshatching is appropriate. A T-square and a triangle are effective in making crosshatch lines within the bars (Exhibit 12-13).
5. The Y axis should begin at zero unless a positive-negative bar graph is used. A break in the axis should be shown if the bars are too high to show numbers continually from zero.
6. Use grid lines only if necessary. The more lines on a graph, the more cluttered and complex the chart appears. (62)
7. Either horizontal or vertical bars may be used. Since far more horizontal than vertical bars can be placed on a standard-size page, however, horizontal bars should be used whenever a large number of bars will appear in a single chart.

To increase your awareness of bar graphs and their use in business reports, you should watch for bar graphs in your reading. In national magazines, business magazines, newspapers, and annual reports you will find bar graphs used very frequently. By studying these graphs you will notice different adaptations and techniques that you can apply in the graphs you will make when preparing reports.

CIRCLE GRAPHS

Circle charts, frequently called pie charts, are used to represent 100 percent of a certain factor; for example, sales, expenses, or workers during a certain period of time could be shown in a circle graph. The subdivisions of the graph would then be shown by several slices in the pie. Exhibit 12-14 illustrates a basic circle graph.

EXHIBIT 12-14
Circle Graph

Percentage Yield of All Divisions for 1978

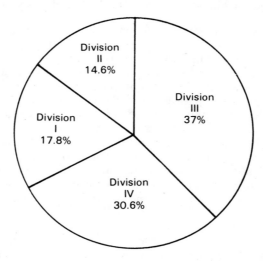

The circle graph can be used to show no more than one "whole" with its subdivisions, and it cannot show change over a period of time. Hence, it is somewhat limited in its use since many graphs must show more information than this.

Guidelines for Constructing Circle Graphs

Circle graphs are relatively simple to construct, but several guidelines should be followed to make them consistent with accepted standards.

1. The first slice in the circle should be drawn from the center of the circle to the top of the circle—12 o'clock position. The several segments of the chart should be arranged in descending order going clockwise around the circle. When one of the segments is labeled as "miscellaneous" or "other," however, it should appear immediately to the left of the 12 o'clock position even if it is not the smallest segment.
2. Segments may be emphasized by crosshatching or coloring or by removing a certain segment from the rest of the circle as is shown in Exhibit 12-15.
3. Each segment of the chart should be identified. If the segment is large enough the identifying words can be typed inside; otherwise, the identifying words can be typed immediately outside with a line connecting them to the appropriate segment.
4. The specific percentage and/or amount of each segment should be identified, usually with the words that identify the segment.
5. Make the size of the circle appropriate to the page. Although there is no recommended size, you must make the chart large enough to be readable yet not so large that it is overbearing.

EXHIBIT 12-15
Circle Graph with Cross-Hatched Segment Removed

Spending Patterns of U.S. Consumers 19--

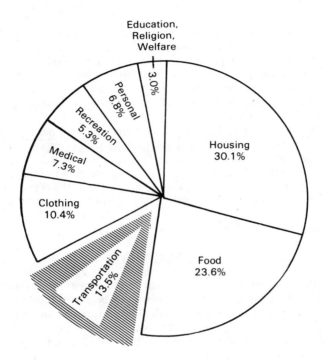

Source: Hypothetical Research Company.

You will find that your use of circle graphs is usually rather limited when compared with line and bar charts. Line and bar charts are more flexible in their applicability, and it is easier visually to compare the length of bars and the height of lines than the area of segments in a circle. Nevertheless, the circle chart can be used effectively when the various subdivisions of a single factor need to be shown. Because the circle chart is so simple and straightforward, its impact can be significant.

GENERAL GUIDELINES FOR GRAPH CONSTRUCTION

Traditionally titles have been placed below the graphs, but an increasing number of report writers are placing the chart titles above the respective charts. Charts in a report should be numbered with arabic numerals (1, 2) consecutively throughout the report. Charts and tables should always be numbered separately, although both tables and charts may use arabic numbering in the same report.

Titles and subtitles should be concise yet descriptive. In as few words as possible, they should identify the appropriate who, what, why, when, where, and how information. The reader should have no questions about the intent of a graph after reading the title. Any required source notes associated with charts should be placed beneath the charts, beginning at or near the left margin.

Charts are frequently set off from the report text which surrounds them by horizontal lines above and below the charts or by a line that forms a complete box around the charts. While neither method is necessary, the ruled frame gives the chart added emphasis and increases reader attention. If rulings are used, at least three blank spaces should be left above and below a chart. If no rulings are used, at least an inch of blank space should be left above and below the charts.

Charts may be placed in the report body and in the appendix. If a graphic presentation makes a significant contribution to the report, it should be placed in the body. If the report body will not be seriously affected by the omission of a chart, however, it should be placed in the appendix. There is no clear-cut guideline for making this determination; the report writer must make this decision based on his or her feeling about the importance of each graph.

SUMMARY

Above all, the report writer should realize the importance of interpreting a chart. Ideally the content of the graph should be mentioned and the graph shown and interpreted. Although physical limitations of standard-size paper often preclude this arrangement, the report writer must not neglect the responsibility of interpreting the chart. Both graphs and tables are rather cold presentations of facts and figures. For example, they might state that sales for the past year were $14,306.780. What they really tell, however, is whether the figures are good, poor, or average. Hence, the report writer must give meaning to the graphs by interpretation and evaluation. Only then can they serve their intended function as a report aid.

Reading 9, "Effective Communication of Financial Data," is an excellent example of the points emphasized in this chapter.

DISCUSSION QUESTIONS AND EXERCISES

1. Which of the following two table numbers is correct? Why?
   TABLE III   TABLE 3
2. What is the major difference between open, ruled, and boxed tables? Under what circumstances would you use each of these styles of tables?
3. If there is insufficient space for a table or chart on the page on which it is first mentioned, where should it be placed?
4. If information is not available at a certain point in a column of a table, what should you do?
5. Complete the following sentence: The Y axis of a line chart is used to show

6. What differences can you notice in a component line chart and a component bar chart?
7. Why is it important for the Y axis of line and bar charts to begin at 0?
8. Why is it possible to misrepresent facts by using disproportionate tick marks on the X and Y axes?
9. What major advantage do line and bar charts have over circle charts?
10. Why should the width of all bars be kept equal in a bar graph?
11. Under what conditions might you use horizontal bars?
12. If you want to graph the change in sales volume for Company X during the years 1970 through 1978, would you use a circle chart? Why?

13

Prefatory and
Appended Sections

When all sections that make up the introduction, body, and conclusion of the report have been written, you are ready to consider the prefatory and appended parts of your report. You must first know their purpose, content, and format.

THE PREFATORY SECTIONS

Since many reports you write will be read by several people (in the business environment this may include people at different administrative levels, some of whom you may not know personally), you frequently will use most of the elements of a long, formal report. These components may include any or all of the following: cover, title fly, title page, letter of transmittal, table of contents, table of illustrations, synopsis, bibliography, and appendix.

Cover

The cover identifies and protects the contents. It also identifies the writer and may carry numeric or alphabetic information for reference purposes. The cover should be as durable as its anticipated or projected use requires and attractive and appealing visually. The title should be clearly legible.

Title Fly

The title fly repeats the title inside the cover. The cover title and title fly should read exactly the same and should adequately describe the contents. Titles of more than one line in length should be arranged in the form of an inverted pyramid; for example:

A STUDY OF THE ASSOCIATION AMONG ECONOMIC UNDER-
STANDING, DOGMATISM, LIBERALISM/CONSERVATISM,
AND OTHER AFFECTIVE ELEMENTS FOR ECONOMICS
STUDENTS IN SELECTED TEXAS HIGH SCHOOLS

The wording of a title should tell on a single reading what is covered in the report since it sets the pattern for the organization of the report. Logically, a complete title cannot be written in one or two words. Thus it is helpful to build your title around the five *W*'s—*who, what, where, when,* and *why.* Try to answer as many of the *W*'s as possible, either by statement or implication. Sometimes *how* may be added to this list.

Title Page

The title page restates the title and provides essential identification. It should give the title of the report, the name of the person(s) submitting the report, the name(s) of the person to whom the report is being submitted, the company name, and the date (Exhibit 13-1). The words "submitted to" and "by" often precede the names. Sometimes the phrases "authorized by" or "approved by" also may appear on the title page.

EXHIBIT 13-1
Title Page

A STUDY OF THE ASSOCIATION AMONG ECONOMIC UNDERSTANDING, DOGMATISM, LIBERALISM/CONSERVATISM, AND OTHER AFFECTIVE ELEMENTS FOR ECONOMIC STUDENTS IN SELECTED TEXAS HIGH SCHOOLS

Submitted to
Educational Resource Associates
Houston, Texas

By
Robin Dial
University of Houston
Houston, Texas 77004
June I, 1976

Letter of Transmittal

The letter of transmittal accompanies and transmits a report to the intended reader. It serves about the same purpose as the preface or foreword in a textbook. This letter is preferably written in a direct style. This prefatory part of the report is generally used to express the writer's feelings about the research project or to provide helpful information about the report.

The letter of transmittal begins with a statement relative to the actual transmission and is followed by a brief reference to the authorization and an identification of the report problem or topic. If a synopsis does not accompany the report, the letter may review briefly the more significant findings, conclusions, or recommendations.

The letter of transmittal may contain a few statements, observations, explanations, or opinions of a personal nature; for example, 1) your attempts to be objective; 2) your surprise, pleasure, or disappointment concerning the outcomes of some of the findings; or 3) an offer to supply additional information or to make further inquiry, should either be desired. The letter should end with some expression of gratitude for having been given the assignment and possibly an offer or willingness to accept future assignments (Exhibit 13-2).

EXHIBIT 13-2
Letter of Transmittal

3801 Cullen Boulevard
Houston, TX 77004
June 1, 1976

Educational Resource Associates
2111 Cedar Street
Houston, TX 77004

Gentlemen:

Here is the study you authorized January 21, 1975, dealing with economic under-standings of Texas high school students.

The primary problem of this study was to determine the changes that occurred in the student as the result of a semester's instruction in economics. After analyzing the data received, I concluded that (a) during the semester of instruction the student's knowledge of economics increased significantly, (b) between the pre- and post-tests for dogmatism the students became significantly less dogmatic, (c) during the semester there was no significant change in opinionation, i.e., liberalism-conservatism.

As you are aware, sound empirical research often requires a combination of efforts on the part of several individuals. With much gratitude, appreciation is expressed to many persons who in one way or another contributed to this research study.

If at any time you wish to discuss certain aspects of this study, you may reach me at the above address. Thank you for the opportunity to complete this project; if I can serve you in the area of research in the future, please do not hesitate to call.

Cordially,

Robin Dial

Some reports enclose a letter of authorization before the letter of trans-mittal. The main purpose of such a letter is to remind the reader that he or she authorized the report.

Table of Contents

The table of contents is actually a polished report outline. It names the major sections or topics and gives the beginning page number of their location in the report. If there is a synopsis, it is usually the first item listed; the appendix is the last (Exhibits 13-3 and 13-4).

EXHIBIT 13-3
Table of Contents—Dissertation

TABLE OF CONTENTS

Table of Illustrations

The table of illustrations lists and gives the page number of all tables and graphic aids. If there are a sufficient number of each type of graphic aid, they may be listed by type. If there are only a few of each, all may be listed as "figures."

The table of illustrations may continue on the same page as the table of contents or it may occupy one or more pages of its own, depending on the number of illustrations and available space (Figure 13-5).

Synopsis

The synopsis is a summary of the main or essential parts of the report. It is the complete report in miniature; its length is from one-tenth to one-twentieth of the whole report. It is designed primarily for the busy individual who may not have time to read the entire report.

EXHIBIT 13-4
Table of Contents—A Business Report

TABLE OF CONTENTS

EXHIBIT 13-5
Table of Illustrations

LIST OF TABLES

All major facts are included in the synopsis. (Other names for material briefly summarizing the report are *abstract, digest, epitome, precis, brief,* and *summary.*) It may begin in natural, normal order by summarizing the introduction, each major section, and summary-conclusion. Or, it may begin with a general recommendation or conclusion (direct approach or deductive reasoning) and then continue with a brief account of material taken from the introduction, conclusion, and major sections of the text (Exhibit 13-6).

EXHIBIT 13-6
Normal Order Versus Direct Order in Writing Synopsis

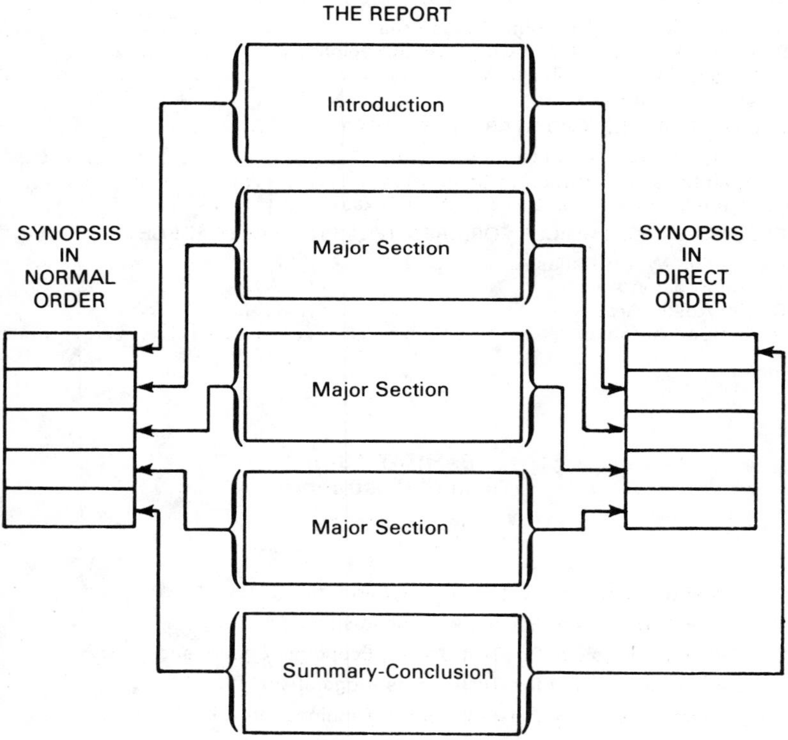

THE REPORT

Source: Boyd, William P. and Raymond V. Lesikar. *Productive Business Writing* (Englewood Cliffs, NJ: Prentice-Hall, Inc., 1959). pg. 433.

After a reader has read through the cover, title fly, title page, letter of transmittal, table of contents, table of illustrations, and synopsis, he or she is ready for Chapter 1 or the introduction to the study. Since the method of writing the major divisions of your research project has already been dealt with in Chapter 11, we will not discuss the introduction, major sections, and conclusions-recommendations in this chapter.

THE APPENDED SECTIONS

Sometimes it is desirable to add special sections to the report—bibliography and appendix, for example. The presence of these components is usually determined by the specific needs of the problem.

Bibliography

Normally only those reports that make extensive use of bibliographical research need a bibliography, which is a list of references relating to a given subject or author. You should consult any standard style guide for information related to the proper construction of such a list. (Exhibit 13-7 provides one example; see the list at the end of this chapter for references to help in preparing a bibliography.)

Appendix

The appendix is a separate part of the report and is used for supplementary information which supports the body of the report but is considered too detailed or of little interest to some readers. Typical appendix content includes: general or summary tables that do not directly support the conclu-

EXHIBIT 13-7
A Sample Bibliography

BIBLIOGRAPHY

Books

Bach, G. L. *Economic Education in the Schools.* New York: Committee for Economic Development, 1961.

Clark, Harold F. *Economic Education.* Washington, D.C.: Eleventh Yearbook of the National Council for Social Studies, 1964.

Fricke, B. G. *Opinion, Attitude and Interest Survey.* Ann Arbor: University of Michigan Press, 1962.

Galbraith, John K. *The Affluent Society.* Boston: Houghton-Mifflin Co., 1958.

Mermelstein, David (Ed.) *Main-Stream Readings and Radical Critiques.* New York: Random House, 1970.

Periodicals

Cummings, H. "Economic Education in the Secondary Schools," *Journal of Educational Sociology,* XXIII (March, 1950), pp. 397-401.

Garwood, John D. "The Need for Economic Education," *School and Society,* XCII (October 17, 1964), pp. 289-291.

Heckman, H. W. "Economic Illiteracy, the New Challenge to Free Enterprise," *Oklahoma State University Newsletter,* Spring, 1969, pp. 1-4.

Hurwitz, H. L. "The Current Revolution in Economics Teaching," *Scholastic Teacher,* LXII, No. 1 (November, 1963), pp. 7-8.

Mann, William R. and Daniel R. Fusfield. "Attitude Sophistication and Effective Teaching in Economics," *The Journal of Economic Education,* I, No 2 (Spring, 1970), pp. 111-129.

Winne, John F. "A Scale of Neuroticism," *Journal of Clinical Psychology,* VII (April, 1951), pp. 117-122.

sions; working papers, including tally sheets; questionnaires; procedures; formulas. Tables and graphic aids that directly support the conclusions or summaries should not be placed in the appendix; they should be in the section of the report to which they apply.

Another element sometimes found in the appended sections is the *index,* which is an alphabetical guide to subject matter contained in the report. However, <u>few business reports will require or justify an index</u>.

SUMMARY

The writing style of all reports is derived from the formal style presented in this chapter. A report, however, may not contain all the sections; for example:

1. You may not receive a formal authorization for the report; the assignment may be made orally.
2. You may decide, under certain circumstances, to combine the letter of transmittal and the synopsis.
3. You may use so few references, if any, that you do not need a bibliography.
4. You may not need an appendix if all supplementary material was needed within the body of your report.

DISCUSSION QUESTIONS AND EXERCISES

1. What are the major components of a long, formal report?
2. What does the report cover identify? Why is color choice important?
3. How should the wording of a title be constructed?
4. Explain the five *Ws.*
5. How does the title page differ from the title fly?
6. What is the purpose and content of a letter of transmittal?
7. How might a letter of authorization and a letter of transmittal be similar? Different?
8. What is the difference between a table of contents and a table of illustrations?
9. When may a table of contents include a table of illustrations?
10. What is the purpose and content of a synopsis?
11. What are some other names besides "synopsis" that may be used to summarize a report?
12. Review Figure 13-5 and explain any differences in the writing of a synopsis.
13. What determines whether there will be appended sections for a report?
14. Do all reports need a bibliography? When is one necessary?
15. What is the purpose and content of an appendix?
16. What are four reasons why a report may not contain all the formal components discussed in this chapter?
17. Prepare all necessary sections discussed in this chapter for your report and then prepare the final draft for typing.

REFERENCES FOR BIBLIOGRAPHY PREPARATION

1. Allen, George R. *The Graduate Students' Guide to Theses and Dissertations—A Practical Manual for Writing and Research* (San Francisco: Jossey-Bass Publishers, 1975).
2. Campbell, William G. *Form and Style in Thesis Writing* (Boston: Houghton Mifflin Co., 1969).
3. Clark, James L. and Lyn Clark. *HOW: A Handbook for Office Workers* (Belmont, CA: Wadsworth Publishing Co., Inc., 1975).
4. Knapper, Arno and Loda I. Newcomb. *A Style Manual for Written Communication* (Columbus, OH: Grid Publishing, Inc., 1974).
5. Turabian, Kate L. *A Manual for Writers of Term Papers, Theses, and Dissertations* (Chicago: The University of Chicago Press, 1973).

14

A Checklist of Requirements for Writing Effective Reports

For your report to achieve its purpose and for your words to be understood, you need a good, detailed plan consistently carried out and carefully checked. The purpose of this book is to develop your skills by guiding you through the process of research methodology and reporting. At each major juncture you have been encouraged to demonstrate your researching and writing skills. (We will look at your oral reporting skills in the next two chapters.) By now you should know why research and reporting processes are important and why your skills are vital to your success.

From the writing standpoint, one step remains. You must evaluate and edit the rough draft prepared after studying the previous three chapters. You must make sure you have fulfilled your objectives and purposes. There are four major areas to check before submitting your report: 1) organization, 2) language style, 3) mechanics and presentation, and 4) content and analysis. These categories are not listed in any special order, since their importance will vary with your abilities and duties. They are not mutually exclusive either. They should, however, provide you with a fairly complete list for personal evaluation of your report before it is presented for reading.

ORGANIZATION OF YOUR REPORT

A well-written report should be so organized that a reader can skim through it and get a good idea of its value and the nature of its contents. Your reader should be able to immediately grasp the total structure and underlying theme. Check the overall organization of your report against the following criteria. Can you answer "yes" to all these questions?

_____ 1. Are first things first?
_____ 2. Is each paragraph a complete, well-developed thought unit?
_____ 3. Are ample subheadings, or other display devises, used to quickly indicate the substances of the paragraphs or sections they begin?
_____ 4. Is each section of the report logical and well-integrated?
_____ 5. Is there variety, originality, and force within the report?

_____ 6. Are facts organized to hold the reader's interest and to carry conviction?

_____ 7. Have all facts and figures been skillfully selected?

_____ 8. Has there been a comprehensive survey of all useful sources?

_____ 9. Has complete documentation been provided?

_____10. Is the development of the report consistent?

_____11. Is an outstanding weighting of the relative importance of the report's components evident?

_____12. Is each major consideration recognized and stressed?

_____13. Are the pros and cons presented in the report well balanced?

_____14. Is there a skillful relation of exhibits to the written text?

_____15. Do all arguments move ahead to a conclusion?

_____16. Is the relationship among pieces of evidence realistic?

_____17. Have all irrelevant details been eliminated?

_____18. Is there a clear synthesis of all data presented?

_____19. Are the main points of the report briefly summarized and displayed?

_____20. Are a summary and conclusion provided at the end of the report?

LANGUAGE STYLE USED IN YOUR REPORT

Readability and a clear style of writing, should be primary concerns. For the report to be readable, you must make it as clear as possible to all those likely to read it. You must give the reader the most for his or her reading time. To insure that your language style leads to successful understanding, be certain you can answer "yes" to the following questions.

_____ 1. Is the structure of each sentence clear?

_____ 2. Do all words express the intended thought?

_____ 3. Is the language adapted to the vocabulary of the reader?

_____ 4. Is good syntax evident; that is, are word forms arranged to show mutual relationships in the sentence?

_____ 5. Are all sentences and paragraphs coherent; that is, do they stick together?

_____ 6. Are transitions provided for orderly procession of ideas?

_____ 7. Are the sentences generally short, with more few-syllabled words then many-syllabled words?

_____ 8. Have repetitions been eliminated?

_____ 9. Have you eliminated words which may be inferred from context or implication?

_____10. Is your report free from antagonistic words or phrases?

_____11. Is your report free from hackneyed or stilted phrases?

_____12. Is the tone of your report authoritative, courteous, and in tune with those receiving it?

_____13. Is the tone calculated to bring about the desired response?

_____14. Is the report easy to read and understand?

_____15. Have you been completely lucid?

MECHANICS AND PRESENTATION OF YOUR REPORT

If feasible, you would like your report to be as short as possible and yet be effective. This requires a neat, orderly appearance and a format consistent in style. If you can answer "yes" to the following questions, you probably have produced an effective report.

_____ 1. Have you prepared a polished, clean final copy?

_____ 2. Does the physical appearance of each page create a favorable impression?

_____ 3. Have you left generous margins and given the reader an "easy eyeful of type"?

_____ 4. Have you used proper grammar and spelling?

_____ 5. Can the reader readily recognize the report's purpose?

_____ 6. Can you state a single purpose for each paragraph?

_____ 7. Can you state a single purpose for each sentence?

_____ 8. Can you state the purpose of each part of every sentence—word, clause, phrase?

_____ 9. Have you given the reader enough information all along the way?

_____10. Are the major divisions of the report (conclusions, recommendations, supporting data) easy to find?

_____11. Have you eliminated or relieved long explanations by a liberal use of illustrations and examples?

_____12. Are all charts, tables, and graphs clear and appropriate?

_____13. Is the report concrete rather than abstract?

_____14. Is a thorough proofreading evident? (Your report should be read, reread, edited, and reedited at least five times.)

CONTENT AND ANALYSIS OF YOUR REPORT

No doubt it is obvious to you that your report should be complete and in depth. It should provide all the information necessary to accomplish the purpose and answer fully all questions likely to be in the reader's mind. The following questions will help you judge the content of the report. Can you answer "yes" to each of these:

_____ 1. Have you included all essential facts and provided sufficient detail?

_____ 2. Do you have adequate illustrative material to cover the points raised in the written text?

_____ 3. Have you made full use of supporting figures?

_____ 4. Are all facts directed to the reader's interest?

_____ 5. Is the accuracy of all factual information substantiated?

_____ 6. Are all statements in conformity with accepted rules and policies?

_____ 7. Has a proper synthesis of all data been made?

_____ 8. Is the report unbiased in its approach, equally for and against?

_____ 9. Are all arguments presented nonoverlapping?

_____10. Have you reached logical conclusions?
_____11. Have you considered all sensible alternatives?
_____12. Is your final summation of superior quality?
_____13. Are your recommendations unambiguous?
_____14. Have you reached a clear, definite decision which follows careful analysis?
_____15. Have all foreseeable consequences of recommended action been fully thought out, explored, discussed?

MISCELLANEOUS CONSIDERATIONS FOR YOUR REPORT

Although the preceding lists are exhaustive, there are a few more items to consider before submitting the final report. Can you answer "yes" to these questions?

_____ 1. Did you know what was wanted and why when you started work on the report? (Always make sure you understand the overall situation.)
_____ 2. Have you dealt with a definite and limited problem?
_____ 3. Did you keep a clearly defined purpose in mind and stick to it?
_____ 4. Did you give serious thought to the need and temperament of the person for whom the report is prepared?
_____ 5. Has the right type of binding or fastening been used?
_____ 6. Does the title express the nature and value of the report and make the receiver want to read it?
_____ 7. Have you provided a table of contents or an index so the reader may quickly locate desired material?
_____ 8. Is the report within an acceptable or a required length?
_____ 9. Have enough copies been made for distribution?

SUMMARY

Providing you with a list of almost eighty items for evaluating your report prior to final typing seems overwhelming. However, *good* report writing is a difficult and arduous process. Only thorough, consistent review of your writing will reap rewards. You are encouraged to check your rough draft copy against each section of this chapter. Your reader is entitled to the best possible product.

Reading number 10, "Reports that Communicate—Reports that Motivate," amplifies several of the points listed in this chapter.

_____ Part IV

The Process of
Oral Reporting

15

The Oral Report
in Business

Reports may be either oral or written. We have dealt primarily with the written report thus far—essentially in a formal format. Oral reports may also be presented formally with visual aids, or they may be simple, informal directives. In both cases the communication will be effective only if it accomplishes its purpose.

Ours is an extremely verbal world. We constantly encounter discussions, conversations, arguments, and speech presentations for one purpose or another. We have discovered over the years that written communication can be slow, expensive, and frequently the least effective means of sending information. Oral communication, on the other hand, provides visual personal contact and the opportunity for a two-way flow of information. Many companies now encourage the use of the telephone for transmitting messages because of its speed, convenience, and economy.

This chapter and the following one will explore the use and importance of the oral report. We have established the crucialness of the written report; however, effective oral communication also is vital to your future success. If you fail to learn oral reporting skills, you are limiting your career possibilities. For example:

> As you move up the career ladder in any field you get paid less and less for personally doing things; but you also get paid more and more for your ability to motivate other people to do things. Therefore, increasingly your success will depend on your ability to communicate with other people. Your *ideas* can only be valuable as your communication is effective. (70)

THE IMPORTANCE OF ORAL COMMUNICATION

Oral communication might be defined as a process in which a speaker interacts verbally with a listener to influence the receiver's behavior. In our basic model of "the process of communication via reports" (Exhibit 3-1), we began with a sender encoding a message and transmitting it to a receiver. That same model is applicable to the oral report. For example, the speaker (manager) decides a new sales quota must be reached. He decides how best to reach the quota, encodes that message, and transmits it to a receiver (subordinate). The receiver translates the symbols heard, interprets the message, and responds (hopefully) by increasing sales.

Any efficient message process in an organization will depend on the communication skills and attitudes of the individuals involved. In the long run, no organization can reach its potential unless its personnel understand the factors of communication and are able to control its variables. Instructions, explanations, and reports occur primarily through the spoken word.

IN BUSINESS

cutting sharp

Spoken, face-to-face communication is important to business operations. As one writer has stated, "incisive speech counts in industry!" (27) Effective speaking is an indispensable tool of management.

There have been several attempts to determine how much time is spent by business people in oral communication. One study reveals that managers spend about 30 percent of their work day speaking. Other communicative activities include writing, 9 percent; reading, 16 percent; and listening, 45 percent. (71) Another estimate suggests that 25 percent of a business person's job is devoted to talking on the telephone; 25 percent to discussing the business with employees, executive associates, superior officers of the company; and 25 percent discussing product problems with prospects and customers. (84)

These statistics support the importance of oral communication. Managers need skill in effective speaking to build goodwill and mutual understanding. If they are to effectively plan, organize, control, motivate, and coordinate, managers must recognize the importance of oral communication. Since they will accomplish their tasks primarily through people, oral communication is the managers' means of influence.

ORAL REPORTING

We established early in this book that reports must help decision making. If a report cannot assist the user, it fails. Basically your report (oral or written) should inform or answer a problem in one of these three categories:

1. *Questions of fact* concerned with the meaning, existence, or truth of something.
2. *Questions of value* concerned with making an evaluation of something measured either in comparison with something else or against some kind of standard.
3. *Questions of policy* concerned with deciding on a practical solution to a problem. (96)

Your report may contain answers to all three of these questions. The objective is to assist the hearer in reaching an efficient, effective decision.

SPECIAL CHARACTERISTICS OF THE ORAL REPORT

Although there are similarities between a written and an oral report, there also are basic differences. For example:

1. *The oral report is intended for a specific audience.* You cannot always be sure who will read a written report because of the possibility of unlimited distribution. You probably know, however, who will hear an oral report.
2. *The oral report is more limited than a written report.* The oral report is limited by time available for presentation. A written report usually includes all the relevant material (within reason) for whatever use the reader wishes to make of it.
3. *Each point of an oral report must be immediately clear to the hearer.*
4. *The oral report is presented face-to-face.* Written reports are impersonal; however, an oral report becomes very personal. (96)

Each of these points lends credence to the idea that a good oral report must benefit the receiver and help in problem solving and decision making.

THE MANAGEMENT REPORT

Since the oral report should aid decision making, there are seven sequential elements to help measure whether your report will be effective. Does your report:

1. Determine the objectives and purposes in terms of increased or sustained operational effectiveness?
2. Define the essential subsystems that comprise the problem to be measured?
3. Identify the key variables that represent each subsystem?
4. Select an appropriate measurement method?
5. Perform the actual measurement?
6. Analyze the data emanating from the measurement?
7. Evaluate the measurement process in terms of how effectively it fulfilled the stated objectives? (55)

Unless you can answer "yes" to these questions, your report may be ineffective.

TYPES OF ORAL COMMUNICATION IN BUSINESS

There are several common types of oral communication with which business people are concerned. Every day instructions are given, explanations are made, and oral reports are presented. Speeches are made to win approval of policies, to promote the sale of products and services, to inspire others, to create goodwill, to praise people and organizations, and to accept offices and

152

rewards. Oral communications take place in various contexts and circumstances. Effective speaking at the home office, public speaking in the field and at conventions, and executive speaking at sales meetings are arenas for oral reporting.

IN THE HOME OFFICE

If the estimate that 75 percent of a business person's job is oral communication is correct, it is easy to see the importance of making a good speaking impression. At the home office of a business enterprise practically all oral reporting will fall into one of the following categories:

1. *Improvement of staff and personnel*—improving the operations of the staff and personnel, inspiring them to undertake certain self-improvement measures. *to make known*
2. *Promulgation of plans and policies*—enlightening employees about company plans and policies.
3. *Developing more skillful techniques*—helping the efficient coordination and activities of all members of the management team.
4. *Increasing the volume of business*—encouraging and inspiring members of the sales organization to increase sales for the company.
5. *More effective handling of distributors, dealers, customers, and the general public*—visiting (constructively) with the many different types of people who must be seen and who constantly make demands. (84)

A company's home office provides many opportunities for sending and receiving oral messages—another reason why you should develop your oral reporting ability.

IN THE FIELD AND AT CONVENTIONS

Just as numerous opportunities are presented in the home office for oral reports, the field and conventions present many more.

Depending on your career choice when you graduate, you may be reporting to many organizations. Some of these organizations will include distributors and dealers, consumer organizations, service and social clubs, welfare associations, business and political clubs, chambers of commerce, and educational institutions. Your opportunities will be limited only by the number of communities your company serves.

During your work lifetime you will probably attend many kinds of conventions—cultural, political, industrial, and business. There you will meet people, make contacts, develop new acquaintances, talk to friends, or make a speech. Each of these activities is a speaking (an oral reporting) occasion, a selling opportunity. You can attract attention by what you say, interest the hearer in your company or product, convince the hearer of your company's ability, and perhaps close a sale. Each of these acts is a vital component of the oral communication process.

AT SALES MEETINGS

Another process depending on oral communication is sales. Many factors are involved in producing an effective meeting. For a sales meeting to be successful, there are four very important ingredients: careful planning, detailed preparation, a highly competent speaker, and a dramatic, successful conclusion. (84) Good meetings of any type do not happen by accident. The person speaking at a sales meeting has the opportunity to sell the company—its products, techniques and strategies—and himself or herself.

Although all these situations offer communicative opportunities, the most common oral reporting situation is the informal business meeting or conference. The following section will discuss this aspect of oral communication in more depth.

BUSINESS MEETINGS, CONFERENCES, AND INTERVIEWS

Business meetings and conferences range from an extremely informal meeting called on the spur-of-the-moment to a very formal conference scheduled by appointment. One factor common to most management personnel is the large amount of time spent in meetings to solve problems. To reach effective decisions, they exchange information, win acceptance of ideas, change and develop attitudes and behavior, or create a favorable organizational climate. To build group cohesiveness, managers must make these opportunities for interaction.

Since many important affairs of business are handled in a meeting, conference, or interview, what is said by the participants is influential in setting policy. Therefore, the principles of business and conversational speech can help you adapt and flow with the conversation, meet new points of view, deal tactfully with objections, and sell your ideas successfully. You must learn also how to efficiently open and close an interview.

BUSINESS MEETINGS AND CONFERENCES

The reasons for a meeting center around management's need for two-way communication, for more facts or opinions, creative ideas, approaches and solutions, better teamwork, or the opportunity to give instructions. The general complaints against group meetings or conferences are that there are too many, they take too much time, and they may not achieve results. Although these negative attitudes persist, meetings within an organizational setting are essential. Similarly, even though conferences can be expensive in terms of wages and salaries, they are a potentially productive management technique. Both management and employees, therefore, must treat the conference and meeting as an important technique that can help the business operate more effectively.

Types of Meetings

Meetings held for problem solving and decision making may be:

1. *Information meetings*—meetings in which all people of authority are informed about development.
2. *Briefing sessions*—meetings to provide members of the organization with the information they need to carry out a program.

3. *Instructional meetings*—meetings to help employees to be more proficient on their jobs, or to provide them with information to enable them to work with greater understanding.
4. *Creative meetings*— meetings to brainstorm new ideas, techniques, or procedures.
5. *Decision-making meetings*—meetings with both the responsibility and authority to solve important problems facing the organization.
6. *Consultation meetings*—meetings in which the leader asks for advice and suggestions before a decision is reached. (14)

Each of these allows the interaction of participants, the development of sales, and the building of group cohesiveness—but only when used properly. Ineffectiveness in planning will result in a waste of everyone's time.

Proper Use of Meetings and Conferences

An agenda can help to insure a productive meeting. The purpose of the meeting is to solve a problem and reach a decision. To be successful a meeting must accomplish four things:

1. It must have a specific purpose and a definite objective.
2. The proper physical and psychological environment must be consistent with the purpose.
3. Interesting speakers who can dramatize and verbally visualize their messages must be procured.
4. The program should be arranged so the speakers deliver their messages in the most effective sequence. (70)

A prepared agenda can help this goal to be attained.

Planning the Meeting

There is a vast difference between *scheduling* a meeting and *planning* for it. Management needs to realize that a conference is only one of several communication tools to share information; the telephone, memorandum, or face-to-face conversation may serve as well or better. Not only should the meeting be absolutely necessary but also it should accomplish something.

The following principles focus on organizational group meetings or conferences. The manager who follows these guidelines will likely achieve positive results:

1. Unless it is absolutely necessary, do not hold a meeting.
2. Use the meeting as a communication tool.
3. Handpick the people who will attend the meeting.
4. Adopt the proper leadership style for the meeting.
5. Utilize results of the meeting. (53)

Properly used, group meetings are a very effective communication device for managers. Two-way communicative interaction should be the rule. The leader must be able to handle and diagnose all contributions and lead the group logically and systematically.

INTERVIEWS

Another oral communicative technique you should develop is how to conduct efficient interviews in organizations. The interview is a valuable device for coordinating the functions and techniques of employees. A skillful interviewer can get more information from a willing, knowledgeable individual in a few minutes of conversation than from several hours of reading and research (Chapter 8).

Ideally, interviews are friendly communicative exchanges of information between two people about a subject they both want or need to explore. To set up this situation, the interviewer should formulate a clear goal, gather sufficient background information, outline some key questions, and develop a proposed solution for discussion. The interviewee should try to answer the questions asked.

Eight specific steps for conducting a successful interview can be established:

1. Structure the interview climate to make the interviewee comfortable.
2. Provide the interviewee with a clear understanding of the reason for the interview.
3. Focus on the interviewee's message.
4. Attempt to relate ideas presented to previous concents stated.
5. Evaluate each statement as it is made.
6. Guide the interviewee from point to point with pertinent questions when necessary.
7. Develop a program of action if the situation demands it.
8. Summarize and close the interview. (53)

While each step is presented in a seemingly lockstep manner, the interview should be flexible. The interviewer should fit the situation to his or her personality.

SUMMARY

Both written and oral reports are essential to business success. Each has its own style, format, and technique. Your responsibility is to gain as much skill as possible in both areas so that when your ideas are presented they will be accepted as valuable contributions. Any type of efficient message processing will depend on your communication skills and attitudes.

Reading number 11, "Characteristics and Organization of the Oral Technical Report," discusses the purpose, organization, and evaluation or oral reports.

DISCUSSION QUESTIONS AND EXERCISES

1. Why is oral reporting important? What effect does it have on the success of an individual?
2. Define oral communication. How does it relate to the basic communication process described in Chapter 3?

3. On what does efficient message processing depend?
4. Why should you be aware of your level of competence and of your current abilities and practices?
5. What are some of the advantages of oral communication over written communication?
6. What is the fundamental role of oral communication in business?
7. How much time does the average manager spend communicating on the job?
8. What percentage of time is spent speaking? Writing? Reading? Listening?
9. Relate the importance of oral communication to planning, organizing, controlling, motivating, and coordination.
10. What is the basic purpose of any report?
11. Explain the three categories that most report questions fall into.
12. What are some of the basic differences between a written and oral report?
13. How can you be sure your report will aid the decision process?
14. Define some of the types of oral communication in business.
15. Where may oral reportings occur? Explain different situations and show where the most common oral report situations occur.
16. Are the general complaints against business meetings justified? Why?
17. Discuss types of business meetings.
18. How can you ensure a successful meeting?
19. Discuss the general rules for conducting an organizational group meeting.
20. Ideally, what should an interview accomplish?
21. Explain the steps for conducting an interview.
22. Assume the leadership of a small group meeting and lead the members in a discussion of a case or topic of your instructor's choosing. Attempt to apply as much knowledge from this chapter as possible.

16

How to Present an Oral Report

Any presentation you make—whether to a small group, at a conference, or to a large number of people—should affect those who hear it. More than any other single factor, your success as a speaker will depend on careful preparation. Everything said in this book about presenting a written report is essential at this point. Sometimes the only difference between a written and oral report is the method of transmitting the message.

PLANNING AND PREPARING ORAL REPORTS

Common steps in planning, preparing, and presenting involve 1) selecting the subject, 2) determining the purpose, 3) analyzing the audience and occasion, 4) gathering the material, 5) arranging and outlining the parts, and 6) practicing the speech aloud for wording and fluency. (63) Each of these topics (except the last) has been discussed in the context of a written report. Therefore, you should refer to Chapters 4, 5, and 11 for a thorough review of these certain preparatory steps, viewing them in an oral reporting sense.

Selecting the Subject

Often the selection of a topic is simple; you may be assigned a subject on which to speak or you may volunteer to speak on a specific topic. However, what do you do when asked to speak on a subject of your choosing? A good principle to remember is that your personal experiences are often the best source of ideas for a talk; it is always easier to talk about firsthand experience. From a business environment context, you often will be given the topic—one with which you are usually familiar—and be instructed to present your data at a given place on a given date.

Determining the Purpose

Your presentation must serve a function; it must have an objective. No doubt the objective will be in terms of a specifically planned audience response. The success of that objective will be apparent in the audience response. To make a truly successful presentation, you must have a positive belief, faith, or conviction translated into a practical objective. (58) Consequently, you need to ask yourself, "Why am I making this report?"

The reason for determining the purpose of your report is to give the audience one thought. Based on the forgetting curves of live audiences (75 percent loss within 48 hours), presenting one main idea in a speech is an effective way to influence your audience.

Gathering the Material

After determining the subject matter of your oral report, the next step is to gather the data to support your subject. This might include examples, statistics, quotations, or analogies—any form of evidence. Chapter 5 discussed this subject, so, you may wish to review that chapter at this time.

Arranging and Outlining the Parts

An outline provides the skeleton structure of your presentation and materials to be used as reinforcements. Guidelines provided for written reports in Chapter 11 are also pertinent to oral reports.

Practicing the Speech Aloud for Wording and Fluency

Often what reads great on paper is just not palatable for the oral presentation. Practicing your speech aloud can indicate sections which need amplification, support, or visual representation. Reading aloud also tests the smoothness of your report. Does it flow? Does it carry your audience with you every step of the way? Are there complex, technical areas where you may lose your listeners? You may even wish to use a test audience.

As a speaker you have certain responsibilities. You must be audible, clear, and understandable. You must be able to ask and answer questions, and you must be willing to restate and clarify your message when needed.

PRESENTING ORAL REPORTS

Several techniques for making the oral presentation are available to you, in addition to certain elementary principles already presented in this chapter. For example, how would you answer the following questions: What are the best means of beginning and ending the speech? How do you phrase the main points to achieve the maximum effectiveness? How can you appeal to the listeners' senses? How can you use gestures and the body to communicate your thoughts?

BEGINNING AND ENDING THE REPORT

Every report, long or short, has a beginning and an end. In fact, the impact of your report usually depends on the way you present your opening and closing remarks. The main points of your report should be tied together into a firm and vigorous conclusion.

Some of the most frequently used means for developing the introduction are: 1) referring to the subject or occasion, 2) using a personal reference or greeting, 3) asking a rhetorical question, 4) making a statement of fact or opinion, 5) using a quotation, 6) telling a humorous anecdote, or 7) using an illustration. (63)

You may conclude your presentation by: 1) issuing a challenge or appeal, 2) summarizing, 3) using a quotation, 4) using an illustration, 5) supplying an additional inducement to belief or action, or 6) stating a personal intention. (63)

These suggestions may help strengthen your reports and maximize audience response.

PHRASING YOUR MAJOR POINTS

To achieve maximum effectiveness in stating major points, keep in mind the following characteristics of good writing: coherence, unity, objectivity, positiveness, emphasis, and readability. Everything mentioned in Chapter 10 about good writing would also be pertinent to good speaking.

APPEALING TO THE LISTENER'S SENSES

Visual and auditory devices allow you to reach a listener directly. Occasionally, however, a listener's senses must be reached indirectly—he or she, through the use of your language, recalls images previously experienced. There are seven types of imagery (seven doorways to the mind) that you can use to create understanding: 1) visual; 2) auditory—hearing; 3) gustatory—taste; 4) olfactory—smell; 5) tactual—texture, pressure, heat and cold; 6) kinesthetic—muscle strain; and 7) organic—internal sensations. (63) The more senses you appeal to, the better your audience will comprehend your topic. For example, some studies show that people retain only 20 percent of what they *hear* but will retain 50 percent of what they *see and hear*.

USING GESTURES AND THE BODY TO COMMUNICATE

What you present and the actions you use during the speech process are intimately related. What we do and how we appear also are related. For example, the gestures you use or the bodily action you demonstrate can reinforce delivery, affect comprehension, or convey feeling. There are at least six ways in which verbal and nonverbal systems interrelate: repeating, contradicting, substituting, complementing, accenting, and regulating. (1) In sum, it is through gestures and body language that people learn when to communicate, what to communicate, and when to listen.

The Use of Gestures

Gestures involve the whole body, not just hands and arms. They are a language all their own and can express many emotions. There are at least four types of common gestures you can use in oral reporting:

- Descriptive Gestures—visual aids useful for describing sizes, shapes, motions, relationships, or directions.

- Emphatic Gestures—reinforcements for ideas which are less concrete and more abstract (raised index finger, pounding on podium, smashing fist into hand).
- Enumerative Gestures—indication of numbers; generally involves one or more fingers.
- Pointing Gestures—use of hand or finger(s) in place of a pointer. (96)

The proper use of gestures will help clarify or emphasize the ideas of your message. To be effective, however, they need to combine the qualities of relaxation, definiteness, and timing.

The Use of Body Language

In addition to gestures, other bodily actions communicate either your intended message or a totally unrelated message. Every movement you make sends a message to someone, and it may not be the one you intend. The principle aspects of bodily action which should concern you as an oral reporter are personal appearance, facial expression, personal manner, speaking position, platform movement, posture, and eye directness. (96)

- Personal Appearance—your general appearance, how you dress, and how you carry yourself. Personal cleanliness, neatness, careful grooming, and appropriate attire create positive initial impressions.
- Facial Expression—the moods of your countenance. Your face is your most easily seen visual representation of your feelings or reactions to statements and situations. Your goal should be to achieve a facial expression that reveals self-assurance, vitality, and warmth.
- Personal Manner—the way you sit and carry yourself. You can reveal a genuine attitude of alertness and courtesy, an air of quiet confidence and eagerness. Or you can appear slouchy, bored, fidgety, and generate no enthusiasm.
- Speaking Position—whether you speak from a position too near or too remote from your listeners. You can easily display attitudes of warmth or aloofness by the distance you choose to maintain from the audience.
- Platform Movement—how you move about. Avoid remaining in the same spot. Proper movements reduce nervous tension, maintain audience attention, relax the listeners emphatically, punctuate and reinforce ideas.
- Posture—how to stand and what to do with your hands. The proper posture is the one that allows you to be comfortably erect and appear alert, confident, and communicative.
- Eye Directness—how you maintain eye contact with listeners. Eye directness is regarded the most important aspect by some authorities. Strive to look directly into the eyes of your listeners. Avoid looking at notes, the floor, the ceiling, the walls, or out the window. Eye contact demonstrates interest in and consideration for your audience.

ANALYZING THE AUDIENCE AND OCCASION

There are at least three reasons for analyzing an audience and the occasion for the speech: 1) to determine the response you might receive, 2) to assess the response you are getting during the presentation, and 3) to determine the impact of your objective upon the audience.

DETERMINING THE RESPONSE YOU MIGHT RECEIVE ✳

First, before you present your report you should know the answers to these questions: What is the demographic composition of the audience? What do you know about them? How much do they know about the subject? What are their fixed beliefs and values? What is their attitude toward you, the speaker? What is their attitude toward your subject? Obviously, this kind of information is not always easy to obtain, but knowing these things ahead of time will promote the success of your speech. In addition, it would be beneficial to know about the occasion for your speech: What is the nature and purpose of the occasion? What rules or customs will prevail? What will precede and/or follow? What will be the physical conditions affecting the occasion?

ASSESSING THE RESPONSE YOU ARE RECEIVING

To determine if your audience is paying attention to you and moving in the direction of the response you want, *eye contact* is extremely important. Thus, you must learn to look *at,* not over, through, or under your listeners. If you are alert to the cues provided by your listeners, you can observe audience attention. For example, if you observe excessive movement in listeners (shuffling of feet, people squirming in their chairs, or general restlessness), you can surmise that they are not listening to your message. If you sense these things happening, you must deal with the question of "How do I get and maintain attention?"

There are at least a dozen ways you can capture and hold interest. If your audience's listening/attention span begins to wander, try one or all of the following to bring them back:

- Tie the Message to a Basic Appeal. Allow the audience to identify with what is being said.
- Develop a Feeling of Mutuality. People are more likely to listen to someone who agrees with their point of view.
- Act Friendly. A smile is still the universal act of warmth and friendliness.
- Use the Audience's Language. An audience identifies more easily with the person who can speak as though he or she is one of them.
- Be Vigorous and Energetic. If the speaker is alive, alert, intense, and enthusiastic, the audience will be unable to keep from paying attention.
- Communicate with People. Be personable; speak directly to individual persons in the audience.
- Eliminate Distraction. Obviously, not all distractive factors can be foreseen or eliminated, but get rid of what you can.

- Furnish Variety and Relief. Alternate speaking with activity; intersperse chalkboard use, demonstration, lecture, and audiovisuals. Some of the most readily available or easily prepared visual aids are actual objects, if they can be handled and displayed, or models or mockups of such objects, or drawings, diagrams, and graphs.
- Be Unequivocal. Do not be afraid to take a stand on any issue; hedging or "beating around the bush" weakens a presentation.
- Use Novelty and Uniqueness. Be innovative; present ideas in a way they have never been said before.
- Make the Audience Curious. Occasionally, a wrapped package, or the unexplained absence or presence of an element in a presentation arouses curiosity. Silence might sometimes be used.
- Let the Audience Participate. Focus the eyes and ears of almost every member of the audience on what you are doing or saying—from an unspoken mental response to actual physical action. (58)

EXHIBIT 16-1
A Checklist for Oral Presentations

ORAL REPORTS PRESENTATION EVALUATION

If you wish your oral report to be effective, you should be able to answer "yes" to all of the following questions regarding your oral presentation:

_____ 1. Did the presentation have an appropriate beginning and ending?
_____ 2. Were the voice qualities (tempo, volume, and pitch) appropriate?
_____ 3. Were the mechanics of speech (grammar, sentence structure, and word usage) proper?
_____ 4. Were you completely prepared to give the presentation?
_____ 5. Did you appear knowledgeable and qualified to the audience?
_____ 6. Did the prepared message represent:
   A. Clarity of purpose?
   B. Logical organization?
   C. Psychological organization?
   D. Suitability to the audience?
   E. Fulfillment of instructions?
_____ 7. Were you able to relate to the audience's background, interests, moods, etc.?
_____ 8. Did you make effective use of visual aids (handouts, charts, tapes, films, pictures, etc.)?
_____ 9. Did you make effective use of note cards and other reference materials?
_____10. Was your nonverbal communication appropriate; that is, were there no observable, bothersome mannerisms?
_____11. Was the entire report presented in an understandable, logical, and easy-to-follow order?
_____12. Did you accomplish your objective(s)?

DETERMINING THE IMPACT UPON YOUR AUDIENCE

To measure success, you should evaluate every presentation after it has been given. How did the audience respond? Did they grasp your central idea? What were the comments you received or heard about your speech? Are there points which should be deleted before making this presentation again? Are there better ways to emphasize certain keypoints of your talk?

By this kind of final analysis you are 1) identifying the exact function you wish your report to serve, 2) eliminating confusing points and establishing the limits and boundaries in which to work, and 3) measuring the success of your report.

SUMMARY

Your success in presenting oral reports depends on careful planning and preparation. Every oral presentation you make must serve a function; it must have an objective. Therefore, you must know why you are giving a report. Once you have identified your goal, you are ready to gather the material, arrange and outline the parts, and practice the speech aloud for wording and fluency. In addition, it will be helpful if you analyze the audience and occasion, assess the response you receive during the speech, and determine the impact upon your audience. Exhibit 16-1 will make sure your oral report is effective.

Reading number 12, "A Good Talk: C.O.D.," discusses the importance of content, organization, and delivery of oral reports.

DISCUSSION QUESTIONS AND EXERCISES

1. Why should any oral presentation you make affect those who hear it?
2. What major factor determines your success as a speaker? Why?
3. What are the more common steps in planning, preparing, and presenting oral reports?
4. Why should every presentation serve a function?
5. What are three reasons for analyzing an audience and the occasion for the oral presentation?
6. Before presenting your report, what information should you know about your audience? Why?
7. Why is eye contact so important?
8. What are the ways to capture and hold an audience's interest?
9. What are three benefits that can be gained from a final analysis of your talk?
10. Why is it that some reports read great on paper but are not palatable for oral presentation?
11. What responsibilities do you have as a speaker?
12. What are the best ways to begin and end a speech?
13. How may major points be phrased to achieve maximum effectiveness?
14. What are some of the ways to appeal to a listener's senses?
15. How can gestures be used to communicate your thoughts?

16. What are some bodily actions (other than gestures) that may be used to communicate thoughts?
17. Prepare a thorough outline of your written report that would be beneficial in making an oral presentation.
18. Practice the report aloud for wording and fluency until you are ready to make an oral presentation before the class.

Part V

Case Studies for Report Writing

AARDVARK, INC.

Aardvark, Incorporated, has had a college tuition refund plan since 1956 for employees aspiring to middle-management positions in the company. Presently, forty employees take advantage of this benefit. During the past five years the company has been losing several of the employees enrolled in the program at graduation. Last year, for example, one-half of those receiving a degree left the company for other jobs. Thus, Aardvark is paying out money for college-trained personnel, but other companies are receiving the benefit of the investment.

You have been asked to research this problem and to make recommendations for easing the situation. Interviews with 25 percent of those who graduated last year have resulted in a compilation of statements such as:

1. I don't owe the company anything; we made no commitment when I started night school.
2. No one ever asked me how I was getting along.
3. No one ever congratulated me when I graduated.
4. My boss never acted as if he knew I was going to school.
5. I thought I would receive either a raise, a promotion, or both when I graduated.

Write a report to Kenneth Matthew in which you define the problems, discuss its implications, and state your recommendations.

AN ACCOUNTING SYSTEMS REPORT

You are an accounting major at The University. Your professor of the accounting systems course has instructed you to conduct a research project about this course. Specifically:

1. What information should be included in reports made for lower levels of management?
2. How much and what type of information should be made available for top management reports?
3. How does one maintain effectiveness of employees relating to changes in accounting firms?

You are to submit a report of your findings, conclusions, and recommendations to Wayne Dye.

BRANCH BANK EXPANSION—
A CASE ANALYSIS

Background

Warren Smith has recently been assigned to direct the systems and expansion department of TIMBERLINE BANK AND TRUST COMPANY. This department has been charged with the responsibility of conducting an internal systems analyses to determine future branch location sites.

TIMBERLINE is a state bank—fifth largest bank in the state. The bank has six branches, mostly concentrated in Pinedale, the major city within Cannon County. Pinedale is bounded on the north and east by mountain ranges. State University is on the east bench of Pinedale and has approximately 25,000 students.

As assistant vice president of the systems and expansion department, Warren supervises Jolene, an administrative secretary, and Ted, a recent graduate from State University. Ted received a degree in management with an emphasis on marketing research. With Jolene's administrative skills, Ted's marketing background, and Warren's MBA and seven years' banking experience, they feel that they have the competence to be a very effective project team.

Because of a recent surge in branch expansion by several major banks in Cannon County, the president of TIMBERLINE, Rockwell Porter, feels that his bank needs to provide greater conveniences for his customers; otherwise, he feels that his customer base may deteriorate within the year. In an effort to attract new customers and to satisfy present customers, he decides to construct a new branch facility in Cannon County.

Porter immediately summons Warren to his office. He asks Warren to recommend the choicest locations for a new branch in Cannon County. Porter wants these choices in order of preference, since the state banking commissioner may not approve his first choice. Naturally, other banks near the proposed locations will fight to persuade the commissioner to disallow this future expansion.

Porter may decide to apply for all three choices if they appear to be backed with sound research studies. Therefore, the reasoning for any proposed site must be developed with great care. Warren is instructed to submit his recommendation in sixty days.

After two weeks of preliminary research, Warren and Ted limit their alternatives to three: Mountain Village Shopping Center, Sandy Hills Shopping Mall, and Tatesville. Warren decides to spend his time analyzing the buy/lease arrangements at these locations. He delegates the economic analysis to Ted.

Within a month Ted hands Warren his staff report on each of the possible locations.

This case was prepared by H. Lon Addams, assistant professor of business communications Northern Illinois University, DeKalb, Illinois.

Tatesville

The boundaries of the market area are as follows: 1) north boundary, 3800 South; 2) south boundary, 5400 South; 3) east boundary, New Fork River; and 4) west boundary, proposed I-215.

Located twenty minutes (by car) from Pinedale, Tatesville lies to the west of Pinedale and is adjacent to a large industrial firm. The majority of the residents are either low-middle or middle-income. The town continues to extend its borders; since 1965 there has been a 30 percent increase. Census figures were taken in 1975 and increased expansion in residential housing has been evident in the past year. Presently there are 18,005 people in this market area of Tatesville. Farmland to the south may be utilized for further housing developments. The natural boundaries—New Fork River and the new freeway—prohibit further expansion in these directions.

The Tatesville market area contains approximately 180 business firms employing over 4500 people. Essentially there are two concentrations of business activity, both on Aspen Road. The proposed branch site for the Tatesville market area is at the intersection of 4800 South and Aspen Road, contiguous to one of the concentrations of business activity.

Most of the Tatesville businesses are located on Aspen Road. Much of the traffic moving north and south uses the Aspen Road, and traffic flowing east and west uses either 4100 South or 4800 South. The K-Mart complex, built in 1975, is located on the northwest corner of 4800 South and Aspen Road and serves community residents as well as commuters to Pinedale and other areas of Cannon County. The daily traffic counts pertinent to this report are shown in the sketch. ("X" indicates proposed branch site.)

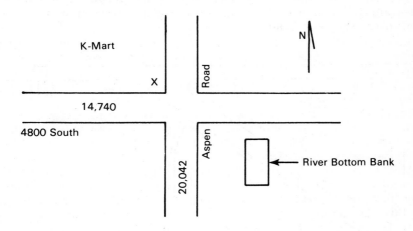

Scattered around this intersection at 4800 South and Aspen Road are a 1) gas station, 2) fast-service food store, 3) drive-in and walk-in restaurants, 4) K-Mart, and 5) River Bottom Bank & Trust Company. One hundred eight people are employed by these firms.

On-site inspection of River Bottom Bank & Trust Company revealed that its one drive-up window was used infrequently and the three inside teller windows were occasionally used. Interviews with K-Mart shoppers indicated a dissatisfaction with the loan officers and branch manager of the bank. Most of those interviewed—nearly all were local residents—expressed their desire for a friendly bank in their area.

Mountain Village Shopping Center

Located within five minutes of State University and ten minutes from downtown Pinedale, Mountain Village Shopping Center services a large residential area. There is very little undeveloped ground because of the sharp-sloping mountains to the east, the university to the north, and continuous residential housing to the west and south. However, condominium and apartment house construction is evident in a few areas nearby. And married-student housing units recently doubled on the university property, only a few minutes from the village.

The percentage increase in population has been 14.1 percent over the 1965 to 1975 period. Census figures reveal that the type of home in the area is predominantly upper-middle income; many well-to-do professional people live nearby on the slopes of the mountains. Generally the village market area contains well-educated, community-minded people. The area surrounding the village is over 70 percent residential and is extremely well kept.

Within the village market area there are over 200 businesses, employing 7,745 people. Since Village Boulevard is a main artery from the foothills to Pinedale, traffic is heavy going west into the downtown area. Nearly 20,000 vehicles pass by the village daily on this boulevard. See sketch.

Approximately 40 percent of the businesses in the village market area are located on Village Boulevard, which suggests the drawing power of the boulevard. One half of the boulevard businesses are clustered in the Mountain Village Shopping Center.

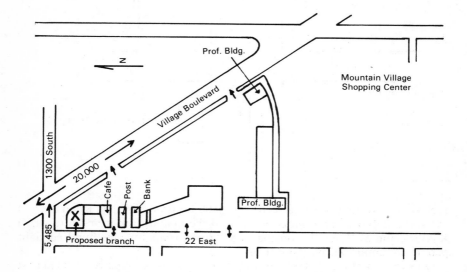

The Mountain Village Shopping Center is located on the southwest corner of 1300 South and Village Boulevard. The complex has grown from 22 businesses in 1969 to 35 establishments with 410 employees at present. The village includes grocery and drug stores, specialty stores, doctor and dental offices, and a major branch bank.

Central Bank is located in the middle of the village. It is the third largest bank in the county, has ten other branches, and is one of the most progressive banks in the county. During the afternoons, long lines typically form at both the drive-up window and the six inside teller windows. It appears that another progressive bank could capitalize on the business generated by this center and surrounding community.

Also, within this market area is Security Bank, the eighth largest bank with three branches. This bank caters to the university crowd because it is located north of the village, practically on the doorstep of the university. It has two drive-up windows and five inside teller windows. The inside teller windows receive constant business, but the drive-up window receives a medium amount of customers.

Sandy Hills Shopping Mall

According to the Sandy Hills City Manager, rapid growth of Sandy Hills City has been assured by the tremendous number of building permits issued by the city in January of 1977. During January, the city issued permits worth two million dollars, which is the heaviest month in the history of the city and nearly equaled the annual total experienced two years ago.

Included in January's permits were 77 residential housing units; 22 four-plex units; one 25-unit apartment house; one 13-unit trailer court, and five business remodeling permits. Farmland south of the market area may give way to future residential housing projects.

Generally the Sandy Hills market area contains average-priced homes and has plenty of room for future growth. According to a recent study by the newspaper agency, the majority of the Sandy residents are either craftsmen or foremen; some hold professional and managerial jobs. The study shows that the typical Sandy resident is in the middle-income bracket.

Census tract information reveals that Sandy Hills has increased from 11,390 residents in 1965 to 21,109 in 1975—an 85 percent increase. Sandy Hills is a well-kept, attractive area. Within the Sandy Hills market area, there are approximately 125 business establishments employing over 2,500 people. Approximately 33 percent of this business activity takes place near the possible branch site in the Sandy Hills Shopping Mall.

The Sandy Hills Shopping Mall is located on the southeast corner of 9400 South and 700 East. Since this is the only major shopping center within five miles in any direction, the Sandy Hills Shopping Mall is quite popular. A major grocery store chain and a well-known drug company provide the nucleus of buying activity.

Traffic counts conducted by the researcher revealed that 9,925 vehicles pass by the mall daily traveling east, and 16,525 vehicles pass by the center daily traveling north toward Pinedale. See sketch.

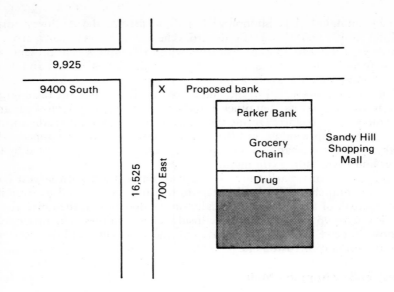

9,925

9400 South   X   Proposed bank

Parker Bank

Grocery Chain

Sandy Hill Shopping Mall

Drug

16,525

700 East

Parker Bank & Trust established a branch in the mall when it first opened in 1965. Parker Bank & Trust is the tenth largest of the twenty-five banks located in Cannon County and has other branches. This branch has one drive-up window, keeps 9:30 to 5:00 banking hours, and is located at the north end of the mall. This is the only bank within the Sandy Hills City limits; as a result, many local residents seem to identify Parker Bank & Trust as "their" bank. Perhaps part of the explanation for this strong loyalty is the bank's free checking policy.

CHURCH MISSION REACHOUT

You are an active member of the Local Church and are concerned with an evangelical outreach program to foreign students. You have been asked by the church leaders to propose a method for teaching the Bible to the campus' 2,000 foreign students.

You have heard of similar programs which have been a great success and have decided to review their programs first. Write and obtain copies of such mission outreach programs, review them for shortcomings and strengths, add your own ideas, and write a recommendation proposal.

Submit the report to Pastor Ramic.

A COMMUNITY COMPUTER CENTER

To determine the possible need for using a community computer center in your town, questionnaires were sent to 2,000 business people. Responses were received from 800 persons, 400 of whom said they had some problems where a computer might help. There were 350 who said they needed no help; 50 were unsure of their need for such a service.

This data corresponds to other information you have seen from similar communities. However, you are not yet convinced of the need for a computer center in your city. Therefore, you have decided to conduct a study into the cost of such a service. You are planning to visit each firm that indicated a need for computer services to see just how much computer time they would need.

Draft a questionnaire or interview schedule to gather the primary data for your decision and conduct a library search to determine computer time costs. If, after your research, you think a community computer center is necessary, write a feasibility study for presentation to your boss.

FOOTBALL PREDICTIONS

You are a member of the athletic staff for your school. The athletic director has asked you to conduct a study on the other football teams in your school's conference. You will want to know such things as:

1. Returning starters
2. Junior college transfers
3. Freshman team returnees
4. New freshmen
5. Win-lose record
6. Physical data on each player
7. Professional data on coaches
8. Alumni support

When you have gathered this information on each league team and analyzed it, gather the same data on your own football team. From this comparison and analysis, you will be able to predict your team's chances of overall success.

Your report should be submitted to Atheno Giles, Athletic Director.

HILLTOP HOTEL, INC.

Early in 1968 the Hilltop Hotel opened its doors for business in Atlanta. This hotel, a 23-story structure, was the first major step toward turning Atlanta into a booming convention city. During the first few years of business, the Hilltop Hotel averaged between 85 and 95 percent occupancy, well above the 60 percent occupancy required to break even.

Hilltop Hotel, Inc., was organized by a group of successful businessmen in the Atlanta area who had felt the need for a major convention facility for several years. After a year of successful operation, the Hilltop Hotel began turning the heads of several international hotel chains. Within five years, five new major hotels were competing for convention business in Atlanta. This increase in hotel growth proved to be more than the city of Atlanta could support and in the eighth year of its operation, Hilltop Hotel is now averaging between 55 and 60 percent occupancy.

Hilltop management feels confident that within the next five years Atlanta will grow to a size that can support the present number of hotels, but now Hilltop is struggling for survival. The immediate objective is to increase the occupancy rate above 60 percent so the organization can at least show a profit. After that point management feels that consistent growth will come as the city grows.

A consulting firm that has worked with Hilltop management has proposed the following three alternatives:

1. Join an international hotel chain, thereby capturing the "free" advertising carried out by such worldwide organizations.
2. Increase the sales staff and expand sales efforts to groups other than just the large groups catered to in the past.
3. Refurbish the hotel and give it a new look. Along with this refurbishing, improve the night shows in an attempt to gain a larger share of the local market.

Although Hilltop management can see that some advantages would accrue as a result of implementing these recommendations, they are also aware of a number of disadvantages.

1. Joining a national or international chain would mean loss of economy and sharing profits with the mother organization.
2. Increasing sales staff to push for different groups would result in an immediate financial drain on the hotel. No assurance can be given that the increased sales staff would pay for itself in higher occupancy rates.
3. Refurbishing the hotel would also be an immediate financial drain on the hotel, and an attempt to gain a significant share of the local market might have a negative impact on the convention goers who come from out of town.

Although Hilltop management could accept and implement all three recommendations, they are not sure that any one is necessarily good for the organization.

Assume that you are an executive in the Hilltop organization. Evaluate the three alternatives and write a report of recommendation to top management. You may recommend any or all of the alternatives, or you may recommend a completely different approach to Hilltop's problem.

THE LEW-BAKE DEPARTMENT STORE

The Lew-Bake Department Store has a large shoe department. Twenty sales clerks have worked in this department for the past ten years. They are a closely knit social group.

Last year the department store hired seven new clerks to work in the shoe department. The newcomers encountered several problems immediately:

1. The former sales clerks take the desirable times for coffee breaks and lunch times.
2. The older sales clerks receive priority from the cashier.
3. The older personnel frequently instruct the new ones to straighten things up (which should be an equal responsibility). The newer clerks sometimes lose sales to the older clerks because of this.

You are the assistant department manager, and the newcomers have complained to you about these problems. Prepare a written report for your manager analyzing the problems. Make justifiable recommendations.

MARKET RESEARCH AND INVESTMENT ANALYSIS

You are a student enrolled in a course called Marketing Research. You have been asked to conduct a research project on one of the following topics:

1. The market for health food items in supermarkets.
2. A suitable site for a shopping center.
3. Investment opportunities in electric utilities.
4. Mutual funds for the small investor.
5. Need for a new men's or ladies' clothing store in your town.

The intent of this project is for you to show initiative, imagination, resourcefulness, and thoroughness in securing and presenting your data. The bulk of your information can be secured through bibliographical research, questionnaires, interviews, or observations.

PROPOSAL REPORT

Assume that you are a regional sales representative for a national firm that operates a large chain of retail outlets (gasoline stations, jewelry stores, pizza shops, hamburger stands, restaurants, motels or hotels, beauty salons, grocery stores, hardware stores, clothing stores, department stores, sporting goods stores, and so forth). You may select the type of retail outlet you want to work with.

You are to assume that lately you have been bothered by the rather careless attitude on the part of many local managers to keep their businesses clean, tidy, and appealing to the public. As a regional sales representative of your firm, you have a responsibility to serve also as an inspecting agent. You feel that you lack the clout needed to enforce your recommendations, however, because the national office has never specified the standards expected of each local outlet.

Design an inspection form for your firm and write a recommendation report to your immediate superior. Explain the background of the problem, state your overall objective, and describe in detail your proposed program (which includes the use of the inspection form).

SELECTION OF ADMINISTRATIVE ASSISTANT TO COUNTY MANAGER

INSTRUCTIONS

Assume that you serve as personnel manager for Dade County, Florida, and that you have been asked to interview applicants for the position of administrative assistant to the county manager. Following your interviews you are to write a memorandum report to Leland G. Price, county manager, analyzing the top three job candidates and ranking these candidates in order of preference.

After performing your analysis of the three candidates, write your memo report in the following order:

1. Statement of objective
2. Presentation of factors (in order of importance)
3. Presentation of alternatives
4. Analysis of alternatives
5. Conclusion and recommendation

Double space your report and use appropriate subheadings. Check your report for coherence, depth, readability, accuracy, and other characteristics expected in high-quality reports.

JOB DESCRIPTION

General Statement of Duties:

Performs varied and independent work in assisting the county manager in the performance of his administrative duties; does related work as required.

Distinguishing Features of the Position:

This is administrative and staff work of a highly responsible nature. The employee in this position is the principal assistant to the county manager in the details of administration. The range of his duties is as wide as the entire county administration, and they are performed through both general and specific delegation by the county manager. In major areas of delegation, the employee has wide latitude for the exercise of independent judgment, limited only by review and general policies determined by the county manager. This employee performs both assigned and independent staff work. He makes recommendations to the county manager in the development of overall administrative policies. He gives policy guidance and interpretation to major department heads. Through frequent daily conferences and contacts with the county manager, he keeps informed and abreast of current and projected developments in the conduct of the county government. This position differs from that of administrative assistant in the more responsible and complex work performed.

Examples of Work: (Illustrative only)

- Receives requests and complaints from the public concerning administrative actions of the various departments, channels the requests to appropriate departments, follows up on the corrective actions and sees that replies to the inquiries are given.
- Reviews incoming correspondence, memoranda, reports, and similar materials for the purpose of summarizing important phases and making recommendations concerning them.
- Confers with them and advises department and division heads in working out detailed plans of functions that the county manager has delegated and on which he had indicated general instructions.
- On direction of the county manager and with general policy guidance, prepares directives to department heads and division heads.
- As directed, performs organizational and procedural analyses in the county departments.
- Initiates research and special studies in needed areas and prepares reports with recommendations for corrective action.
- Coordinates the preparation of background materials and agenda for the board of supervisors.
- Attends meetings of the board of supervisors, conferences and committee and staff meetings to provide assistance to the county manager and make recommendations on subjects under discussion.

- Represents the county manager at meetings he is unable to attend.
- Prepares detailed budget requests for the board of supervisors, county manager's office, volunteer rescue squad and miscellaneous activities; supervises central filing system and library.
- Serves as liaison between county and general assembly during sessions.

Required Knowledge, Skills, and Abilities:

Comprehensive knowledge of the principles and practices of local governmental administration; considerable knowledge of public administration; considerable knowledge of local finance administration; good knowledge of sources of information related to problems of local government; ability to write clear and concise reports, memoranda, directives and letters; ability to develop comprehensive plans from general instructions; ability to accomplish assigned administrative tasks with a minimum of supervision and with only general directions; ability to meet the public and to discuss problems and complaints tactfully, courteously and effectively; ability to establish and maintain satisfactory work relationships with department heads as well as with other county employees; good physical condition.

Acceptable Experience and Training:

Extensive experience of an increasingly responsible nature in local governmental administration and graduation from an accredited college or university, with a master's degree in public administration; or any equivalent combination of experience and training which provides the required knowledge, skills and abilities.

Candidate #1: Leon W. Howard

Personal Data:	Married with one child Age: 26 U.S. Citizen Place of birth: Ohio
Education:	MPA, 1976 Syracuse University; GPA, 3.6 Certificate Training in Municipal Administration of the International City Management Association 1975 BA, 1974, Ohio State University, in Political Science
Experience:	Planning Development Coordinator for County in Ohio; 1 year Research Assistant for Professor at Ohio State University; 1 year Sales Representative for Encyclopedia Sales, Inc.; 1 year
Other Data:	Put self through college; interested in reading, sports, and debating
Interview Notes:	Seems mature in thinking and in actions; communicates quite well orally, but admitted having a bit of difficulty in English-related courses

Candidate #2: Rudolph K. Hernandez

Personal Data:	Single Age: 24 Mexican ancestors; U.S. Citizen Place of birth: Georgia
Education:	MPA, 1976 University of Georgia; GPA, 3.4 BA, 1974, Georgia State University, in Communications
Experience:	Teaching Aid for GSU Communications Professor; 1 semester Administrative intern with City of Atlanta for 1 summer, personnel department
Other Data:	Received aid from government for school support; member of Intercollegiate Knights; Student Body Vice President at GSU, 1973-1974; Editor of MPA Newsletter at University of Georgia; Interested in people and traveling
Interview Notes:	Seems like a go-getter; a good communicator both in oral and writing situations; not quite as mature and level-headed as Howard, but no problem anticipated here

Candidate #3: Virginia Foust

Personal Data:	Divorced, three children Age: 36 U.S. Citizen Place of birth: Louisiana
Education:	BA, Louisiana State University, 1962, in English and Journalism; GPA, 3.9
Experience:	Administrative Assistant to Senator in Washington, D.C.; 4 years Administrative Assistant to Mayor of mid-sized town in Louisiana; 3 years
Other Data:	Interested in reading and creative writing; desires to relocate in Florida near her sister and brother-in-law.
Interview Notes:	Has had some outstanding experience in her past jobs, although she has been more a private secretary than an administrative assistant; her work has involved relatively little work with other groups of people; seems relatively stable; it is obvious that she would be coming to Florida for her sister rather than for the job; communicates quite well orally and has published three short stories.

STUDENT COUNSELING PROGRAM

You are the assistant dean of women at The University, which has an enrollment of approximately 20,000 students. The dean of women has asked you to conduct a survey on the life, activities, problems, and responsibilities of the undergraduate female student so that a new counseling program for women can be established.

You will need to:

1. Prepare a questionnaire regarding the needs of female college students.
2. Solicit support of the project, explain the purpose, and show how the results will serve female students.
3. Compile results and submit a memorandum report to the dean.

REGISTRATION HEADACHES

Registration for coursework at most colleges and universities is a headache. You have been appointed to an ad-hoc Student Advisory Council for recommending changes to the current procedure.

Your research will review the present registration method, its advantages and disadvantages. An analysis of the data you gather will suggest changes that need to be made.

Submit your report with recommendations to George Salenger, Registrar.

REVIEWING YOUR PROGRESS

At this point you have completed the major part of this text. Review your progress in researching and reporting procedures. Write down your weaknesses and strengths and draw a conclusion as to your growth. Submit your discoveries and conclusions about your progress in this course to your instructor.

_____   Part VI

Readings

Improving the Effectiveness of Management Reports

The undertaking of processing data, keeping books and records, and churning out reports is not a penny ante poker game. A typical business probably spends upwards to five cents out of every sales dollar on these functions. This amount increases in significance when we consider the fact that this could be half as much as the company's annual earnings.

Despite the significant expenditure for management information, it is surprising how many financial organizations fall short of providing *meaningful* information that can be used effectively for profit-oriented decision making. Often, after thousands of man-hours and dollars are spent turning out the product, the ball is dropped on the goal line because the information is not presented in such a way that it will be acted upon. Too often information is generated for its own sake rather than for the sake of the individual who is going to put it to use. Unfortunately, this occupational hazard applies particularly to financial management.

My purpose, therefore, is to review some of the concepts and management reporting techniques that have proven effective in helping executives maximize the profitability of professionally managed businesses. I will refer to certain recognized guidelines for effective management reporting and will illustrate how these concepts and guidelines have been applied successfully in achieving this objective.

MANAGEMENT BY OBJECTIVES

The experience of many successfully managed companies has demonstrated that profitability is best achieved by applying the principles of management by objectives. This process consists of assigning the responsibility and accountability for making a profit or controlling costs to specific individuals, asking each manager to establish revenue, cost, and profitability goals, measuring results against these goals, and then taking corrective action when reported results vary from goals. This style of doing business, of

Allen H. Seed, "Improving the Effectiveness of Management Reports," *Financial Executive* (September, 1969). With permission of the publisher.

course, requires professional management and a willingness to take risks and accept mistakes. Although management may not be successful with this approach in every case, it is held that this philosophy more often than not produces superior results in the long run.

MANAGEMENT ACCOUNTING

The implementation of the principles of management by objectives naturally requires a structure of management information which is designed to help the professional manager manage his business. In this connection, there are five related management accounting concepts that should be applied to make "management by objectives" something more than a catch phrase in the spectrum of contemporary business jargon. They are as follows:

- *Standard costs* to develop *(a)* measures of the profitability of products before they are manufactured, *(b)* the basis for measuring the profitability of sales territories and customers, and *(c)* tools for controlling manufacturing costs.
- *Budgeting and profit planning* to provide meaningful yardsticks for decision making and appraising operating performance.
- *Responsibility accounting* to provide managers with reports of actual results compared to plan, so that they can determine those things they can do something about.
- *Contribution reporting* to assure that profits are contributed *up* through the organization rather than expenses charged *down*.
- *Return on investment* to provide a measure of how well a manager employs his capital.

In my opinion, all of these concepts are fundamental to effective management reporting and apply to just about every profit-oriented business situation.

APPLICATION OF CONCEPTS

In order to relate these concepts to practical management reports, let me show you how they have been applied in my own company.

I should first describe the division in question: the Container Division. It converts and sells corrugated shipping containers. On the one hand, it might be considered to be a large business because it includes 26 plants that do well over $100 million a year worth of business. On the other hand, it could also be considered to be a collection of small businesses because each plant is largely an autonomous operation serving a specific geographic market. So, although it may be a big business, it has many of the same problems and opportunities of small businesses.

Each plant, for example, has its own plant general manager, plant production manager, plant sales manager, and plant controller. Each plant general manager's primary assignment is to maximize the profitability of his operation. He has the capacity to do this because he has his own sales force, can price his own products, runs his own shop, and has his own plant controller.

The following is an explanation of the summary statement of operating results that the plant general manager receives on the fifth working day following the end of the month.

* * *

STANDARD COSTS

The use of standard costs forms the foundation of the summary statement. Standards consist of materials, conversion, and out-freight, and corresponding variances from standard are reported. To those who may believe that standard costs are not practical in a job-shop situation, let me say that the Container Division is really in the custom-tailoring business. Each shipping container is cut and printed to customer's specifications. Each plant sells about a thousand different containers a month, and separate standard costs are developed for each container. These standards are used primarily for pricing purposes, but they are also used to determine standard costs of sales on our operating statement.

BUDGETING AND PROFIT PLANNING

Secondly, the statement of operating results compares actual results with budgeted or planned results. It contains a "current plan" and an "annual plan." The "current plan" is the latest budget that was established by the plant general manager for his plant. The "annual plan" is the plan that was originally developed at the beginning of the year. This approach recognizes that planning is a continuous process and that plans should therefore be revised from time to time. However, it is important not to lose sight of the "annual plan" which is this Division's basic commitment to corporate management.

In no case are results compared with last year or prior periods. In our opinion, to compare current results with previous periods is casting backward, not forward, and is inconsistent with the philosophy of management by objectives.

RESPONSIBILITY ACCOUNTING

I would call your attention to the fact that the plant general manager's name should appear on the operating statement. Including his name is the essence of responsibility accounting, which simply requires that every element in a financial statement be identified with a specific individual and that only items controlled by an individual be reported to that individual. The plant general manager is responsible for all of the operating results that are reported.

CONTRIBUTION REPORTING

The concept of contribution reporting also is employed in the statement. First of all, standard direct costs and variances from direct costs are separated from so-called "constant expense." Direct costs are those manufacturing costs that vary with production. They are the incremental costs of producing more or less product. Constant expenses, on the other hand, are largely a function of time. They are budgeted on a fixed monthly basis and do not tend to vary with production.

This separation of fixed and variable costs has several important advantages from a management control point-of-view. First of all, it allows a manager to identify quickly the price-cost relationship of his product mix, which in this case is the responsibility of the plant sales manager. Secondly, it makes breakeven determinations and a lot of other "what if" calculations easy to make.

For example, this plant's breakeven point is approximately $495,000 (constant expense of $99,000 divided by an actual contribution of 20 percent of net sales). Similarly, if this plant increases sales by $100,000, earnings would be increased by $20,000 (20 percent of $100,000).

Finally, it is easy to understand (no terms like "over- and under-absorbed burden") and easy to install (direct costs are budgeted on a variable basis, and constant expense is budgeted on a fixed basis). As you well know, simplicity is often the key to stimulating constructive action on the part of operating management.

Plant earnings before taxes, the plant "contribution" to divisional and corporate earnings, are reported on the plant operations statement. Divisional or corporate overhead is not prorated to the plants because these expenses cannot be controlled by the plant general manager. It is amazing how this has helped managers zero in on the problems that they can do something about by avoiding useless conversations about expenses beyond their control.

RETURN ON INVESTMENT

The fifth concept is the measure of return on investment which is called "capital employed." This return is calculated by dividing annualized plant earnings by total capital employed. Capital employed is defined in this case as the sum of cash accounts receivable, inventories, and the cost of plant equipment. The use of this measure permits a manager to evaluate the overall economic impact of trade-offs and alternative courses of action. The long-term objective here is *not* to maximize the percentage return on investment as such, but rather to optimize the dollar profit contribution after obtaining a minimum return on capital employed.

REPORTING TECHNIQUES

Let me turn now to some of the techniques that can be easily applied to improve the effectiveness of management reports. They fall into four general categories.

- What should be included in management reports?
- When should information be reported?
- To whom should information be sent?
- How should information be presented?

REPORT CONTENTS

- Focus attention on key controllable items that the executive concerned can do something about. The critical areas that each manager can do something about and that have an important bearing on the results reported have to be identified. In the case before us, for example, the critical factors are identified as being:

   a. Sales volume—utilizing the practical capacity of the plant.
   b. Standard profitability—obtaining an adequate return on the invest-ment employed by achieving standard gross margin objectives.
   c. Waste control—insuring the maximum utilization of materials and minimizing spoilage.
   d. Direct labor performance—productivity standards for the people who work on machines.
   e. Indirect labor control—organizing and staffing the plant to minimize the number of material handlers, shippers, janitors, etc. that are re-quired for production.
   f. Expense control-controlling expenditures for factory supplies, dies, travel, warehousing, etc., and organizing and staffing selling and ad-ministrative functions to maximize profitability.

- Compare actual results reported with a plan, budget, or standard so that information reported may be evaluated in relation to objectives. Num-bers that are compared to nothing in a report are usually quite useless and can be extremely frustrating to an operating manager.
- Include significant ratios and unit costs on reports so that quantitative results may be related to activity levels. The statement of operating results, for example, should show ratios such as percentage of net sales in addition to percentage of return on capital employed. Such ratios as percentages of waste, direct labor, performance, capacity operated, cost per standard di-rect-labor hour and calendar days sales for inventories are shown on other reports.
- Highlight trends and tendencies for planning purposes so that unfa-vorable trends may be checked and favorable trends capitalized upon. Con-tainer Division control reports are supplemented with five-year trend charts of the key ratios in each plant.
- Show non-accounting information on accounting reports so that the reports will contain the whole story. Many financial executives have a tendency to shy away from reporting information that is not in the books. I think that this is a mistake that leads to short-changing the manager who can put this information to use. So, unit information, as well as accounting information, is reported.

- Comment on what happened, why it happened, what is being done about it, and when it will be done to insure that action is taken based on the reported results. The monthly commentary prepared by plant general managers has turned out to be one of the most valuable control tools in this division. In addition to serving as a vehicle for communicating with higher levels of management, these commentaries have the special merit of forcing each plant general manager to think through the critical aspects of the operation each month and to become quite proficient in understanding the business arithmetic that applies to his type of operation.

WHEN TO REPORT?

- Relate the frequency of reports to the frequency of the action that can be taken because of the results reported. There is nothing magic about a month. Some things, such as direct labor performance and waste, lend themselves to daily control. Capital expenditure reports, on the other hand, might be prepared quarterly, semi-annually, or even, in some cases, annually.
- Distribute reports promptly after the close of the period reported so that action may be taken while the "horse is still in the barn." In this case, monthly operating statements are prepared and distributed by the fifth working day following the end of the month. Daily reports are distributed on the next day. A "fearless forecast" is even distributed on the fifth working day before the end of the month. All of this, of course, requires making up a schedule and sticking to it.

RECIPIENT OF REPORT

- Limit the distribution of reports to persons who actually act on the information contained in the reports, not only to reduce the cost of preparation, but, most importantly, to utilize more effectively the time of the recipients. I am sure that every business has certain reports that have certain special status. Ten copies are prepared and everybody receives them, including the cop on the beat. Each person on the list looks at them and comments occasionally but only a few people actually do something because of the results reported. This is a constant problem and it is, unfortunately, a very sensitive area.
- Summarize and interpret results for higher levels of management so that attention will be focused on results obtained. The reports should indicate that subordinate levels of management will furnish detailed explanations and plans for corrective action as required. In International Paper's corrugated shipping container plants, for example, the foremen receive the daily details of direct labor performance by machine and shift for their department. However, the plant production manager and plant general manager receive only a one-page summary for the entire plant. Senior levels of management not only do not have the time to plow through details, but, more importantly, they will never develop their subordinates. The philosophy of management by objectives will not work if they fuss around with all of the nuts and bolts of the business.

PRESENTATION

- Simplify reports so that they are understood by the recipient and so that too much information will not bury the key information. I think that presenting too much information is one of the important failings of many management accounting systems. The typical operating executive is not grounded in finance and statistics, and too much information tends to confuse him.

- Establish a uniform format for all reports in order to make it easy for an executive to follow from one report to another. In many respects, this is what separates the professionals from the amateurs. The professional recognizes the impact of good design and a uniform format in getting his message across. The amateur thinks his job is over when the numbers are put on a report. However, in all fairness, I think that some professionally designed reports fall short because, even though they look good in their initial presentations, they are extremely difficult to produce on a regular basis.

- Confine each report to one 8½ x 11 page wherever practical. Use plenty of white space to improve readership and assist with filing. The important thing that we have to remember here is that reports should be user-oriented and not accounting-oriented. These little techniques will also help the user.

- Distribute tab runs on pre-printed forms, decollated and placed in binders wherever practical, because tab runs can be cumbersome and difficult to work with. I have noticed that data centers commonly fail in this regard. These long, accordion tab runs can be very difficult for an executive to work with.

- Break up columns of numerical data by placing captions in the middle of the report. If you have ever watched an executive go down a report with a ruler you will know what I mean by this point.

- Identify each report with the name of the individual responsible and accountable for the results shown, thereby personalizing the report and causing it to receive more attention. This also tends to insure that the report structure follows the organization. As previously discussed, this is also what "responsibility accounting" is all about.

- Report only significant figures. Omit the pennies and show in thousands or millions, wherever applicable. Although this point may seem self-evident, it is amazing how many large corporations report to the nearest penny, usually because it makes it "easier to balance" at the expense of the user, of course.

In summary, I believe that a tremendous opportunity exists to improve the profitability of our respective organizations by applying a few simple concepts and techniques to our reporting structure. This is not an easy undertaking because of the many habits, biases, and personality factors involved in every organization. However, the experience of many successful businesses testifies to the fact that efforts along these lines usually pay off handsomely in the long run.

Reading 2

Research in Business and Economics

The role of business and economics is central in our society, and then many aspects have therefore been subjected to a great deal of study. Some of this research is carried out in academic institutions, some in government and private agencies, and some in business firms. In all such studies, the data obtained must be recorded, analyzed, organized, and presented in a form that is useful.

CHARACTERISTICS OF AMERICAN BUSINESS

Today (1971) American Gross National Product is nearing the $1,000 billion level and is increasing by about 4 percent each year. The businesses contributing to this tremendous quantity of goods and services range from the American Telephone & Telegraph Company, with its $25 billion in assets, to individuals operating "out of their hats." It is an economic system characterized by change, by an increasingly high level of technology, by mass production and mass consumption, and by steadily increasing capital investment in each worker. The range of capital investment, for example, runs from about $4,000 per worker in the apparel industry to $103,000 per worker in the petroleum industry.[1] Such huge investments are, of course, repaid in high productivity of the industries in which they are made. Today the average worker produces about six times the output of his counterpart a century ago.[2] We have every reason to expect that productivity will continue to increase; in fact, raising the national standard of living depends upon such an increase.

THE NEED FOR RESEARCH

Research is the basis on which business firms and society analyze existing situations and initiate change. The success of the economic system depends upon the ability of its members to conduct that research satisfactorily.[3]

Fortunately, there has been emphasis not only upon product and technological research (which accounted for expenditures of $24 billion in 1967) but also upon business and economic research. It has been estimated, for example, that in marketing research alone, expenditures have grown from $24 million in 1940 to $100 million in 1950 to $300 million in 1960, to $425 million in 1965, and to more than $700 million in 1970. In fact, in recent years marketing-research expenditures have grown about twice as fast as GNP.[4] Economic researchers are also in great demand, and at present there is a considerable shortage of good research economists. Business and government organizations are being structured to depend more and more heavily upon their research staffs for guidance in all their planning programs.

Universities have recognized this increased emphasis upon research, and for degrees in business and economics many of them now require research reports from their students. On the undergraduate level this requirement includes specific course papers and, for honors courses and seminars, usually longer research reports nearly equivalent to master's theses. Master's programs in business and economics often require formal theses, as well as research papers of various lengths and levels of sophistication in other courses. On the doctoral level, each student must write a dissertation that demonstrates a high level of competence in the investigation of a problem; in addition, he too must satisfy the usual course requirements for term papers and reports.

ENDNOTES

1. Theodore J. Sielaff and John W. Aberle, *Introduction to Business: American Enterprise in Action* (2nd ed., Belmont, CA: Wadsworth Publishing Co., Inc., 1966), pp. 5-20.
2. Vernon A. Musselman and Eugene H. Hughes, *Introduction to Modern Business: Analysis and Interpretation* (4th ed., Englewood Cliffs, NJ: Prentice-Hall, Inc., 1964), p. 35.
3. Robert Ferber and P. J. Verdoorn, *Research Methods in Economics and Business* (NY: The MacMillan Co., 1962), pp. 3, 7.
4. Albert Blankenship and Joseph B. Doyle, *Marketing Research Management* (NY: American Management Association, 1965), pp. 12-15.

Reports that Communicate

Modern accounting reports range far beyond the textbook classifications of balance sheet, income statement, and annual report. Much emphasis is being placed on preparation of reports that are highly analytical and inter- pretive. Today's accountant must be more than a gatherer of figures, more than an allocator of costs. Today's accountant must be a "management accountant." That is, he must have not only highly developed accounting skills and knowledge of accounting principles but also a far greater insight into the overall functioning of the business than ever before.

To meet the needs of modern business, management is challenging the accountant to produce more reports, bigger reports, and better reports. The greatest challenge lies not in gathering the varied data, not in analyzing for hidden trends, but rather in being able to transmit this data with all its pertinent meanings to management. Liken the accountant to the football spotter. From his vantage point the spotter watches the game. He sees a weakness in the opposing backfield. This information in the hands of his quarterback may mean the difference between victory and defeat. He picks up his telephone and relays the information to the bench. But on the bench the coach hears only static. There has been no communication. The key play is lost.

In the same way a business play can also end in a loss. For the accountant to have information and be aware of a trend is not enough. To be able to communicate rather than just present is becoming a good accountant's prime skill. If he has this ability, he can increase the effectiveness of a management group by giving it the best tools possible with which to do its work.

SCOPE OF ACCOUNTING REPORTS

Accounting reports can be divided into three major groups or types: statistical reports, financial reports, and narrative reports. Under the head-

Michael J. Reiter, "Reports that Communicate," *Management Services* (January-February, 1967), pp. 27-30. Copyright 1967 by the American Institute of Certified Public Accountants, Inc.

ing of statistical reports we find reports on such facts as units produced, number of complaints versus sales, and waste. The financial report group includes reports of receivables, budget reports, and, that statesman of the accounting world, the annual report. The final group includes the research report and variance expalanations.[1]

Accounting reports for management could instead be divided on a frequency basis—into periodic reports of performance and special reports for planning and policy making. The periodic reports, such as budget reports, monthly statements, and sales reports, have become fairly fixed in form and content through accounting convention and company policy. Most organizations have standardized these reports to the point of presenting them on printed forms. Although this practice may sacrifice some communication effectiveness, the volume of periodic reports necessitates some degree of standardization.

PYRAMID STRUCTURE

The essential feature of periodic reports is that each is a supporting part of the report at the next higher level. Such an integrated system permits management by exception. A division manager can see which area of his organization—production, sales, or advertising—is causing a deviation. The production manager can pinpoint an off-budget department, and the general foreman can locate the specific part of the plant where the deviation occurs. In each instance the individual can direct his attention to the persons or operations at fault and initiate corrective action promptly.

Special reports are designed to give detailed information on specific operations or problems about which management decisions must be made. The special report should expand or supplement data that may be found only in part in various periodic reports. Special reports may be required to give comparisons of performance data other than those comparisons generally used. These reports deal as much in "how" and "why" as they do in "how much."

Many long-range planning decisions, for expansion or for changes in product mix, for example, cannot be made on the basis of the information given in the periodic reports. The special studies required to obtain the needed data must be thorough, and their presentation must be highly communicative. In selecting the format and reporting style the accountant must take into consideration the end use of the report, the complexity of the problem being studied, and the needs and temperament of the person who will receive it.[2]

PROBLEMS OF RECEPTION

All of us, whether accountants, engineers, or managers, tend to assume that when we report data we have gathered or state even a simple opinion it will be understood exactly as we meant it. Modern-day research in the field of communication clearly disproves this normal assumption.

Claude E. Shannon in 1948 presented a paper entitled "A Mathematical Theory of Communication" that laid the groundwork for the modern-day study of information theory or communication theory. This new field of study has shown us how much, or perhaps how little, we actually do communicate with our fellow man. Its theories, although enlightening, do not solve our communication problems for us. They do, however, point out the areas of difficulty and strongly emphasize the need for skill in the art of communicating with others.

Communication theory provides, in the "bit," a universal measure of the amount of information we can pass on to someone else. It tells us how many of these "bits" can be sent per second over different channels, be the channel oral or visual. Communication theory shows us how to state, or "encode," messages efficiently and how to avoid errors in transmission. This last is of great value to us; how to say what we mean.[3]

Communication theory tells us that the amount of information conveyed by a message is directly related to the receiver's uncertainty about what the source of the message will say. Here is an example: If you see what is obviously a one-dollar bill and a man tells you it is a one-dollar bill, the amount of information conveyed is negligible. If you see what looks like some kind of engine and are told its type, use, and other particulars, the amount of information conveyed is greater. The amount of information transmitted, then, depends in part on how uncertain the receiver is of what he will receive.

Of what value are these abstract theories and generalizations to the accountant who must write a report? How can an accountant apply such concepts as "transmitter," "receiver," and "noise" to his work? How can he better communicate?

KNOW THE "NOISES"

The first step to better communication through reports is to know what "noises" cause poor reports. These "noises" may be personal traits, lack of communication skills, or outside distortions. Accountants of one major company were accused by a top executive of "using a pattern of rubberstamp expressions. They write badly and their reports are complicated, obscure, and tiresome."[4] Such a comment is not one that an accountant should be proud of. Yet it does point up a common "noise" in the form of shopworn expression and poor writing style.

"Noise" can take various forms. For example, you are a sales manager whose orders are not being filled because of production processing problems. You receive a report that reads like a technical dictionary. Buried somewhere in the "noisy" veriage may be the length of time required for solution of the problem and the anticipated level of production until then, the facts you need to know. Yet you may tire long before you reach the page on which they are hidden. You are a victim of "noise." Another common example of "noise" is the qualified sentence: "Production is good, all things considered" or "Costs were fairly low, despite minor scrap problems."

Such distortions often result from accountants' lack of training in basic report writing. Many times such training on the high school and college level is relegated to the few courses in English that everyone is obliged to take. Courses in the field of accounting tend to deal with method and cover reporting only in terms of standardized forms. With more special reports to be done, the managerial accountant finds that not only are the figures important but so are the narrative comments on those figures.

Fear of authority and the "cover-up" attitude also produce distortions. Just how detailed should an accountant's analysis be? Information may well be lost because of fear of uncovering a skeleton in someone's business closet.

Distortion can also occur on the receiving end. The mere quantity of reports received may have become more important to the receiver than what the reports say; he rates a job by the poundage of paper produced. Or a manager may look upon a periodic report not as information on performance but as a prescription for conduct. This is especially likely to occur with budgets and variance reports. The tendency is to change performance so as to have a better report without trying to get at the real cause of a variance.

The managerial accountant, as "transmitter," must tune himself to perform his reporting function well. Of prime importance is his ability to put himself in the place of the manager or executive who will use the report. The accountant must be able to envisage what the report is supposed to do. He must be aware of the problem involved, be it expansion or new products or whatever. He must detail the narration of his report to answer as many as possible of the foreseeable questions. The scope of his study must be such that all factors involved in and affected by the decision management will make are completely covered.

To achieve this high degree of problem orientation, the accountant must have a close working relationship with both the receiver of the report and those from whom background information and primary data are obtained. He must think in the frame of reference of the receiver. Semantic issues must be settled before the narrative section of the report is written. When the narrative discusses overhead, asset, or discount, will the executive reading the report include the same items under these headings as the accountant who writes the report? To avoid confusion the accountant must become an extension of the person requesting the report.

Assuming that you have the requisites of a good "transmitter" and that you are alert to possible distortion factors, you have only to pick the proper "signals." Your "signals" will consist of the format used for data tables and charts, the key segments of the analysis narrative, and, most important, the words and style used.

Data tables may be large or may be in small segments, each dealing with one cost segment or area of the report. The prime requisite here is to keep tables in meaningful order and readable. Charts may run the gamut from line charts through bar graphs to pie segment charts, depending on which will best convey the significance of the data presented. Clutter should be avoided. Charts and graphs should be easy to interpret and clearly labeled.

Words and style are of great importance, particularly in the special reports. A foundation of good grammar is essential for good reports. Another handy tool is an unabridged dictionary. Reports such as accountants prepare cannot be polished by the average secretary.

The standard writing techniques for tone setting, proper flow, emphasis, and phrasing are as basic to accounting reports as to any other writing. Reader attention will be held if the basic principles are followed. Brevity and conciseness are also essential. Many an important fact is lost in a mass of verbiage. The use of new and different words and phrases will give life to reports. The same old worn-out statements can be an anesthetic rather than a stimulant to action.

GUIDEPOSTS TO GOOD REPORTS

A good report is not a matter of chance but almost a work of art. All of the rules in the many books written about reporting can be summed up in six key words. Good reports should possess clarity. They are clear and concise, are written in good style, and are easy to read. Good reports have consistency. They stay in the problem area and do not deviate. Meanings and terms do not change in midreport. Good reports display adequacy. They are complete in all respects. Coverage is not slipshod. Good reports possess timeliness. Their data and interpretation are in the light of present circumstances and practices. Good reports have adaptability. They show recognition of the possible different viewpoints on the problem at hand by presenting data to analyze these views. And, lastly, a good report has interest. Gone are the rubber-stamp phrases and mire of useless words. The report takes and holds the reader's attention. It not only shows but it also tells.

The managerial accountant, in properly fulfilling his reporting function, displays skills in composition, human relations, general business knowledge, and communication as well as accounting. He must communicate the necessary information in the proper manner so as to achieve the best end result. He must be a dynamic part of the decision-making team.

ENDNOTES

1. C. E. Redfield, *Communication in Management* (Chicago: University of Chicago Press, 1958), p. 164.
2. W.C. Himstreet and W. M. Baty, *Business Communications* (Belmont, California: Wadsworth Publishing Co., 1964), p. 319.
3. J.R. Pierce, *Signals, Symbols and Noise* (New York: Harper & Row, 1961), pp. 1-9.
4. P. Douglass, *Communication through Reports* (Englewood Cliffs, New Jersey: Prentice-Hall, Inc., 1957), p. 379.

The Business Decision Maker

Most every business report, sooner or later, makes an impact on a business decision. This destiny of the report is its rationale, its reason for being in the organization . . . .

The ways in which reports serve business decision makers vary widely, of course . . . . an informational report may serve merely as a repository of information . . . . The examinational report . . . may serve a "define and explain" function. This function helps the decision maker build insight about the problem which creates the need for his decision. And, finally, the analytical report may give full-blown comprehensive treatment to the problem to be solved and the associated decision or decisions to be made. As far as a report's ultimate destiny is concerned, it matters little what the report is called or what its appearance reveals; the one thing all reports should have in common is a vital relationship to decision making in the organization. . . .[1]

INFORMATION AS A BASIS FOR DECISIONS

. . . the manager first and foremost is a decision maker . . . .

As we can see in Figure 1, the manager, as a decision center, is the human counterpart of an electronic computer. . . .

. . . let us first consider briefly, in two classes, the nature of information: (1) observational information, and (2) inferential information. *Observational* information, as the words suggest, is information which the manager gathers on the basis of his direct observation of physical phenomena in his environment. *Inferential* information is that which comes to the manager indirectly through other people and from his direct observation of a few relative to many sources. Also included under the heading of inferential information is that which the manager generates and projects within himself after his direct observations of the world about him—the manager's conclusions, for example . . . .

Adapted from David M. Robinson, *Writing Reports for Management Decisions* (Columbus, OH; Charles E. Merrill Publishing Co., 1969), pp. 365-373. With permission of the publisher.

FIGURE 1
The Manager as a Decision Center in the Organization

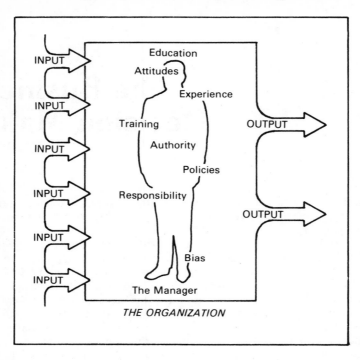

... The accuracy, reliability, appropriateness, and completeness of a manager's decisions are functions of the accuracy, reliability, appropriateness, and completeness of the information on which the decisions are based. To be sure, the skill of the manager as a decision maker—influenced by such factors as his ability to be objective, his perceptive ability, his learning ability, and, certainly, his general intelligence—has a direct bearing on the effectiveness of his decisions. However, the business report, which frequently is the primary medium of communication on which a manager's final decision is based, is particularly vulnerable to criticism when the decision is defective in some manner. . . .

THE DECISION-MAKING PROCESS

As is the case with any abstract expression which serves as a label for a complex idea, *decision making* does not lend itself to easy definition. . . . Decision making . . . is the process by which a manager—

Frames the tentative hypotheses bearing on the problem and its possible solutions;
Tests (or verifies) the hypotheses in some acceptable manner, preferably by conducting objective research;

Establishes the alternatives for the problem solution and *selects* that alternative which he concludes is best under the circumstances; and *Communicates* the selected alternative to secure its acceptance as a decision.

The sophistication of the approach a manager takes to make a decision according to this plan varies considerably, of course, with such factors as the general significance of the problem and the time and resources available to solve the problem. In some instances, for example, we can expect a manager to frame his tentative hypotheses on the basis of nothing more than casual thought. In other instances, we might find a manager who conceives a fairly well-thought-out plan for gathering objective data with which to frame the tentative hypotheses.

In any event, this framework for the intellectual activities associated with decision making provides us a means by which we can relate the process to the nature and scope of report writing. We can see very quickly, for example, that an analytical report actually could contain within its covers total treatment of a decision-making event. Such a report could present a line of reasoning which sought and discovered tentative alternatives (possible problem solutions) and expressed such alternatives in the form of untested or unverified hypotheses. Then the report could present the results of associated testing by relating the information gathered through a reliable research methodology to each of the alternatives. The report could then present a conclusion as to which was the best alternative among those considered and, then, finally, stimulate those affected to accept this alternative as a decision with merit. In a comprehensive report-writing situation all of these factors might well be accounted for in a single report. . . .

ENDNOTE

1. In this chapter we are concerned with placing decision making into a broad perspective which will help us see its relationship to business report preparation. Thus a detailed treatment of the subject is beyond our needs here. We should note, however, that decision making—as both an art and a science—has been commanding a great deal of attention in the management literature in recent years. For those readers who would like to consider this subject in depth, we recommend as an excellent source William T. Morris, *Management Science in Action,* Richard D. Irwin, Homewood, Illinois, 1963.

Planning for Effective Researching and Reporting

PLANNING PROCEDURES

So far . . . you have familiarized yourself with preliminary information about definitions, uses, classifications, illustrations, and trends of modern business reporting. By learning what business reports are expected to be and to do, you have prepared yourself for *planning* these messages effectively. But *how* should you plan? What *procedures* will lead you to developing and presenting effective reports?

The major steps that we recommend involve a work plan as well as a report outline. . . . The work plan includes questions which, when answered clearly and specifically, will produce a research proposal.

Concerning business research and reporting, these communication factors require your attention:

1. Authorization
2. Identification
3. Purpose
4. Scope, Limitations, and Design
5. Schedule and Budget
6. Justification and Additional Considerations

A UNIFIED MESSAGE

Now let us see how the factors of your work plan easily fit into a unified format. Study carefully the work plan illustrated in Figure 2. Note that the work-plan format is flexible. Its parts may easily be rearranged to accommodate the writer's and the reader's preferences. Moreover, the plan offered to you here has been used successfully to propose and to guide research in businesses, industries, government agencies, sciences, and arts. Application

---

Condensed from Morris Philip Wolf and Robert R. Aurner, *Effective Communication in Business* (Cincinnati: South-Western Publishing Co., 1974, pages 499, 504, 505, 508, 509. With permission of the publisher.

FIGURE 2
The Work Plan

A WORK PLAN FOR EFFECTIVE RESEARCH AND REPORTING

1. **Authorization**— What person, people, policies, regulations, or circumstances permit you to undertake your report project?
2. **Identification**— What is the topic of your study? the title of your project?
3. **Purpose**—What is (are) the objective(s) of your project?
4. **Scope**—What are the major areas of your study?
5. **Limitations**—How do you propose to confine your scope? What factors probably will modify or restrict your study?
6. **Design**—How do you intend to build and conduct your study?
   a. Assumptions: What ideas or concepts do you hypothesize initially without proof?
   b. Tentative Conclusions: What kinds of results are likely products of your study?
   c. How do you propose to separate your project into its related issues or subtopics? Concerning those issues or subtopics, what kinds of data do you seek? How do you plan to collect and evaluate the data?
      (1) Sources. What people, publications, records, and other references pertain to your study? Which of the pertinent references are available to you? Which of the available, pertinent references do you intend to use?
      (2) Data Collection. How do you intend to acquire information from the available, pertinent sources? Through readings, observations, interviews, questionnaires, experiments, other means? In what sequence do you expect to use the methods of acquiring information?
      (3) Previous Findings. What earlier work is related—directly or indirectly—to your project? What have earlier studies revealed?
      (4) Data Use. How do you plan to process the data that you collect? How do you propose to analyze, synthesize, and interpret the information?
      (5) Report Format. What kind of message do you expect to produce? Is your report to be written—a memorandum, a letter, a many-paged document, a publication? Is your report to be oral—an extemporaneous, a textual, a memorized message? What style and tone of writing or speaking do you intend to use? What method of report reproduction—typewriting, hectographing, Mimeographing, Xerographing,printing, filming, tape recording, other means—do you anticipate?
7. **Schedule and Budget**—What are the "due dates" for intermediate phases of your study? What is the "deadline" for presenting your final report? How much time, money, and other resources does every major phase of your proposal require? How much of these resources does your total project require?
8. **Justification**—Of what potential value is your project? Who is apt to benefit from your report? What kinds of benefits are likely to result? Why does your project merit the investment of time, money, and other resources?
9. **Additional Remarks**—What relevant considerations are omitted from the preceding categories of your work plan?

Note: According to writer and reader preferences, the parts of this plan may easily be rearranged while retaining logical unity. For example: Authorization, Identification, Purpose, Justification, Scope, Limitations, Design, Schedule and Budget, Additional Remarks.

of this plan has produced useful reports that range from letters and memos to term papers, monographs, master's theses, and doctoral dissertations.

Please bear in mind that we have explored ONE kind of work plan. Other types may be used and, even within the form that we have suggested here, items may be arranged in an order other than the one we have discussed. Remember to build your plan according to the directions of your employer or instructor. . . .

Remember, also, that the temptation to begin composing a report without adequate planning is strong. You may be tempted to plunge immediately into drafting the text; but surrendering to this temptation is likely to cause needless expense, confusion, and misunderstanding. For these reasons we have described a comprehensive and flexible blueprint for a planning *process*. . . .

You may need to prepare several revisions of your first work plan before your proposal is approved. Welcome the opportunity for revision. Changing a work plan is certainly better than having to rewrite—or to risk rejection of—your final report. You will find that the more detailed your work plan becomes, the easier the phases of data collection, data processing, and final composition are likely to be. . . .

Ten Commandments for Effective Written Communications

WHO IS THE FINAL JUDGE OF YOUR WRITING?

Most business transactions, from start to finish, are activated by some form of communication, usually written—letters, memos, reports. The objective of these communications is to get some person or persons to do what should be done to complete the transaction.

Always remember, therefore, that the *reader* of your communication—*not you*—is the judge of your writing. He will decide from what you say and how you say it whether the communication will accomplish its purpose.

The responsibility, then, for getting favorable action rests upon your shoulders. How will you discharge that responsibility?

- First, you must sincerely want to write clearly and convincingly—to serve your reader as well as your company.
- Second, you must set up specific writing standards.
- Third, you must constantly strive to attain these standards.
- Fourth, you must check each communication against the standards to be sure that you have achieved them.

THE FIRST COMMANDMENT

Keep average sentence length within 18 words and use no more than 10 long words in each 100 words.

An overuse of long sentences and long words forces your reader to spend more time than he should in understanding your message. Your writing will accomplish little unless it can be read easily and quickly. Your reader will thank you if he doesn't have to wade through long, rambling sentences.

Clyde Blanchard. Reprinted with permission, *Ideas for Management*, 1971 Ed. published by the Association for Systems Management.

204

Test Your Own Writing

Select a passage of at least 100 words, but not more than 250. Count the words in the passage. Then apply the Gunning formula:

1. Count the number of sentences in the passage. Then find the average length. For example, if you have 6 sentences in a passage of 120 words, the average sentence length is 20 words.
2. Count the number of long words, excluding those for which no satisfactory substitute exists.

Gunning defines a long word (for this purpose) as a word of three or more syllables for which a suitable shorter word can be substituted.

If you find that the average length of your sentences is not more than 18 and that you haven't used more than 10 long words in each 100 words, then your writing is readable to anyone who has at least an eleventh-grade education.

This formula, which Gunning calls the "Fog Index," does not measure the *quality* of your writing. Although it may be easy to read, it can still be worthless. You must have worthwhile content to start with.

Suppose, however, that you find that you are using too many long sentences and too many long words. What to do? Let's consider first how to shorten those sentences that are unnecessarily long.

How to Shorten Long Sentences

Many too-long sentences can be shortened by adhering to the definition of a sentence. Webster defines a sentence as "a group of words expressing *one* completed step in a course of thinking."

Many long sentences violate this definition. The writer has expressed two or more complete steps in his thinking. In so doing, he has strung together these steps with the connectives *and* or *but* instead of ending each one with a period. Here's an example:

Thank you for your order of October 20, and we shall make the drawing at once, and we will send it to you for your approval.

This sentence expresses three thoughts. If the reader is a skillful writer, he will get the impression that you are not. This impression may adversely affect his reaction to your entire letter.

To avoid this unfavorable reaction, recast your sentence, adhering to the definition of a sentence:

Thank you for your order of October 20. We will make the drawing at once. When it is completed, we will mail it to you for your approval.

We must use both long and short sentences to avoid monotony. But, long or short, each sentence must conform to rule.

You will, of course, have to write some sentences containing two clauses connected by *and* or *but*. Why? Because the information contained in the two clauses is needed to complete the thought you are expressing. Here's an example:

> We are enclosing our check for $490, *and* we will send you the balance on May 2.

Here's another:

> I will give you $5 now, but I won't give you another cent this month.

Note that the two statements in each example are essential to complete the writer's thought.

We set as a standard for the average length of a sentence 18 words and showed how to maintain this standard. We emphasized that the mere shortness of a sentence, however, does not guarantee its clarity. A long sentence may be clearer than a short sentence. We should use both short and long sentences to avoid monotony.

Too Many Long Words

Goethe once said, "Everyone hears but what he understands." The Bible, 1 Corinthians 14-9, has this verse: "So likewise ye, except ye utter by the tongue words easy to understand, how shall it be known what is spoken? for ye shall speak into the air."

About 50% of the words you will use will consist of short words, such as: a, an, the, at, for, is, was, were, will, can, not, but, as, so, has, have, it, we. Conesford reminds us: "Never forget that English is rich in monosyllables. If this wealth is used and the short words are made the backbone of speech and writing, they can give them simplicity, strength, and beauty."

If, however, we were to use only short words, our writing would be choppy and void of reader interest. It would have no warmth, no color. We must, therefore, use enough long words to avoid this defect.

We get into trouble from the point of view of readability only when we use too many long words for which shorter ones would suffice.

Some have said: "Complexity is not the badge of wisdom; wisdom goes hand in hand with simplicity."

If your "Fog Index" (described in the first installment) is too high because you are using too many long words, here are some examples of what to do:

Instead of Using	Use
abundance	plenty
accumulate	gather
affix a signature	sign
commence	start
communication	letter, wire, etc.
compensate	pay, reward
conveyance	car, truck, etc.
demonstrate	show
encounter	meet
locality	place

modification	change
objectives	aims
terminate	end
unavailability	lack
utilization	use

You can see from these examples that it is easy to get rid of long words. But you would be making a mistake if you concluded that you should never use the long words in the first column. Use them by all means, but don't overuse them.

The essential point to remember is that it is more important to use the right word than the short word. So, if the right word is a long word, use it.

To find the right word, you will need at least two reference books close at hand—a dictionary and a book of synonyms.

THE SECOND COMMANDMENT

Don't waste words; make each word pay its own way.

Use only those words needed to convey your thoughts clearly, convincingly, and in a spirit of empathy. *Empathy:* The imaginative projection of one's own consciousness into another's. The prime requisite of successful communication.

If the words are heaped up, the thoughts become more and more obscure . . .
. . . A word too much defeats its purpose . . . True brevity of expression consists of everywhere saying only what is worth saying, and in avoiding tedious details about things every man can supply for himself.

—Schopenhauer

As it is the mark of great minds to say many things in few words, so it is that of little minds to use many words to say nothing.

—La Rouchefoucauld's Maxims

Words are like leaves; and
where they most abound,
Much fruit of sense beneath is rarely found.

—Alexander Pope

How to Cut Letter Costs

In 1957 the cost of the average business letter was $1.70, according to a survey conducted by *American Business*. The cost has risen to more than $3 today (1971).

The average letter is from 20 to 50% longer than is necessary. These letters are costing from 30 to 75 cents more than they should. What to do? Cut out all wasted words.

Suppose you received a letter that started with this expression:

"I have your letter of May 6 and in reply would say . . . ." Would you be annoyed at having to read these 12 words before you found out what the writer was going to tell you? Of course you would. The writer has wasted his company's money and your time. He has also given you an unfavorable opinion of himself as an up-to-date businessman. You are likely to say to yourself: "Maybe his firm is as out of date as he is."

Now you can see the damage that may be done by writing letters that contain words that say nothing of importance. The skillful writer would probably say: "Here's the information you requested." You are telling your reader in the fewest possible words what he wants to hear. You are writing economically.

Wasting One Word Really Wastes Six

George Allen, a salesman for an office supply store, met a customer, Jim Jones, on the sidewalk and stopped for a chat. Just before they departed, George said: "You use a lot of our columnar pads, Jim. We've got them on sale at half price the rest of this month. How many shall I send you?"

"Oh, I could use at least two dozen," replied Jim. George conveyed his message in 28 short words. And he got the order. "That was easy," he thought to himself, "I'll write a letter to several of our customers; we'll get rid of the entire lot in no time." So, as soon as he got back to the office, George called in his stenographer and dictated a letter.

The letter George dictated:

> Dear Sam:
> Our records show that you are a regular user of our columnar pads, which have been selling at $2 a dozen, as you know.
> We find that we are overstocked on this item just before inventory time, so, for the rest of this month, we are going to price these pads at half price, only $1 a dozen, as long as our present supply lasts.
> This is a real bargain, so I suggest that you take advantage of it and stock up. I'll be looking for your order by return mail, or, better still, just give it to me over the phone.
> Sincerely yours,   (108 words)

The 28 words that George used in selling Jim have now grown to 108—an increase of 260% Why?

Why did George use 80 more words in writing than he did in talking?

The only reason he wrote a letter was that he didn't have time to talk to each customer. Is this reason a valid one for using 80 more words? Emphatically not. If we were to ask George why, he would give us the stock answer of thousands of dictators: "When you write, you should use a different style than when you talk."

If asked whether he knew the cost of a letter, George would tell you that he hadn't given any thought to cost. Today, as the cost of paperwork, which includes letters, is eating up profits at an alarming rate, we must be conscious of the cost of letters and especially of the cost of wasted words.

Let's consider the cost of those 80 wasted words in George's letter:

George dictated	80 wasted words
His steno wrote	80 wasted words
She transcribed	80 wasted words

```
She proofread ............................80 wasted words
George proofread ........................80 wasted words
Sam read................................80 wasted words
     Making a total of .................... 480 wasted words!
```

Why Say the Obvious?

One type of thoughtless writing is giving your reader information he already knows—saying the obvious.

Another type is telling him to do something he would do without your telling him—again, saying the obvious.

For example:

We *have your letter informing us that* . . . .
You can't answer a letter of a request without having received it. Your reader knows that.
We have *checked our records* and find . . . .
Will you please *consult your records* and . . . .
How else will you find except by checking or consulting your records.
Enclosed *you will find* our new catalog.
The enclosed catalog will be found by your reader without your telling him.

Why Don't You?

Ask yourself "Why don't we?" as you read these sentences:

We *desire to* acknowledge your letter.
     (Well, why don't we?)
We *should like to* ask you to . . . .
     (Well, why don't we?)
We *wish* to thank you for . . . .
     (Well, why don't we?)
We *want to* acknowledge receipt of your check.
     (Well, why don't we?)

Why Say It Twice?

Saying it twice is called *doubling*. The writer who doubles thinks he is being emphatic. He is, but without any need to be. Learn to depend upon the meaning of a word. Don't feel that its meaning always needs to be strengthened by adding another word that means the same. Here are some common forms of doubling:

Don't Say	Say
the sole and only purpose	either one
true facts	facts
assistance and service	either one
necessary steps required	either one

even more complete	complete
manufactured in the past	manufactured
separate and apart	either one
still continues	continues
same identical	identical
larger in size	larger
just recently	recently
basic principles	principles
important essentials	essentials
first began to	began to
exactly equal	equal
ask the questions	ask
surplus left over	surplus
mutual cooperation	cooperation
enclosed herewith	enclosed
look forward with anticipation	anticipate
grossly exaggerated	exaggerated
consensus of opinion	consensus
at the present time	omit
a new innovation	an innovation
eye-witness	witness
fell down	fell
past history	history
hollow tube	tube
most unique	unique
absolutely finished	finished
personal opinion	opinion

The technical name for doubling is tautology. Tautology is but one of several weaknesses of the unskilled writer. If you have this weakness, get rid of it—now.

Watch Out for Wordy Phrases

Here are some wordy phrases that the average writer uses because he isn't cost conscious. Now that you have become so, you will spot the wasted words at once. But, don't stop there; put those phrases on your "Don't Use" list.

Don't Use These Wordy Phrases	Use Instead
for the purpose of	for
for the reason that	since
in order to	to
in the event that	if
with reference to	about
pursuant to your request	as requested
prior to	before
subsequent to	after
along the lines of	like or about

from the point of view of	from
in as much as	since, because
in accordance with	as
in the case of	in
in the neighborhood of	about
on the grounds that	since, because
with a view to	to
with the result that	so that
with the regard to	about
in other words	omit
in the amount of	for
at a later time	later
at the present time	now or omit
due to the fact that	because, since
in the near future	soon
in view of the fact that	since, because
payments of a similar nature	similar payments
within a period of one year	within one year
to make a decision	to decide
take into consideration	consider
care must be exercised	be careful
large number of	many

How many of these wordy expressions do you use? If used over and over, how much do they cost your company in wasted words a year? Can you afford circumlocution?

THE THIRD COMMANDMENT

Write so that your reader can't misunderstand you and will believe you.

Misunderstandings in letters usually arise from a lack of knowledge of semantics—the science of the meaning of words. Most misunderstandings are caused by:

1. The use of abstract words, which may have one meaning for the writer and another for the reader.
2. The use of shop talk, trade jargon, and alphabetese when writing to the uninitiated.
3. A lack of coherence—the words aren't put together in the correct sequence.

Words have two kinds of meaning. The dictionary meaning (denotation) and the meaning based on one's experience with the words (connotation). Misunderstandings often arise from this second kind of meaning—connotation. For example, a supervisor says to one of his men: "Your work isn't *satisfactory.*"

The worker replies: "I don't understand; I think my work is *satisfactory.*"

A misunderstanding has arisen. Why? Because the two men interpret the word *satisfactory* differently. To make himself clear, the supervisor replies:

"You have been late six times this month; you made four mistakes in the last report; and you forgot to order those new forms we need."

Now the two men understand each other. That one word *satisfactory* caused all the trouble. Words that can be interpreted differently by the writer and the reader are known as abstract words. Don't use them unless you wish to keep specific facts from your reader.

Abstract Words

Compare specific, label words with these expressions: quite a little, a little longer, too many, as soon as possible, within a reasonable time, unsuitable, inadequate, conditions, facilities, extravagant, difficulties, unsatisfactory.

Whenever you use these and other abstract expressions, you must realize that your reader may interpret them differently from you. To avoid misunderstandings, then, use specific words—words that appeal to your reader's senses: his sight, touch, hearing, smell.

Beware Shop Talk

COIK is the abbreviation for the expression, "clear only if known." You can't expect your reader to understand you when you're telling him about something of which he has no knowledge. Business writers often forget that others outside their business aren't familiar with shop talk, including coined abbreviations.

Think of your reader; ask yourself—Will he understand my message? Will he, through his experience with words, place the same meaning on the words I am using as I do?

> Girl: I'll have you know I don't go out with perfect strangers.
> Sailor: Calm yourself; I'm not perfect.

Write So That Your Reader Will Believe You

Your reader may understand every word you use and yet not believe you. In business it is essential that seller and buyer believe in each other.

Millions of dollars are wasted in communication because the writer ignores the beliefs of his reader.

Never "duck" the issue. When you are wrong, admit your mistake. Your reader will spot hypocrisy and evasion every time.

THE FOURTH COMMANDMENT

Write in a friendly, informal style whenever feasible.

> Think first of your reader's feelings.
> Give him an honest reason why.
> Be friendly, direct, sincere.
> —Gustave Flaubert

In nearly every letter you write you are asking your reader to agree to something or to act in a way you want him to act.

You write many letters only because you can't talk to the recipient.

The more nearly your writing style approaches your informal, friendly conversational style, the more effective your letters will be.

Four rules to follow

1. Do not place the blame on your reader.
2. Don't sound superior.
3. Don't sound bossy.
4. Don't be too positive.

Friendly letters pay big dividends. An ill-chosen word or phrase, a cold, formal letter, too many *I's* and *We's* and too few *You's*—these are the things that kill good will.

Unfriendly Expressions

Many mistakes and misunderstandings occur in transacting business. Some credit applications cannot be granted. A firm has to say "No" at times to its customers and to its employees. Mistakes have to be rectified.

The skillful writer, following the Golden Rule, finds a friendly way to avoid offending his reader under these difficult circumstances. He doesn't write such tactless and selfish expressions as these:

- We are in receipt of your complaint.
- We can't understand your position.
- We are sorry you didn't understand our letter.
- We shall be happy to survey the damage.
- We have no record of receiving your letter.
- We are in receipt of your letter about the possible damaged roof.
- We shall be pleased to receive your order.
- We can't seem to please you.
- Please describe in detail your alleged accident.

The writer of these expressions was thinking more about his company than about the reader. Too much "We" and not enough "You."

Contractions Help

In conversation you use contractions often. You say "it's" for "it is" and "let's" for "let us." Sprinkle a few contractions through your writing; they will add informality to your letters.

A French proverb

He who leaves your company pleased with himself is surely pleased with you.

Keep this proverb in mind as you construct the closing paragraph. Write an ending that is appropriate. Then you won't need a complimentary closing.

THE FIFTH COMMANDMENT

Use words of action when you want action and when you want your reader to know that you are taking the action he desires.

Most business letters report actions or request the reader to take action. Your letters may be easy to read, concise, understood, and yet not get the action you want. Why? Because you do not use words of actions.

Words of Action

Words of action are mainly verbs. Verbs are divided into *active* and *passive* verbs. Active verbs are strong; passive verbs are weak. You can always spot a passive verb; it is composed of some form of *to be* and the *past participle* of another verb. Examples:

be bought, is needed, was taken, has been followed, is desired, was approved, have been completed

Here is a sentence with two passive verbs:

Your truck will *be bought* by us as soon as it *is needed.*

With active verbs:

We will *buy* your truck as soon as we *need* it.

Note the lack of action in the first sentence. Also note that you use more words with the passive form. Here are more examples:

Passive: The enclosed form is to be signed and returned by you as soon as possible.
Active: Please sign and return the enclosed form by Wednesday of next week.

Now you are positively requesting action and you have *dated* this action— by Wednesday of next week. Dated Action means being specific as to *when* the action is to be taken. Dated Action is much more effective than such abstract expressions as *as soon as possible.*

Verbal Nouns

A verbal noun is a noun formed from a verb. Here is a list of some common verbal nouns:

Verbal Noun	Verb
improvement	improve
operation	operate
resumption	resume
attention	attend
announcement	announce
elimination	eliminate

Note that most verbal nouns end in *ion, tion,* and *ment.* They also are long words and are usually used with the passive verb. All verbal nouns are useful words. You will, however, usually strengthen your sentence by using the verb form for the noun. Here's an illustration:

> Verbal Noun: An *improvement* in our system has been made.
> Verb: We have *improved* our system.
> Verbal Noun: *Consideration* of your claim is being given by our credit manager.
> Verb: Our credit manager is *considering* your claim.

Positive Closing

When you request action, use the strongest possible closing consistent with good business practices. Beware the four words, *hope, trust, may,* and *if.* Their use in your closing paragragh gives your reader the loophole he may be looking for—the chance to delay or take no action. Illustrations:

> We *hope* that you will send your check soon.

Merely hoping won't get action. You must ask for it:

> We shall expect your check by return mail for the balance due on your account.

Here's another weak closing:

> *If* you will send us the information needed, we will be able to complete our estimate and send you the quotation requested. .

Now let's get rid of that weak word *if:*

> We will complete our estimate and send you the quotation as soon as we receive the needed information. Won't you please send it by return mail?

Test Each Use of a Verb

You will use active and passive verbs correctly if you will test each use of a verb by asking yourself this question: Do I want action in this sentence? If your answer is Yes, then you will use an active verb. If your answer is No, then you may choose whichever form best fits the thought you are expressing. In this way you will develop a style that will enable you to mix the two forms effectively.

Action verbs get action. Dated action brings quicker and surer action than does the use of abstract expressions such as *as soon as possible* or *at your earliest convenience.* Beware passive verbs. Use them only when you *don't* want action.

THE SIXTH COMMANDMENT

Write so that your words and sentences will stick together.

You have had the experience of listening to someone talk in a rambling way. You found it almost impossible to follow his thinking. He was talking incoherently. Coherence (sticking together) is a must in business writing. You must link your words, sentences, and paragraghs in logical order so that your reader will follow your thinking easily.

You have already learned to use only those words that are needed to convey your meaning. Your next problem is to use only those thoughts that are needed and to arrange them in a logical, one-two-three order.

Logical Arrangement

Only the skillful writer can write or dictate an effective letter or report without first jotting down all the thoughts he needs to include and then arranging them in the right order.

Stick to the major thoughts you wish to express. Don't be tempted to inject incidental thoughts. Thought detours will cause your reader to stray from the main thought and may also confuse him.

Misplaced Word or Phrase

The misplaced word or phrase is a common violation of coherence. Here are two illustrations:

Wanted: Young man to run hardware store out of town.

Mrs. Smith was presented a bouquet of roses for being the mother of the most children by Mr. Jones.

Misplaced words cause a lot of trouble in business writing. Check this mistake by reading your letter to yourself or to someone else before signing it.

Be very careful with the placement of the word *only*. Note how the position of this word affects the meaning of the sentence:

Only we said that he could sell cars.
We *only* said that he could sell cars.
We said that *only* he could sell cars.
We said that he could *only* sell cars.
We said that he could sell *only* cars.

Pronouns

Another cause of incoherence is the misplaced or incorrectly used pronoun. A pronoun stands for a noun. It is used to avoid monotony that comes from the repetition of the noun. The noun to which a pronoun refers is called the antecedent of the pronoun. The pronoun should refer to the noun *immediately preceding* the pronoun unless the meaning is absolutely clear. For example, consider this sentence:

Mr. Jones told Mr. Smith that he had not ordered enough to meet *his* needs.

Who did the ordering, Mr. Jones or Mr. Smith? Whose needs, Mr. Jones's or Mr. Smith's? If Mr. Smith did the ordering to meet his own needs, the sentence is correct. Since three interpretations of this sentence are possible, the writer must make his meaning unmistakenly clear.

Do not use a pronoun for a noun that occurs in a preceding paragraph. Keep all antecedents within the paragraph and keep each one within the sentence in which the pronoun occurs unless you are sure that your meaning is clear when the antecedent is in a preceding sentence.

Word Links

All sentences in a paragraph should express closely related thoughts. To show this close relationship, use word or phrase *links*. In so doing, you enable your reader to follow your chain of thought easily.

Here is a paragraph with no word links connecting the sentences:

Nearly all business transactions start, progress, and finish with written communications. Business writing skill is essential to success. Few business correspondents are skillful writers. Few business firms have set writing standards. Few have any control over the quality or cost of their letters.

As this paragraph is constructed, every sentence appears to have equal importance. None of them is linked to the following sentence. Note the improvement in coherence when these sentences are linked together.

Nearly all business transactions start, progress, and finish with written communications. *For this reason,* business writing skill is essential to success. Few business correspondents, *however,* are skillful writers. *Furthermore,* few business firms have writing standards or controls over the quality or cost of their letters.

The links are italicized. They hold the main thought together throughout the paragraph. Prepare a list of word and phrase links to use in your own writing. Insert them as needed, but don't force them into sentences just to have a link when one may not be needed.

Coherence involves many other factors, but space does not permit a complete treatment. Always remember that disorder annoys most readers because it confuses them. Strive to keep your thread of thought unbroken from start to finish. You can do this by making your words stick together logically.

THE SEVENTH COMMANDMENT

Use variety of expressions to avoid monotony and to increase reader interest.

Letters that are merely factual and that have a monotonous sameness in vocabulary and style will build little, if any, good will. The reader will feel that you, the writer, have done only the minimum in composing your letter. On the other hand, he will feel complimented if you go to the trouble of injecting variety of expression.

Variety's still the very spice of life. Cowper stated a principle of psychology that's as true today as it was in his time. Still the spice of life for you, the writer, as for the reader. You, too, will benefit by using variety; you will enjoy writing much more than you have in the past.

In expressing your thought, you have many words and many sentence constructions to choose from. Take the trouble to discard your worn-out expressions; in their stead use new ones. Let's start with the salutation; it's long overdue for a change. For example, instead of always writing *Gentlemen,* you might start your letter this way:

This letter, Gentlemen . . .
> is a request for your catalog.

Instead of *Dear Mr. Smith,* write:

Thank you, Mr. Smith . . .
> for your prompt attention to my request of April 20.

or:

You were thoughtful, Mr. Smith . . .
> to send me a notice of an increase in your prices.

You can get rid of the worn-out complimentary closing in a similar way. It isn't needed if your closing paragraph is friendly and to the point. So write your closing paragraph so that your reader finishes reading your letter with a friendly feeling toward you and your company. Too much We attitude may nullify the effect of all the rest of your letter. The YOU attitude honestly expressed in the closing paragraph makes a complimentary closing unnecessary. Leave it out.

To give you an inkling of the potential wealth of the English Language, here are excerpts from a source book that should be on your desk. It is the *Word Finder,* published by Rodale Books, Inc., Emmaus, Pa.

Let us suppose that you had included the following sentence in a letter: Our business suffered a severe loss last year.

What other words could you have used to inject variety into the sentence? Let's start with the word *business.* The *Word Finder* suggests these words: Occupation, trade, concern, enterprise, industry, work, commerce.

For the expression *suffered a loss,* the *Word Finder* has: droops, expires, falters, founders, simmers, succumbs.

After studying these words, you recast your sentence:

> Our enterprise is foundering because of a lack of capital.

or:

> Our concern will expire unless we reorganize at once.

If you have been using the same old words and expressions for years, it's a safe bet that you are writing without variety and not getting any fun out of it. Remember, as someone has put it, there are no routine letters, only routine letter writers.

Variety of Sentence Openings

The first sentence structure learned in school is *Subject* followed by *Verb* followed by *Object*. Many unskilled writers never vary this order. Yet we have eight other beginnings from which to choose in varying your style. Here they are: The original sentence:

> The Writer (subject) should grasp (verb) every opportunity (object) to use variety.

1. With a clause: "If you will employ variety at every opportunity, you will write more effectively."
2. With a phrase: "By employing variety you will write more effectively."
3. With a verb: "Don't miss the opportunity to build good will by using variety in your writing."
4. With a correlative: "Not only brevity and friendliness but also variety is an essential factor in good writing."
5. With an adverb: "Always use variety in your letters to increase their effectiveness."
6. With an adjective: "Skillful writers employ variety at every opportunity."
7. With an infinitive: "To be a successful writer, you must use variety of sentence structure and vocabulary."
8. With a participle: "Following the advice of skillful writers, he used variety in his business letters."

Use Picture Words

As you read, be on the lookout for picture words. When you come across one, jot it down. You will be able to use some of these picture words in your own writing. You can adapt others. As your interest grows, you will coin your own.

Here are some picture words taken from current reading:

We *stumbled* into another *pitfall.*
This kind of treatment is hard to *root out.*
He used *hard-headed* common sense.
Management's freedom is being *whittled away.*

He passed the *baton* to his unit heads.
Happy Motoring on the *sunny side of the road.*

Variety in Words

The English language is a gold mine of words. In seeking the right word, finding it, and using it, you are taking a major step toward skillful writing. You are eliminating monotony.

THE EIGHTH COMMANDMENT

Acquire proficiency as a dictator.

Proficiency in dictating letters to a stenographer or by means of a dictating machine is not easy to acquire. Writers who have a little trouble in composing letters in solitude are often unable to dictate letters to someone else. The presence of another person, or even a recording machine, is a disturbing influence. And yet, for speed and economy of production, most business letters must be dictated. So, in addition to becoming a skillful composer of letters, you must become a proficient dictator of letters.

Organize Before You Dictate

We are all familiar with the saying: "An ounce of prevention is worth a pound of cure." Organizing your letter before you dictate it is that ounce of prevention. A poorly organized letter is not clear; it usually isn't accurate or complete; it impresses the reader unfavorably; and it often destroys good will.

Specific Procedures to Follow

Here are some specific procedures to follow before answering a letter:

1. As you read the letter you are to answer, underline the points you should include in the answer. Make marginal notes of pertinent thoughts that occur to you.
2. Have your secretary gather all the information you will need before dictating, such as file copies of previous correspondence, data from other departments, enclosures, etc.
3. Select a subject line that is specific and complete.
4. Prepare a short, friendly opening that will get the attention of your reader at once.
5. Arrange the sequence of your thoughts in a logical, coherent, smooth-reading order.
6. Plan a closing that is short and friendly. If action is desired, ask for it. Don't put too much *We* in the closing. Readers do what you want them to do because *they* will benefit, not you.
7. Check to make sure that you have included all the information that the reader should have and that the information is accurate.

THE NINTH COMMANDMENT

Make sure that the physical appearance of your letter will impress your reader favorably.

Having assured yourself that your letter is well written as measured by the goals we have set for you, you are now ready to take the next step: Make sure that the physical appearance of your letter will impress your reader favorably.

Although the expression "Fine feathers make fine birds" is not always true, it applies to your letters provided they are well written.

The Fine Feathers of a Business Letter

The fine feathers of a business letter are:

- An attractive appearance, as indicated by the letterhead, the envelope, the placement of the letter, the even touch of the typist.
- Good taste in the selection of paper and type and in the display of the information that makes up the letterhead.
- Correct punctuation, spelling, capitalization, and syllabication.
- Adherence to established rules of styling.

Why a Subject Line?

In correspondence between two business firms, we urge the use of a subject line. Why? Because a subject line placed after the name and address tells the reader at once what the letter is about.

Here is an example:

Panhandle Fair Association
P.O. Box 1529
Lubbock, Texas

Subject: Price of Sash for Fair Building
Gentlemen:

If the mail of this association is first opened by its mail clerk, as is often the procedure in large organizations, he knows by reading the subject line to what department or individual to forward the letter. He doesn't have to waste his time reading the whole letter.

The writer of the letter, by deciding what is to be the specific subject to write about *before* he writes the letter, refrains from including other matters in the letter. Should he need to write the company about another matter, he writes another letter.

Answering a letter containing two or more subjects slows the service a company wishes to render because the letter has to travel from one department to another before it is completely answered.

Use a subject line, therefore, but be sure that it is specific. Suppose the subject line in the illustration had read just *Sash;* it might refer to many things. The mail clerk would have to read the letter to find out to which department to send it.

Paragraphs

Short paragraphs are easier to read than long ones. In business letters the paragraph should not be longer than eight lines. Four to six lines are preferable.

Run-In Items Make Reading Difficult—Tabulate Them

Here's an example of run-in items:

The 80′ x 80′ x 14′ truss-type grain storage building weighs 76,430 pounds, sells for $13,560 fob our shop, will store 91,286 bushels, and can be filled to 11′, 10″ high on the sidewalls. It would include four 12′ x 13′ double sliding doors, four 4′ x 4′ louvers; and would have a bulkhead in the end for loading and unloading. The erection would cost $3,400 without foundations.

Tabulated Items

Here is the description of our truss-type grain storage building:

Dimensions	80′x80′x14′
Capacity	91,286
Weight	76,430 pounds
Cost fob our shop	$13,560
Erection cost	
without foundation	$3,400

This building can be filled to 11′, 10″ high on the sidewalls. It would have—

4 double-sliding doors	12′x13′
4 louvers	4′x4′
1 bulkhead in end for	
loading and unloading	

Is there any doubt in your mind as to which style is more readable and easier to check? The format is often as important as the message.

THE TENTH COMMANDMENT

Continue to improve the thought content of your writing and to enrich your diction.

Dwight Van Avery, a member of General Electric's Educational Staff gives his company's views regarding the ability to express ideas:

The ability to express ideas is perhaps the most important of all the skills a man can possess.
Every day you will be called upon to speak and write; and when you open

your mouth or write, you will be advertising your progress and potential worth.

What you write and what you say will determine in part your rate of climb.

As you strive to improve your writing skill, you will constantly search for the right words. In so doing you will be improving your *diction*.

Diction

Diction, as defined by Webster, means the choice of words to express ideas; the use of language with regard to clearness, accuracy, and variety. It differs from vocabulary, which refers to all the words in the English language. Yet, without a large, rich vocabulary, your diction will be limited. The larger your vocabulary, the more words you command from which to choose those that will best express your thoughts.

Relation of Vocabulary to Success

Johnson O'Connor, founder of the Human Engineering Laboratory, through years of research, has proved that a large vocabulary is a significant factor of business success.

"Words," says O'Connor, "are the instruments by means of which men grasp the thoughts of others and with which they do much of their own thinking. Words, therefore, are the tools of thought."

O'Connor found through many tests of executives that the large vocabularies of successful businessmen come before their success rather than after. So, unless you are sure that your working vocabulary is growing continuously, you are lacking this vital aid to your own progress.

Have you any idea of the number of words in your own vocabulary? Here are some figures that will help you estimate its size:

The average eighth-grade pupil knows around 10,000 words. Upon graduation from high school his vocabulary has grown to about 15,000. The college graduate has added 5,000 more. These 20,000 words make up his *recognition,* his reading vocabulary. His actual working vocabulary is usually much smaller. Why? Because he is lazy in the use of words; and because he does not realize the worth to him of a rich, varied vocabulary.

How many working words have you added this month? This year? Unless you are the exception, your answer will prove to you that you are stuck with the vocabulary you had when you left school. Your vocabulary doesn't grow much unless you form the habit of adding words regularly—say, one or two words a week.

To build this invaluable habit isn't so easy as it seems. You must first select a *useful* word. Then, you must study its definition or definitions, for many words have several meanings. Next, you must study its synonyms, if any, to enable you to select the word that accurately expresses the exact shade of meaning you wish to convey. Finally, you must use the word over and over until it becomes fixed in your vocabulary.

In addition to a dictionary and a synonym book, you will find "Mark My Words," by John B. Opdycke (Harper) a fascinating and rewarding source book. In it you will find the exact word you are looking for and the reasons why, also the part that the word plays in the family of words to which it belongs. Get this book and study one family of words a week.

The Dale Plan

Edgar Dale, of Ohio State University, recommends this plan for improving your vocabulary and your diction:

1. Improve the range and depth of your experiences.
2. Work at your vocabulary a little every day.
3. Read more.
4. Use some of your new words in your conversation as well as in your writing.
5. Read aloud to find out whether you can pronounce your new words correctly.
6. Learn the meaning of key roots of words and the important prefixes and suffixes.
7. Develop an abiding interest in the origin of words.

If you do not have a plan to increase your vocabulary and your diction, try Dale's. And stick to your plan with the tenacity of a bull dog; the reward is worth far more than the effort you will expend.

Build a Reference Library

Build a reference library for constant use. Not many books; just a few, well read and well digested. You have many excellent books from which to choose; here's a suggested list:

- Menning and Wilkinson, *Writing Business Letters,* Richard D. Irwin, 1955.
- Janis, J. Harold, *Business Communication Reader,* Harper and Brothers, 1958.
- Douglass, Paul, *Communication through Reports,* Prentice Hall, 1957.
- Thomas, J. D., *Composition for Technical Students,* Scribners, 1959.
- Flesch and Lass, *The Way to Write,* McGraw-Hill, 1955.
- Gunning, Robert, *The Technique of Clear Writing,* McGraw-Hill, 1952.

Lincoln on Writing

In the "Lincoln Treasury," edited by Caroline Harnsberger, is this inspirational quotation:

> Writing, the art of communicating thoughts to the mind through the eye, is the greatest invention of the world—great in enabling us to converse with the dead, the absent, the unborn; and great, not only in its direct benefits, but greatest help to all other inventions.

Seek worthwhile thoughts; organize them for clear, smooth reading; choose the right words and put them together coherently, and write always for your reader.

Gamesmanship in Written Communication

Consider the following note to a department head. What does it tell you?

> Attached for your review is a proposed position paper regarding a draft of a staff presentation on current problems.

A first glance may tell you only that its author is a bad communicator. Actually, he is probably a much better communicator than he is a manager. He is a product of a school of communication that is becoming as widespread as insincerity and evasiveness. This is the school of "*deliberate obfuscation.*"

The memo may not say much, but the supervisor who wrote it didn't want it to. It was designed to keep him off the hook for anything the report said. The tools were three words—"review," "proposed," and "draft"—used to protect the writer from any semblance of self-commitment and to convey a sort of permanent tentativeness.

So the memo actually tells us that its author is a weasel. Unfortunately, its readers, put off by the lack of clarity or because they are too busy to take time for the analysis that we just made, probably will not glean this message. They will react in a way that the writer intended them to react—and, somewhere in the back of their minds, they will credit him if the proposal is good or remember that it was only a "review" of a "draft" of a "proposed position" if it is bad.

In communication dealing solely with fact, such gamesmanship is seldom practiced. It is when the writer is expressing a judgment or opinion or putting forth new ideas that he may take cover. One person described this maneuver with the comment, "That's where I tiptoe through the tulips."

Mary C. Bromage, "Gamesmanship in Written Communication." Reprinted by permission of the publisher from *Supervisory Management* (May, 1972), pp. 14-17. Copyright 1972 by American Management Association, Inc.

SILENCE IS GOLDEN

Perhaps the simplest game is noncommunication. Not inadvertent non-communication, either. Silence may become a strategy in itself.

A refinement on silence is delay. This also serves the purpose of indicating disinterest or disagreement. And there is always the possibility that the potential message-recipient, while waiting, will arrive at his own conclusions—again keeping the writer off the hook.

Besides delaying by failing to communicate, the writer may delay through indirectness—another gambit in the game of communication. Instead of pinpointing the problem and putting forth a solution in the beginning of a communication, the writer may hold back his answer, sometimes leaving it to the puzzled reader to pick the answer out of the air.

THE CIRCULATION PROBLEM

Since the invention of the copier, a message once prepared for only one person's eyes with, at most, one copy for the file, may now travel far and wide—to friend and foe alike—on the organizational chart. A list of c.c.'s on a paper inhibits the writer's sense of directness and candor—and most worrisome of all to the writer are the people who are not listed but who will receive the letter, report, or memo by the underground route.

So the sender, doubtful about the extent of his message's distribution, resorts to a slow, inductive approach: He identifies his subject gingerly, fills in background detail copiously, reaches his apparent conclusion circuitously, and ends irrelevantly. The prose that results has been reduced to the level of the lowest common denominator of the probable recipients. If doubt about the reception of his message mounts high enough, the writer may never unwrap his point from its swaddling clothes.

Thus, while wide circulation of a message reassures co-workers that they know everything that's going on—and carbon copies on file serve as security blankets for those who receive them—it leaves the message's originator less secure about controlling the effects of what has been said. Putting forth an idea or point of view in the face of innumerable unknown interests invites danger, especially where upward communication is concerned. One manager, preparing a report by command for his vice-president, said, "It is unpleasant to take an authoritative position and direct action on a subject that is usually better understood by the recipient than myself." Another businessman noted, "Much writing is done to answer a request. After traveling through many levels of management, its original purpose is lost."

WHAT?

The strategies of silence, delay, and indirectness are not the only games that are played with paper and pencil; certain stylistic devices—all impeding the clarity and conciseness of the written word—also are used. These practices are neither new nor unknown, having been employed by professional writers when they wished to create a sense of mystery, mood, and illusion.

For example:

Abstract words require the reader to visualize a concept and thus result in less clear-cut delineation of meaning:

> We will determine the potential benefits to be derived from implementation of an improved system in broad terms and assign priorities for proceeding with the installation of the individual project areas, based upon our evaluation of the advantages to be obtained versus the time and cost required for implementation and operation of the new application.

(But are you going to help us increase the production of nuts and bolts?)

Generalities and imprecise phraseology allow more emotive and personalized interpretation than does objective wording:

> A budget should vary with the expected workload, so that it will be accepted as fair by the plant people who are influential.

(How much money is needed to do each job? How much do the plant people expect?)

Passive voice hides the identity of the doer of an action, thus reducing the amount of information contained in the communication:

> The effect of the work that was done in the quality control department, which had been slowed up by the major service interruption, was discussed with all the major departmental supervisors who were included.

(Who actually said what to whom?)

Bland language may be substituted for that which might offend the readers:

> His performance record is consistent with his ability as reflected by the completion of his formal education at the grade-school level.

(But is he qualified for the job?)

Clichés, which are trite expressions used repeatedly for a multitude of occasions, are not tailormade to any one occasion:

> With regard to your request as to my experience and background qualifications in computer work, I would like to indicate to you that I have had minimal exposure. Please feel free to contact me for details.

(What? Write him again?)

Jargon contrived to make the simple seem complex may impress, but it does not enlighten:

> In taking advantage of this opportunity to get in touch with a group of students, I want to relate the news of our plant's being selected as the sole source for parts originally released to outside vendors. The parts henceforth will be conformed with standard company specifications. The data will come from our formatted files.

("Released?" "Conformed?" "Formatted?")

Long sentences often leave a blur in the reader's mind, demanding that he reconstruct everything between the subject and the period to arrive at the meaning:

> It has been our objective to review the audit work performed by the internal audit staff in order to attempt to establish the degree of assurance that can be placed on the account data system, to the extent that it completely and accurately processes data based on the testing method employed.

(Just what is the objective?)

These examples are typical of a style that withholds more than it gives to the reader. The complete catalog of such devices is long and probably growing, so great is human ingenuity under the pressures of organizational stresses and strains.

"I CALL IT POLITICS"

If the tactics of obfuscation are knowingly adopted, then gamesmanship is the result. In an article in *The New York Times,* Vice President Spiro Agnew, explaining his own choice of words, whether for the sake of clarity or the converse, is quoted as saying, "I suppose if you want to get a point across, you say it in exciting language, and then bland out everything else."

Whether the game can be won by deliberate noncommunication is a matter for the sender to decide. "I call it politics," one industrial supervisor replied to a question about the reasons for vagueness.

Only the individual, closely dug into his working environment, can, if he will, fully explain why he writes as he does, and he is quick to do so when his writing is criticized for being circuitous or foggy. It is the sender's situation that underlies the style of whatever he writes, and the guiding factor for his writing is not rulebook principles of good writing but the achievement of his ultimate managerial ends. What, after all, do lack of clarity, excessive length, and indirectness imply? Do such qualities point the way to win the game?

Deliberate obfuscation is not necessarily a winning tactic when words are the pawns and business is the board on which the game is played. Once the reader sees where the moves are leading, the writer is undone, and the repercussions may be greater than those that would have resulted from forthrightness itself.

How to Develop a Presentation Objective

THE PRESENTATION MUST SERVE A FUNCTION

A presentation must serve a function: there is no other reason for making one. If it does not, nothing has been accomplished. That function is always the same: to affect human beings—to set others to respond or change in some way. The change itself may take many forms. It can be a temporary or permanent audience response, a single decision or act. It can range from the highest intellectual or emotional communion to simple entertainment . . . .

. . .without exception, the objective of a technical presentation should be stated as a *specific* mental, physical, or emotional *activity* on the part of the audience. Once a presenter identifies the function of his presentation in this manner, he takes his efforts out of the generalized realm of simply dispensing information. He acquires the main tool for making his presentation actually *do something*—for making it functional.

THE STEPS IN OBJECTIVE DEVELOPMENT

Proper objective development actually includes every major phase of the presentation itself. If the job is done right, the whole presentation *is* a process of developing an objective.

1. The presenter begins with the right perspective . . . . This includes his own motivation and sense of purpose.
2. He engages in a process of clinical analysis, using his knowledge and understanding of audiences in general.
3. He determines precisely the audience response he desires, the function that this particular presentation is to perform.
4. He actually states *this* objective.
5. He converts his objective to a thesis in a form suitable for revelation to his audience.

Adapted from W. A. Mambert, *Presenting Technical Ideas* (NY: John Wiley and Sons, Inc., 1968), pp. 43-54. Copyright 1968 by John Wiley and Sons. Reprinted by permission of the publisher.

6. To support this thesis, he selects a single basic thought pattern, reinforced by appropriate psychological and physical "patterns."
7. Using his written objective as a guide, he then proceeds to gather information and select the supporting information and material which will best help him to accomplish this objective.
8. He composes his presentation and integrates all of this information and material toward one objective: the stated audience response.
9. He then delivers the presentation to the audience with his specific objective as the foremost thought in his mind.
10. When he finishes his presentation, he concludes with an attempt either to get the desired audience response or to obtain evidence that it has taken place.
11. His final step is to compare the actual response or lack of response on the part of his audience with his stated objective. If the two are identical, he has accomplished his objective. If not, he has failed.

The mere stating of an objective is only one step in a process which makes objective development the main force in making a presentation a deliberate act. A properly formulated, stated, and developed objective permeates the entire presentation situation. It touches on *everything* the presenter thinks, says, and does. It is the main guiding force for his own motivation. It dictates the basic structure of his ideas. It tells him what to include or omit in the body of his presentation. It will govern how he delivers his message to the audience, it will influence their reactions, and it will provide the only valid measurement of the presentation's success or failure.

It should be a smooth and flowing process . . . .

. . . It is almost impossible to make a truly successful presentation without a positive belief, faith, or conviction translated into a practical objective. It is also true that the more deliberately and scientifically the objective is calculated and devised, the better are the chances of the sense of purpose coming to fruition. But attitude and objective remain inseparably intertwined. To reduce both into something which in fact can be accomplished is the aim of the objective development process.

THE OBJECTIVE SHOULD BE WRITTEN DOWN

If a presenter is not using a written statement of purpose for his presentations now, a pleasant surprise awaits him in the considerable help it will give him in such tasks as planning and outlining, properly limiting treatment, choosing specific devices, stating a thesis, being sure of himself and generally saying precisely what he wants to say. There is a reality about putting the words down in "hardened" form that is lacking in merely having an objective "in mind." Once the statement is on paper, it can be examined more objectively . . . . Every major point, every detail, every planned phrase, and every aid contemplated can then be laid beside it and a single question asked—and answered:

"Does this contribute to the accomplishment of the stated objective?" . . .

THE CHARACTERISTICS OF A TRUE OBJECTIVE

. . . By attempting to reduce the specific function to a defined audience response, to specific audience behavior, the presenter has three important factors working for him:

1. He has narrowed his presentation to something that he can see and handle by identifying exactly what function he wants it to serve.
2. He has established limits and boundaries within which to operate, thus eliminating much confusion and uncertainty.
3. He has a means of measuring his success, simply by comparing what he stated in the beginning with what comes out at the end. . . .

Every presentation will, of course, take place within the framework of a *general* purpose such as to sell, to teach, to train, to inform, or to persuade. This general atmosphere dictates matters such as level of formality, the kind of language used, and other aspects of the basic relationship between the presenter and his audience. . . .

CONVERT THE OBJECTIVE TO A THESIS

Thesis is the main idea or central thought of the presentation itself. It is the presenter's private objective converted for public consumption. . . . The thesis also is motivationally reinforced by linking it to a basic emotional channel. Intellectually it uses a cause and effect pattern. The outcome is behavioral.

Usually a thesis can be stated in a single sentence. It normally is the most generalized statement the presenter makes to his audience; it announces what he is going to prove—or what he has proven. . . .

A SINGLE THOUGHT SEQUENCE PATTERN

The key point here for the technical presenter is to think in terms of *giving the audience a single main thought,* based upon his objective. Since most technical presentations are designed to *reveal* the idea as quickly as possible, and not to build suspense, this main thought almost always should be stated at the beginning, and every opportunity taken to re-express it throughout the presentation. Often by its nature, the thesis will give a strong indication of what the structure, or thought sequence pattern, of the presentation will be. . . . The thesis indicates that a cause and effect pattern is probably the most logical thought sequence along which to direct the audience.

. . . Presenters tend to ignore the "forgetting curve" of live audiences. . . . Therefore the only hope of making a lasting presentation is to reduce it to a form in which it can be remembered. The best way to do this is "single-thought" presentation. . . .

GOAL-DIRECTED DELIVERY

. . . Much of what is meant by goal-directed delivery can be inferred by the reader based on what already has been said about the presenter's perspective. But it also rightfully belongs here as an integral part of the objective development process. In the simplest terms, it is the presenter's manipulation of *himself* as a part of the single-thought presentation. In goal-directed delivery, he makes a concentrated effort to keep one thought constantly in his own mind as he speaks. . . .

. . . Just as thesis is a refinement of objective, goal-directed delivery is a refinement and application of the concept of *awareness*—in this case, awareness of objective. . . .

MEASUREMENT DURING THE PRESENTATION

Most presenters also want to know whether they are accomplishing their objective during the presentation. Audience feedback provides some measurement, but the presenter can use this feedback more deliberately by building intermediate responses into his presentation. . . .

. . . questions can be subtly interwoven into a presentation to the extent that a hearer is not even aware that he is gradually weaving an affirmative net around himself, from which it will become increasingly difficult for him to extricate himself without "losing face"— a form of ego involvement.

A similar type of response point is that of developing a kind of "Cumulative affirmation," . . . . The point here is to ask objective-oriented, generalized questions to which any normal person must answer with a "yes" and to reinforce the questions by actually giving the expected answers. The natural result is the creation of an affirmative atmosphere. . . .

THE ACTION STEP

An action step is an attempt by the presenter either to precipitate the audience's response or to obtain a manifestation of objective accomplishment. . . . It is the final response point of the presentation, and the first step in the audience's response. . . . The action step thus has two basic functions:

1. To evoke behavior.
2. To verify that a response has occurred.

The following are some suggested methods of initiating an audience action step:

- *Direct statement or question.* Tell or ask the audience outright what they must do. . . .
- *Performance test.* Please name the six major elements of functional presenting.
- *A "starter" statement.* "Gentlemen, the first thing you must do is to arrange for your engineering representatives to meet with our designers."

- *A choice question.* "Do you prefer a one or two-year maintenance contract?"
- *Presenter action.* The presenter can start to do something which the hearer must stop him from doing in order to avoid his own action. . . .
- *Name an alternate time.* This is a variation of the double question method. Commitment for a future time is easier to get than an immediate action.
- *Direct use of motive appeal.* Remembering all of the rules of subtlety, the presenter ties his action step directly to one of the basic motive forces. "Now, let's see you prove that you can do it." . . .

THE ESSENTIAL COMPARISON

. . . evaluation of objective accomplishment. . . is also the culminating step in the objective development process. . . .

PRESENTER AND PRESENTATION INTEGRITY

In more ways than one, the word integrity is an ideal one for summing up both the theory and application of the kind of purposeful objective-oriented presenting just described . . . . A good presenter keeps irrelevant information out of his presentation. He also drives aggressively toward his objective, but he never compromises the integrity of his character. . . . Mastery of the art of presentation may get a hearer for his ideas, but always it will be primarily the *man* to whom the audience *listens.*

Effective Communication
of Financial Data

Accountants are often faced with the problem of communicating financial data to executives who are too busy to examine line by line all reports reaching their desks.

There are obvious communication problems when the recipient of a report is not familiar enough with terminology, implicit assumptions, or inherent limitations of accounting statements. Less obvious and perhaps more serious communication problems exist when reports demand too much time and concentration from the reader.

We propose to deal with the problem of management reports which the recipient does not read on time or does not read at all; in many cases both the preparer and the recipient are unaware of the shortcomings of such a report.

The customary evaluation of statements and reports is based on the assumption that the recipient has ample time to study the data carefully. This leads to reports which can be compared to telephone directories. They contain all the information which the user could possibly want, the information is arranged in a logical manner and the reports are objective because the preparer does not have to decide which information is important. Like telephone directories, such reports will serve for reference purposes; they are excellent for finding specific items of information, but they have little news value, since the more important data are likely to be obscured by masses of less important data.

A report can be considered an effective medium of communication when the recipient picks it up as soon as it reaches his desk and is able to get the gist at first glance. He can then make an informed decision whether further study of the report is warranted. Conversely, poor communication will be due to the unwillingness of the reader to waste time studying a report which in all probability may not require any action. Routine reports, by their very nature, contain mostly data which fall within the expected limits, and the recipient should therefore be able to see at once whether there are any

Bergwerk, Rudolph J. "Effective Communication of Financial Data," *The Journal of Accountancy* (February, 1970), pp. 47-54. Copyright 1970 by the American Institute of Certified Public Accountants, Inc.

developments which require his attention or whether a detailed study of the report is unnecessary.

It is obvious that the amount of data which can be comprehended at a single reading is limited, but it is far from obvious how one can determine this limit of comprehension. A questionnaire type of survey would be useless because people will be reluctant to admit that their comprehension is limited. Training and familiarity with the subject and with the presentation enable the reader to pick out the important data and to skip the others. This obscures the problem because it can be argued that the segregation of data into highlights and back-up information should be done by the preparer rather than by the reader. Furthermore, the limits of comprehension under actual conditions may be considerably lower than those under ideal conditions. Laboratory testing would have to duplicate conditions under which people normally read reports. These conditions will depend at least partly on the judgment of the reader how important the contents of a report are for him. If he considers the study of a report essential he will probably evaluate carefully every bit of information, regardless of the manner of presentation.

Most of the time the preparer of management reports cannot count on an attentive audience; on the contrary, internal reports usually have one thing in common with annual reports to stockholders; if a report demands too much concentration from a prospective reader, it will most probably remain unread.

HIGHLIGHTS

Many annual reports of listed companies feature so-called highlights, a two- or three-period comparison of the most important data. Highlights are an effective means of stressing important data, provided there are not too many items. The problem is to find the best number of items to be highlighted. If there are too few items, a valuable communications aid is wasted; if there are too many, the effectiveness of the highlights is impaired. Accountants are usually reluctant to classify an item as unimportant and it is therefore advisable to determine in advance how many items should be highlighted. The decision will then be which information is more important rather than which information is unimportant.

The purpose of our research was the establishment of norms. Persons who are responsible for the preparation of reports can decide whether they want to be guided by the norms or whether they consider a deviation appropriate.

We decided to base our research on the composite judgment of 250 teams of experts in the field of communication of financial data. The *Financial World* issue of October 26, 1966, lists the names of 291 corporations as winners and runners up of the *Financial World* 26th Annual Report awards. These reports were selected by a panel of security analysts and others as best, second best, and third best of 97 industry categories from among 5,000 entries. We requested copies of all 291 annual reports and based our research on 250 reports on a first-come basis.

Some reports had only 5 or 6-line highlights, others had 26 lines and more. The median number of lines was 14. About one-half of the reports (125 out of 240) had highlights of between 11 and 17 lines. (Table 1 gives the full frequency distribution.)

TABLE 1
Highlights

No. of Elements (lines)	No. of Reports
5	3
6	10
7	6
8	10
9	10
10	19
11	12
12	26
13	22
14	18
15	17
16	18
17	12
18	14
19	8
20	7
21	3
22	10
23	6
24	3
25	3
26 and over	3
240	

The question can be raised whether internal reports should have formal highlights; since the format of these reports remains constant, the recipient should know where to find the information which he needs. The answer would be in the affirmative. Modern data processing equipment tends to turn out lengthy reports and it is therefore helpful if the important data are separated from the back-up information. From a practical point of view one report may have to satisfy several recipients who have different information needs. In lieu of tailoring a statement to the requirements of the recipient, one can have individualized highlights. Last but not least, the search for the 14 most important data is likely to result in a better understanding of the needs of the recipient of a report.

It is noteworthy that highlights do not have any horizontal lines in order to indicate totals and differences. This raises the question whether readers find quantitative information more meaningful in the context of a statement, or whether they have more confidence in the accuracy of the data because they can check a few simple additions and subtractions. Items described by the word "other," such as "other expenses" usually have little meaning to the reader; balancing a statement is often the only function of such items. Similarly, when sales are given, a reader may be interested either in the cost of sales, or in the gross profit because either information makes the other one redundant.

Highlights are not restricted to financial data; quite often we find information pertaining to physical capacity or quantities, such as number of units produced or sold. From an accountant's vantage point, dollar information is often more readily accessible than unit information, but in many cases it is not possible to measure and evaluate past performance solely in dollars.

GRAPHS FOR REPORTING
DATA TO MANAGEMENT

Graphs can show data in proper perspective. Many data can be evaluated only by comparison with prior periods. The most common statement presentation is in the form of two columns, one column for the current period and one for a prior period. Such two-period comparisons tend to over-emphasize sudden changes which may not have any lasting significance; at the same time gradual developments may escape notice when the change from one period to the next is comparatively small. One can expend two-period comparisons by tabulating the data for a number of periods but this is not very satisfactory because the study of such a tabulation demands time and concentration. Graphs can solve this problem. Most readers find it hard to discern a trend from a tabulation of, perhaps, ten annual data; on a graph a trend becomes quite obvious.

Below is a tabulation of net income (in thousands) for ten years:

1956	$3,626
1957	5,192
1958	2,046
1959	1,814
1960	2,221
1961	1,727
1962	3,434
1963	3,450
1964	4,165
1965	4,805

Our vertical presentation makes a comparison somewhat easier; most of the time the recipient of a report can get these data only by reading across ten columns and he has to be sufficiently interested in order to take the time to visualize the trend. A chart can convey this information without imposing on the time and concentration of the reader.

Many reports are submitted to management every month. Monthly data can be charted in the same manner as annual data but we may make the discovery that there are heavy fluctuations from month to month which make it difficult to discern a trend or pattern. Such fluctuations are an indication that a month, taken by itself, is too short a period for evaluation.

When charts have to be updated every month it often becomes necessary to smooth out random fluctuations. There are several methods available, but if we want to reduce the risk of using an inappropriate base period or inappropriate weights for past performance, we have to use a method which is readily understood by the reader. Performance for the preceding 12 months is such a method. When we use a bar chart we add each month a bar representing the performance for the 12 months then ended. This has the added advantage that the data are of the same magnitude as the annual performance.

FIGURE 3

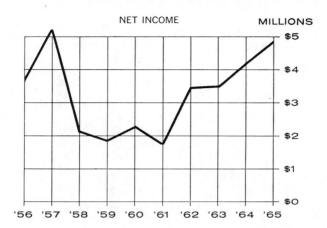

NET INCOME   MILLIONS

Figure 4 represents the monthly sales of Salesman Able. Because of circumstances beyond his control his sales vary considerably from month to month. A study of this chart will disclose that this salesman had a number of poor months in 1967, but the heavy fluctuations make it difficult to discern a trend. The same data can be presented in a more meaningful manner and Figure 5 shows sales for the preceding 12 months. A glance at this chart tells us that something happened on or before December 1966, which caused sales to slip and that from September 1967 onward sales showed again an upward movement.

The year-to-date cumulative deviation from the budget or from last year's performance offers another satisfactory solution to the problem of seasonal and random fluctuations. Such charts indicate how much the current year's performance is ahead or behind the plan and whether the gap has widened or narrowed during the month under review. Year-to-date cumulative is particularly useful when we are interested in such small deviations that data for 12 months' total performance would require too large a chart.

FIGURE 4
Salesman Able—Monthly Sales

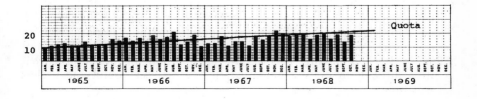

238

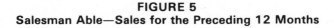

FIGURE 5
Salesman Able—Sales for the Preceding 12 Months

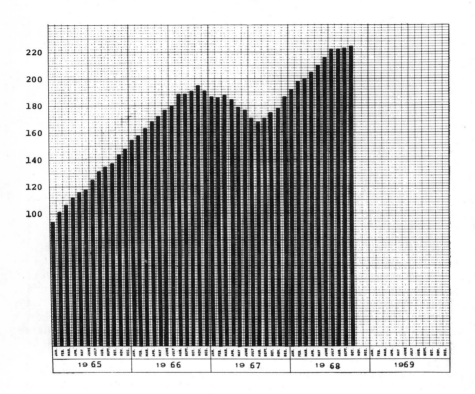

Figure 6 again shows the performance of Salesman Able. Month by month his year-to-date actual performance is compared with his quota and the difference is shown on the chart as per cent deviation. Able was given a long-range quota based on an equal monthly increment in sales. He exceeded his quota in 1965 and 1966; later on he fell behind. Normally, we would show each year on a separate chart, but four years are shown on Figure 6 for comparison with Figures 4 and 5.

GRAPHS FOR DECISION MAKING

It is generally assumed that internal reports are to inform management. This is a misleading concept because not all information is useful; a voluminous report may appear very impressive but its usefulness will depend on its value for decision making. This is self-evident although in actual practice it is often difficult to draw a demarcation line between useful and useless information.

FIGURE 6
Performance of Salesman Able—Year-to-Date
Cumulative Deviation from Quota

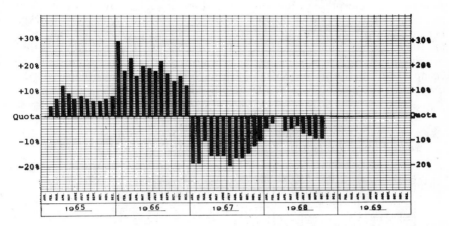

Accounting reports contain quantitative data. In most cases the recipient has to convert, at least mentally, quantitative data into qualitative data such as "good" or "bad," "satisfactory" or "unsatisfactory," "no action required" or "action required."

If an action is required, the reader has to decide what action should be taken. Financial data indicate the effect; management has first to seek the cause and then find a remedy. If sales are down, management has to find out why, and even the most detailed sales statistics may not tell us why sales are down. Elaborate statistics can be used to test hypotheses why certain sales are up and others are down, but we cannot expect accountants to show management how to boost sales. The purpose of routine reports should be to flash a warning whenever management should take some (unspecified) action. Any additional information may divert the reader from the purpose of the report.

Well-designed graphs can reduce the mental effort which is needed to convert objective quantitative data to subjective quantitative data, e.g., "action required" or "no action required."

The most effective graphs have one single element, either a curve or a row of columns. In case of revenue "up" is "good" and "down" is "bad"; with expenses the opposite holds true. An appropriate scale has to be selected: it has to be large enough to show all significant deviations or changes, but it should not be too large because too large a scale will tend to mislead a reader by showing a sharp rise (or fall) which on analysis will turn out to be a normal fluctuation.

The classification into "up" or "down" is inadequate when there is a budget. Sales can be up, yet they may fall short of the target. It will therefore be necessary to add a second element to the chart. The second curve or row of columns will represent the plan or budget. In a service industry the cost of labor is very important and a two-element chart can be used to show both labor and sales. Using different scales for labor and for sales we can have two columns which will be of equal height when the cost of labor is normal. A higher sales column will indicate increased efficiency and, vice versa, a taller labor column will indicate low efficiency. Figure 7 illustrates such a chart. This two-element presentation implies that management can lay off workers as soon as business slows down. This is not true in a tight labor market, because laid-off workers can find a steadier job with some other employer. On the contrary, it may be necessary to hire good workers as and when they become available, even when business is slow. Under such circumstances a comparison of payroll and sales is a third element because anticipated sales may affect the payroll as much as actual sales.

FIGURE 7
Sales and Direct Labor
Scale Shows Breakeven When Direct Labor Cost Is 30% of Sales

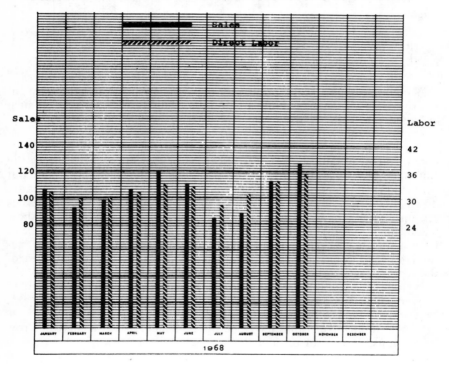

Figure 8 illustrates a three-element chart. A multicolored original chart has more contrast than the black and white reproduction shown here, but it is obvious that a three-element chart makes greater demands on the concentration of the reader than a two-element chart. Therefore one should ask the question whether the third element is really necessary. Charts with more than three elements are not desirable. The objective of a chart is to tell the reader at once whether any action is required. Too many elements defeat this purpose.

FIGURE 8
Projected Sales, Actual Sales and Direct Labor
Scale Shows Breakeven When Direct Labor Cost Is 30% of Sales

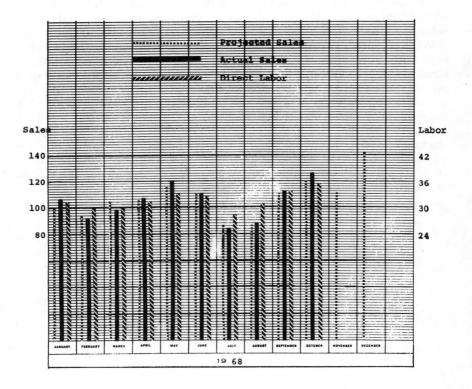

Our aforementioned study of 250 award-winning annual reports confirms that experts on communication of financial data prefer one-element or two-element charts. Most of these annual reports were lavish multicolor productions and contrasting any desired number of elements was therefore no problem. Nevertheless there were only a few charts with three or more elements. Table 2 gives the actual frequency distribution.

TABLE 2
Frequency Distribution of Various Graphs in
Award-winning Annual Reports

One-element graphs	663	57%
Two-element graphs	338	29%
Three-element graphs	113	10%
Four-or-more-element graphs	44	4%
	1158	100%

The usefulness of graphs for decision making depends on proper spade-work; first of all, it has to be determined which data are good barometers of performance. Second, it has to be determined whether "up" or "down" is good enough, or whether a comparison should be made with another time series, with the budget, or with both. Finally, it has to be determined beforehand what is to be considered a significant change or deviation.

When we determine what is significant we have to accept the risk that apparently insignificant information may at some time become important. Headlines are no substitute for the full story; similarly, highlights and graphs cannot convey all the information available. Effective communication requires continuing close co-operation between preparer and user, because information requirements change. In theory a manager should be able to explain which data are the best barometers of performance and which changes or deviations should trigger an action on his part. In actual practice we usually find that evaluation of data is subjective and not consistent. Any attempt to define information requirements can be considered as a step in the right direction for better management.

Reports that Communicate—Reports that Motivate

There has been much talk recently about the future role of the financial executive. Some seem to feel that the comptroller's status will decline because operating managers will come to rely more and more on information supplied by a new department. This need not be! Traditionally the comptroller has been the source of information flowing to management. Even where the actual data processing is under another head, it is our responsibility to assure that there are proper internal controls in the source data and in the machine processing. If we have been doing our job properly, there is no reason to assume that those involved with the compilation of the figures are in any better position to explain the content and variations to management than those in the financial area.

It is the financial man with his knowledge of operating conditions who can provide management information in such a way that it will tie up completely with the financial statements. If we are to do this, we must be able to speak in management terms, we must report clearly, completely and yet concisely. Our reports must communicate pertinent facts organized in such a way as to motivate. We must engender a feedback to ensure that the information provided is in the form required by the recipient and that it gives all the details he needs for appropriate action.

How do we write reports that communicate and motivate? There are many different types of reports, but the following principles are in general terms applicable to all. Although we will concern ourselves to some extent with reports that are in statement form, we will deal more particularly with the commentary report which may accompany a statement or be issued on its own.

WHY THAT REPORT?

The operating man—the manager—is constantly seeking information. You as the accountant must be on the alert to supply what he needs. But you

Spence, C. G., R.I.A., "Reports that Communicate—Reports that Motivate," *Cost and Management* (July-August, 1971), pp. 53-56. With permission of the publisher. Condensation of an address presented to a number of SIA chapters.

cannot do so unless you determine how the information will be used. If a report is being prepared for a manager on a number of his departments, you may want to suggest that the details be supplied initially for a pilot area for the manager's review before any specific decision is made as to how it will be developed further. In this way you can determine the effectiveness of that type of report.

You can often help a manager by suggesting the type of report which you think will assist him. But you should not impose it on him. Each manager is different, each has his own ideas, each has his own way of operating, so you must find out what he wants, why he wants it, and then determine how you can satisfy his needs.

Then there is the area that has a computer. Operating people tend to ask for considerable information because it is, no doubt, available. This is all well and good on occasion but frequently when a report has once been issued, it is automatically prepared month by month thereafter. This can be costly in terms of machine use and clerical time. Obviously, no report should be commenced on a regular basis without careful consideration. Periodically all reports must be reviewed to determine if any have fallen into disuse. Information only has value insofar as it is used.

HAVE WE ALL THE FACTS?

Our reports would be much more complete if we would consider them in the light of the What, the Why, the When, the How, the Where, and the Who. Far too often we see reports which are nothing more than a detailing of what has happened. How can anyone expect this type of report to be useful to senior management? The "why" is omitted. Factual commentary is necessary but to be of practical value, it must be accompanied by an explanation of what brought it about. Even in those areas where the individual operating manager is expected to answer directly to top management, the accountant must be available to help him determine reasons for variances.

If our reports are going to be complete, we must collect all the pertinent facts. It's surprising how often something which is not available in the normal course does become available by a degree of prodding and querying. You can't write a complete report concisely without first having a mass of information which you can analyze to make sure you have all the facts. You must also think of the attitudes of people and how one person tends to emphasize one thing more than another. Because of this, you will soon learn to query people in different ways to make sure that all pertinent facts have been disclosed.

Most situations require that the quantitative data be supplemented by qualitative data such as manpower, plant utilization, and inventory changes. It is really only in this way that it becomes truly informative.

Don't rely on old data until it has been checked out as completely applicable. Make sure it is clear and in a form which does not necessitate the recipient putting it in a different form or seeking a further analysis from someone else.

IS THIS THE BEST FORM FOR THAT REPORT?

Every report must take into account the responsibility level of the recipient. Reports at each level must dovetail into the reports at the next level which may well present the same information in a different way because of the differences in responsibility.

Reporting at the lowest level will be in considerable detail to permit the overseer or foreman to take appropriate action in relation to labor, materials, etc. Detailed reports on labor might well be prepared daily with other reports on less critical elements being prepared weekly. This will depend on the nature of the business and the significance of the various elements of the operation.

There is a principle of reporting to the next higher level which can be effectively employed: roll up reports with the summary for one level becoming part of the back-up to a summary for the next highest level.

At the corporate level the summary report received from each division must be supported with sufficient background information so that the commentary prepared by the division can be supported by an independent review of the ancillary statements. This enables the corporate comptroller's area to substantiate the reports which must be issued for the corporation as a whole and be in a position to explain the background.

Each report should be designed to provide the information which the respective manager needs to carry out his responsibility. As these reports are consolidated for use at the next higher level, they provide the superior with a basis for evaluating the performance of each manager responsible to him. It is obviously important that the information be in a form which is eminently fair. Remember this spells "control" and many people tend to resist being controlled in any form.

In developing any report, keep in mind the knowledge and background of the recipient. And try to relate any change to the specifics of the present. People grasp the significance of change much more quickly if it is explained in terms of existing procedures.

Assure that the form of the report meets the needs of the immediate unit for which it is being prepared and also keep in mind that it must meet the needs of consolidation into divisional or corporate reports so that there will be no problem in understanding how they relate to one another.

Break up the report with suitable sub-headings, provide a table of contents and consider, too, whether you should have some kind of a recommendation at the beginning of the report which will interest the reader in the general content.

Another approach is to prepare a brief—one-page—report supported by a series of schedules to provide necessary detail for those who want further background.

Don't hesitate to make the body of the report as bright and interesting as possible. Any officer reading a report will be more willing to do so if he finds it as interesting as the sports columnist's account of last night's hockey game.

SHOULD THE FORM BE CHANGED?

In reporting don't stick to one drab uniform approach. Be daring! Use different methods. You might not click one way but you are apt to click in another. The form of explanatory comments may be constantly changing depending on the emphasis needed. But be careful not to alter the form of the statements without the complete understanding of the recipients. When they get used to one format they know where to look for specific details and a change might be upsetting.

Remember there is no "one best way" which should be constantly followed although it is important to be consistent in the content to assure comparability.

If you are annoyed because you have written the same type of report month after month and seen no reaction to it, you will no doubt feel like writing a snooty report. Perhaps you should. It will help you to appreciate more fully all aspects of the problem. Then tear it up and write a calm, tactful but forceful report giving fair emphasis to the problems.

We can make ordinary reports appealing, but not on the basis of humdrum reporting. Consider, how can this report be improved?

DID WE SAY WHAT WE MEANT?

It is very important to use words that mean exactly what we want to say. Make sure, too, that your reports do not have a double meaning as exemplified by the comment of a father who said to his son: "I don't care if the basement is cracking, don't keep telling everyone you come from a broken home."

And when you have to quote from someone else be careful to quote in context. It's often wise to read the quote back to that person before letting the report go out.

In private discussion it is often possible to go tactfully into the details of a serious critical comment but extreme care must be taken as to the way such an item is included in a report. Don't be overly blunt and subject the object of your comment to unfair criticism.

Then, too, you must be careful how you report to certain people. Some jump to conclusions and immediately want to dash off to initiate some action as soon as they receive the preliminary report. This should make us recognize the need for tact, to be cautious but not necessarily to stifle a truthful presentation of what has to be done.

IS THE REPORT CONCISE?

How often have you heard someone say, "Give him and him and him a copy—paper is cheap." But the time to read it is not cheap. Just consider the time expended by those to whom you send an "extra copy" of the report— just for information.

More pertinent is the time required of a busy executive to read a long, involved report when it should have been "boiled down" to a few pithy paragraphs. A report which would communicate must be written in a form that an executive can easily digest and understand. It must be brief and to the point.

Where a concise summary or a historical outline is necessary, this should be done with no more detail than is absolutely essential. An excellent example of a summary report appears in Acts. 13: vs. 17-37 of the Bible which in those few verses gives a resume of the travels of the Israelites and their succeeding history.

Victor Hugo in writing to a friend at some length concluded with, "Forgive the length of this letter, I didn't have time to write a short one." It is a recognized fact that it takes time to organize your thoughts and express them accurately but briefly.

However, do not forfeit accuracy for brevity. In a complex operation a certain amount of detail may well be necessary but don't make this your excuse for failing to be as brief as possible, to spend the time necessary to present the matter concisely.

Be careful, too, that statistical reports do not bury important elements of the whole. If you are reporting on a group of operating centers, one of which is over budget by $50,000 and another under budget by $50,000, don't let the apparent overall equality with budget pass without pointing out the two exceptions and including reasons for the respective variances. As Willard Wirtz, United States Secretary of Labor, once remarked, the law of averages is that composition which says that if a man is standing with one foot on a hot stove and the other in a refrigerator he is, on average, comfortable.

REPORT BY EXCEPTION

Much has been said in recent years about reporting by exception. Normally this would seem to be a good method of approach, particularly on control reports or that type of weekly or monthly report that is issued specifically for the sake of giving an operating manager an opportunity to take corrective action.

Even in a year-end "wrap up," there is an advantage in setting out in an introduction those items which require attention so that they will be forcibly brought to the attention of the individual operating man. Even though he may be interested in a fairly detailed report covering the operations in a general way, an abbreviated summary or a letter report covering the main items should be provided to permit the type of action which he will want to take immediately upon receipt of the report.

In an area where there are many items it is quite likely a small number of the items represent a big portion of the volume. It is quite possible that proper control over the few big items will accurately control the "whole." This is often true of working capital tied up in inventories, and of sales where one or two items are of prime importance. Design an exception report that disregards the mass of detail and carefully discloses changes in the few important items.

USE CHARTS AND GRAPHS

It has been said that one picture is worth a thousand words. The same may be said of charts or graphs which can convey the pertinent information at a glance. There are a number of forms—bar charts, pie charts, graphs, etc. But it takes careful study to decide on the right type of presentation for each requirement.

Reports can also be enhanced by the use of various types of statistics such as historical trends and relationships of one area to another or one period to another. Introduce factors such as average cost per man hour or machine hour, percentage of overtime to salary, and percentage utilization. These, too, may be used to compare departments or factories or to indicate corporate trends. Such things as levels of accounts receivables and inventories are very susceptible to graphic presentation.

IS THE REPORT TIMELY?

Accountants often do not recognize their importance on the management team. Consequently, they don't see the need to get information into the hands of operating people as fast as possible. Speed of presentation is probably one of the greatest essentials, combined with an appreciation of the degree of accuracy required. Extreme accuracy in a report which is several days too late for appropriate action negates the value of the report completely.

Let us not forget, too, that formal reports may be supplemented and at times replaced by informal communications which provide pertinent data immediately by direct contact, possibly by phone.

Get at the root cause of delays in preparing a specific report. Do you have problems in your own office? Is there inefficient staff? Do you obtain the information from the operating centers in time? Are there obstructions put in the way of the accounting people in getting information for the report or are there constant delays in getting what is needed?

There are various ways that the flow of information can be surveyed and speeded up. Flow chart the incoming information and by critical path analysis determine where your hold-ups are.

Whether the fault is in your own office or not, you will still be blamed if reports are delayed. You may well have to arrange to provide estimates for missing areas.

RISE TO THE CHALLENGE

The better we serve operating management by providing the information they want, in the way they want it, at the time they want it, the more they are going to look to accounting and the less inclined they will be to rely on other "cuff records" which some areas seem determined to maintain for themselves or on the other outside sources of information.

To satisfy these requirements, our whole reporting procedure must be flexible. Above all, maintain backup working papers, properly indexed and neatly filed for reference and further development of any of the details which may be called for.

We may well be subjected to competition by the computer but you have one of the first computers—the human brain. Use it to rise to today's reporting challenge and yours will not be "the report that failed."

Characteristics and Organization of the Oral Technical Report

MAIN PURPOSE OF ORAL TECHNICAL REPORT: TO INFORM

A speaker may attempt to secure any one of three basic responses from his audience. He may want them to be entertained or interested (as in the case of the after-dinner speaker); to believe or act differently (as in the case of a safety talk); or to understand (as in the case of directions on how to operate a machine). Basically, the oral technical report is expository or informational. The speaker should strive for all three basic responses, but his main purpose is to advance the audience's understanding of the topic under discussion.

If the main purpose of the oral technical report is to inform, the speaker must be objective and impartial towards his material. Even though he may present strong advantages in favor of some recommendations, he scrupulously presents its disadvantages as well. The speaker stops short of playing the role of the advocate arguing for the adoption of a special point of view. He is more like a scientist reporting his latest findings to a group of fellow scientists.

In keeping with the objective point of view, the development of the oral technical report is primarily factual. Although an occasional anecdote may be valuable for illustration or enlivenment, the body of the report should consist of such objective data as explanations, descriptions, definitions, statistics, and expert opinion. Any conclusions offered should be based strictly on the facts available.

Yet, the speaker must take care that emphasis on the data does not obscure understanding of what the data support. An example of this is the speaker who is so preoccupied with explaining certain equations employed in his study that he never makes clear what his equations were intended to prove, nor what results they produced.

Although an oral technical report does not necessarily need the use of visual aids, they are usually recommended. Graphs, diagrams, models, and samples are employed freely for such purposes as explaining mechanisms and processes, presenting statistics, and stating objectives or listing main points. Because it is so easy to use visual aids ineptly, a few suggestions are:

- Charts and diagrams should normally be prepared before instead of during the presentation, when valuable time may be needlessly consumed.
- Aids should be kept simple, focusing only on what is most pertinent.
- Each drawing or chart should be adequately titled and labeled.
- Diagrams and labels should be large enough to be fully legible to those seated farthest away.
- Charts should have a professional look. Drawings and lettering not neat in appearance detract from the report.
- Normally, materials should not be distributed during the presentation since they divert attention from the speaker.
- Aids should not be revealed until they become pertinent in the presentation.

PROPER ORGANIZATION IMPORTANT FOR EFFECTIVE REPORT

As in any form of communication, the pattern of development is very important. The organization of the oral technical report can be most conveniently discussed in terms of the three major divisions of the report: body, introduction, and conclusion.

The body is normally organized in terms of the steps involved in the problem-solution sequence. They include (a) an analysis of the problem to show what is wrong (the evidences of effects of the problem), the conditions which brought about the problem (the causes), and a statement of what is desired (the criteria or expectations); and (b) an explanation and analysis of one or more solutions in terms of their advantages and disadvantages in solving the problem and meeting the criteria.

The report need not always follow the entire sequence. Sometimes it may only analyze the causes of a problem or explain and evaluate a solution to a problem. The discussion of each phase of the analysis should close with a statement showing the subconclusions arrived at during the phase.

The introduction prepares the audience for the body of the report. This is done by motivating the listener to want to hear what the speaker has to say and orienting the listener as to what the report contains.

Motivating the audience depends on two steps. First, the speaker should dwell briefly on the importance of the problems so the listener will have the feeling, "Here's something I want to find out about." Second, the speaker should establish the distinct impression that he has something worthwhile to offer on this subject. This can be done indirectly by referring to the speaker's interest and background concerning the problem and particularly to the amount of time spent and methods used in his investigation. Another way is to create an impression of competence, both in the introduction and throughout the report.

252

Orienting the listener is accomplished by *(a)* identifying and defining the problem by showing its relationship to the area from which it was taken, making clear what phases of the problem will be included in the report, and being explicit as to the exact purpose of the report; *(b)* providing whatever background is necessary concerning how the problem arose; and *(c)* giving a preview of what the main divisions of the report will contain.

When the introduction is completed, the listener should be motivated to want to listen to the report and should know what it will cover and in what order.

The conclusion normally fulfills three main functions. First, the various subconclusions presented during the report at the close of each unit are summarized. Second, general conclusions, in the form of generalizations drawn from the subconclusions, are presented. And finally, any recommendations, arising from the general conclusions are offered.

Evaluation of the Oral Report

YES | NO

Introduction

_____|_____ Did the speaker effectively capture the interest and attention of his review group right from the start?
_____|_____ Did the speaker give the necessary explanation of the background from which the problem derived?
_____|_____ Did the speaker clearly state and explain his problem?
_____|_____ Did the speaker indicate the method(s) used to solve the problem?
_____|_____ Did the speaker suggest the order in which he would report?

Organization

_____|_____ Was the plan of organization recognizable through the use of:
_____|_____ (a) Sufficient introductory information
_____|_____ (b) Successful use of transitions from one main part to the next and between points of the speech
_____|_____ (c) Appropriate use of summary statements and restatements?
_____|_____ Were the main ideas of the report clearly distinguishable from one another?
_____|_____ Was there a recognizable progression of ideas that naturally led to the conclusion?

Content

_____|_____ Did the speaker have adequate supporting data to substantiate what he said?
_____|_____ Was all the content meaningful in terms of the problem and its solution? (Avoidance of extraneous material.)
_____|_____ Did the speaker present his supporting data understandably in terms of the ideas or concepts he was trying to communicate?
_____|_____ Were the methods of the investigation clearly presented?

Visual Aid
Supports
———|———   Did the speaker effectively use charts, graphs, or
———|———   diagrams to present his statistical data?
Did the speaker use clear drawings, charts, diagrams
or blackboard aids to make his facts or explanations vivid to the review group?
———|———   Did the visual aids fit naturally into the presentation?
———|———   Did the speaker give evidence of complete familiarity
with each visual aid used?
———|———   Did the speaker clutter his report with too many
visual aids?

Conclusion
———|———   Did the speaker conclude his report with finality in
terms of one or more of the following:
(a) The conclusions reached
———|———   (b) The problem solved
———|———   (c) The results obtained
———|———   (d) The value of such findings to the corporation
or industry at large
———|———   (e) Recommendations offered?

The Question
Period
———|———   Did the speaker give evidence of intelligent listening
in interpreting the questions?
———|———   Were the speaker's answers organized in terms of a
summary statement, explanation, and supporting
example?
———|———   Did the speaker show freedom in adapting or impro-
vising visual aids in answering questions?

Delivery
———|———   Did the speaker use a natural, communicative
delivery?
———|———   Did the speaker use adequate eye contact in main-
taining a natural, communicative delivery?
———|———   Did the speaker use sufficient movement and ges-
tures?
———|———   Did the speaker use good clear diction to express
himself?
———|———   Could the speaker be heard easily by everyone?
———|———   Was the speaker confident and convincing?
Did the speaker display enthusiasm when communicating his ideas?

A Good Talk: C.O.D. (Content, Organization, Delivery)

One afternoon a Roman emperor was entertaining himself at the Colosseum by feeding Christians to the lions. Several Christians were sacrificed and the crowd screamed for more.

The next martyr said something to the lion, and the beast slunk away. Then a second lion; same result. And a third. The amazed throng began to shift its sympathies to the Christian. The Emperor announced that the Christian's life would be spared. He insisted, however, that the martyr appear before him.

"I am sparing your life," said the Emperor, "but before I release you, I demand to know what it was that you said to those beasts."

"I merely said to each lion: 'After dinner, of course, you'll be expected to say a few words.'"

As community-minded adults, each of us faces a pretty good likelihood he will be "asked to say a few words" at least once during the coming year. The audience may be eight or eight hundred—or more likely—forty, a typical community group audience. How do you feel about it? When someone says to you, "Of course, we'll expect you to say a few words after dinner," do you—like the lions—run in dismay? You shouldn't. You should welcome the opportunity. Here are some helps.

FIMP—FOR INSTANCES MEAT AND POTATOES: CONTENT

Speech content, what the speaker says, really consists of two things; the topic and the supporting particulars. The most effective particulars are "for instances"; they become the meat and potatoes that put flesh on the speech outline skeleton.

TOPICS

The topic may be assigned or it may be left to the speaker's choice. It may be narrowly defined, even specifically phrased, or it may be suggested in the most general sort of way. The speaker may believe the more strictly he limits the topic the more he simplifies his assignment. This is not necessarily true. The decision must be made on the basis of analysis of the audience and commitment to meeting its believed needs.

If the speaker believes a general introduction to the subject is the most useful for the audience, then he will conceive of his topic as a broad survey. He may, on the other hand, determine he will be more helpful if he limits the topic to a narrow aspect and then will develop it in depth.

In the early stages of preparation he should approach the topic comprehensively, but keeping in mind the audience's believed interest. Later on, especially when phrasing his central idea (to be described later), he will sharpen his concept of the topic, covering only what he wishes to cover and taking into account the response he hopes to win from his hearers.

SUPPORTING PARTICULARS

Now, regarding supporting particulars amplifying details, specifics, or FIMP, let us ask; What forms do they take? How do we go about finding them? How do we select them for inclusion?

Types. Following is a list of types of particulars. It is not exhaustive, but illustrates the possibilities:

Instances
Case histories
Events
Examples, illustrations: real or hypothetical
Narratives: true or ficititious; serious or humorous
Definition
Description
Contrast/comparison
Enumeration/listing
Figures/statistics
Humor: quip, pun, repartee
Quotation: witness testimony, authority opinion
Figure of speech: allegory, personification
Audio-visual aid

Sources. The speaker should be active in four ways in conducting his research: *reflection* (taking stock of what he already knows); *reading* (reviewing all types of printed material); *conversation* (formal and informal talks with experts and lay people, informal polls or questionnaires); *observa-*

tion (some topics lend themselves to direct investigation, e.g., community improvements, institutions, organizations, landmarks, nature).

Some tips: begin with *reflection*. Almost always we will surprise ourselves on what we already know on any given topic. Jot down notes during this inventory-taking. Second, do at least some or all of the first three, and—if at all possible—the fourth. Varied research activities provide both perspective and riches of specifics. Third, gather materials voraciously. Our speaker should wind up with at least four times as much material as time will allow him to include in the talk.

Criteria. As our speaker sits down with his voluminous notes, he needs guidelines on what to include and what to reject. Here are four standards:

1. **Relevance.** No matter how dramatic and appealing the narrative may be, how compelling the instance, it is not worthy of inclusion if it does not amplify the point under consideration. This, therefore, must always be the first test: Is it pertinent? Does it apply?

2. **Accuracy.** When we are satisfied that the specific applies, then we must satisfy ourselves that it serves truth. Is it representative, typical? In argumentation (speaking to convince), we must concern ourselves with documentation, revelation of sources. Information has a way of being as good as its source. Conversely, highly respected sources have a way of giving credence to data, e.g., "If it came from *Enclyclopedia Britannica* it must be true." To that end, we will be careful to note details on printed and spoken sources; person, place, data, time, other circumstances; publication, date, page, etc.

3. **Human interest.** On a logical basis, relevance and accuracy certainly are the overriding criteria for good speech materials. On a psychological basis, human interest factors rise to the top. "No matter how good your data are," a pragmatist might say, "if they don't capture listeners' attention, they are wasted."

   Here are some of the time-honored factors of attention and interest: narrative ("once upon a time . . . "), action, conflict, variety, novelty, the familiar in an unusual context (unexpectedly encountering a neighbor 1000 miles from home), humor, the bizarre or abnormal.

   Dr. Russell Conwell, who founded Temple University, was famous for his "Acres of Diamonds" lecture. By giving this talk 7000 times, he earned seven million dollars, many of which were devoted to the education of deserving young men at Temple University. "Acres of Diamonds" is made up of *one story after another,* developing his theme that opportunity lies everywhere about us if we will scratch the surface. Like a skilled composer, Dr. Conwell lost no opportunity to develop his theme.

4. **Adequacy.** This is a tough criterion. When do we have enough specifics—enough for our listeners' understanding, conviction, motiva-

tion? This can only be answered in the crucible of actual speaking.

We can offer a suggestion on the length of a talk, however. A veteran pastor was asked by his new assistant, "How long should I preach when I give my first sermon next Sunday?" "That's up to you," came the reply, "but we feel we don't save any souls after twenty minutes."

Also, we can suggest a formula: "Balance the specific with the general." Use the case history or specific instance, thus providing narrative quality and something with which the listener can identify. Then, lest the listener charge that the specific is atypical or unrepresentative, the speaker advances the appropriate statistic or authority opinion to demonstrate that what is true in the instance cited is generally true. Balance the specific with the general.

Show and Tell: Audio-Visual Aids. A special type of FIMP is audio-visual aids: maps, graphs, charts, tape recordings, phonograph records, flannelboards, etc. They are special because they simply present other types of specifics in audible or visual form, e.g., statistics on a graph, description on a photo, authority opinion on a tape recording, etc.

Use of a molecular model in a talk about prescription drugs illustrates many of the principles of effective visual aids. The speaker begins with the octagonal "benzine ring," representing the volatile, poisonous industrial solvent benzine. Then the speaker adds a cluster of red and yellow atoms at the top of the octagon and he has another compound: this time a food preservative for catsup and jellies—benzoic acid. Then the speaker adds another group of atoms and the compound is not volatile or poisonous, not harmful in ordinary doses, but remarkable in pain-killing properties: *aspirin*.

The molecular model illustrates some "RSVP" principles of effective audiovisual aids usage:

Relevant: The aid visually depicts the exact point under discussion: the significance of tiny molecular changes in pharmaceutical research.
Subordinate: The aid is an aid. Too often audio-visual aids dominate, making the speech an audio-aid to a demonstration. A good test is: the point can be made successfully without the aid, but is better because of it.
Visible (audible): Too often, aids are too small, too faint or too complex to be fully clear to all members of the audience. Simplicity and boldness should prevail. Also, the aid should be in sight only while in use. The red, black, and yellow balls of the molecular model made it adequately visible for an audience of 800. Further, it offered the great advantage of the speaker keeping it between the audience and himself, keeping unity in focus of attention.
Portable: Most talks are presented in public meeting places. The speaker must get his aids there and back. Huge billboards, bulky models, weighty devices become big problems. Imaginative use of paper, cloth and slide or filmstrip projections can provide size with minimal inconvenience.

The molecular model also illustrates some of the following desirable practices:

Action: Adding to, or taking away from the aid heightens interest; marking up a map or graph achieves the same.

Use a modest number: A good rule of thumb is one aid per main point. No talk should have more than five main points.

Use a variety of aids: A chart listing main points, a map, a model, a statistical graph, a tape recording.

"Roll your own": Personally created aids can achieve the simplicity and boldness desired. What they lack in polished artistry may be more than made up for by relevance and impact.

Stow the visual out of sight when not in use. Otherwise it is a distraction, competing for attention. For the same reason, *only in exceptional cases* should aids be distributed to members of audiences. (Handouts may be distributed *after* the talk.)(An exception on aids being stowed out of sight is the so-called "organizational visual." This is a card, blackboard, flannelboard or other device listing the main headings of the talk. This visual is introduced when the speaker previews his main headings, kept in sight and referred to as each main point is introduced, and used for the final summary, then put down out of sight before the "haymaker.")

TELL, TELL, AND TELL: ORGANIZATION

Some authorities regard *organization* as the basis of truly versatile eloquence. Let us consider *schema, central ideas, main headings,* and *transitions.*

Schema

We may properly think of almost any communication in this simple schematic:

The long first line represents the *central idea.* If the communication has unity, it should have a single major theme, thesis, controlling purpose or thrust. Then this central idea should be based systematically on appropriate *main headings,* here represented by the three shorter lines. There should be not fewer than two main headings nor more than five, and the most typical number is three.

Central Idea

How does the speaker come up with the central idea? It may be automatic. He is asked to speak on his opposition to a sales tax for his state. His thesis declares itself: "We must defeat the proposed state sales tax."

Equally often, however, his central idea will be elusive. He is asked to speak on state finances. What does he wish to say? Does he wish to praise or find fault? Does he wish to inform, convince, motivate, inspire, entertain? Does he wish to discuss the broad topic or some limited part? Does he wish his listeners to do something about his recommended program?

When the central idea is elusive, the speaker should give long and hard thought. He may ask himself, "After the sound and the fury, the tumult and the shouting have died, and the details have faded, what is the ultimate 'residue' I would like my listeners to retain?" When he can answer that in a simple declarative sentence, he probably will have his central idea.

Incidentally, when the central idea is simple exposition ("The Community College movement is expanding rapidly"), we call it a *theme*. When it takes sides on a controversial issue ("U.S. should pull its military forces out of Southeast Asia"), we call it a *thesis*. Theses may be stated in different ways calling for different patterns of main headings.

Even if the central idea pretty well decides itself, give it long thought, especially in terms of the response wanted from the audience.

Main Headings

When the central idea has been declared, it is usually relatively easy to come up with the main headings (main points). We wish to wind up with not fewer than two nor more than five: fewer than two, we are not subdividing; more than five, we are not grouping properly. A major purpose of grouping is to serve memory—the audience's *and the speaker's*. Also, almost any central idea will subdivide itself very nicely into two, three, four, or five main headings that cover the subject and are parallel. The most frequent number, as you will see, is three. Some persons trace this to the religious Trinity; others to the fact that any continuum has two extremes and a middle ground.

Items, events, and phenomena in our universe tend to organize themselves into four major patterns. Following are those four with illustrative "stock designs" for each:

1. Chronological or time sequence: past, present, future

   Lincoln's Gettysburg Address, which had its 100th anniversary on November 19, 1964, is a classic example: "Fourscore and seven years ago . . . Now we are engaged in a great civil war . . . It is for us, the living, rather to be dedicated here . . . "

2. Spatial (topographical or geographic)

   Federal, state, local metropolitan, suburban, rural inside, outside near, mid-distant, far left, center, right forward, midships, aft top, middle, bottom East Coast, Midwest, Rockies, Southwest, Far West, Cook County, Downstate Illinois, upper peninsula, lower peninsula, land surfaces, water surfaces

3. Topical (distributive or classification)

   Who, what, where, when, how, why (sometimes) theory, practice, quality, price, service, beauty background, problem, methodology, findings, implications, flora, fauna, animal, vegetable, mineral

A very useful device for preliminary analysis of a complex subject and later selection of main headings is the so-called decachotomy: political, social, economic, religious/moral/ethical, philosophical, educational, scientific, cultural/esthetic, military, psychological. If we were to investigate a subject such as electoral college reform, we might use this list to decide that the most important implications are political, social, and philosophical. Later, in making the talk, we might elect the same three as the best main headings.

4. Logical

Problem, damage (consequences), solution, need, desirability, practicality, cause, effect

There is good reason to believe that the most used stock design is the chronological (past, present, future). This is not surprising. When we consider almost any topic, it is natural to reflect: "What is the background; how did we get into this? Where do we find ourselves now? What is the next step?"

The most-used stock design probably should be problem, damage, solution. This is because we speak purposefully, to meet needs, to resolve problems, to achieve progress. Damage is included because it is the springboard of audience involvement. If, for example, we develop the problem of the electorate's persistent defeats of proposals to fluoridate the public water supply, and the recommended solution is to enlighten the electorate by a program of education, the listener might nod his head in agreement. "Yes; quite right; good sense"; but all at arm's length. If, on the other hand, the speaker drives home incontrovertibly that while this problem continues, *it is these very listeners* and *their children who pay the consequences* (dental decay, pain, cosmetic unattractiveness, inconvenience, financial cost), the listener not only agrees but is ready to act—no longer arm's length, now shoulder-to-shoulder.

The problem-solution design, of course, is a foreshortening of educational philosopher John Dewey's reflective process: define the problem—nature, extent, cause(s); list all plausible alternative solutions; weigh and evaluate each alternative solution; select the best alternative solution (or best compromise or combination); recommend action to implement the solution selected. Then, at that point, reflection ceases and action begins.

Occasionally we hear of a fifth pattern of analysis, called the "psychological." Here the intent is to match the listener's reaction, meeting his interest (or disinterest) as we predictably will find it, and moving ahead as it (human nature) would. Richard Borden's "Ho Hum" formula is a good example:

> Ho hum
> Why bring that up?
> For instance
> So what?

The "AIDA" formula for successful advertising is another: attention, interest, desire, and action. Purdue University's Alan Monroe advanced a "motivated sequence," blending the logical problem-solution with psychological factors: attention step, need step, satisfaction step, visualization step, and action step.

Earlier we referred to central ideas that develop partisan stands on controversial issues being called theses. And we said that when these are stated in certain ways, they call for the development of main headings (contentions or arguments) in corresponding patterns. A thesis may be stated as a question of fact, quality, degree, or policy. When we argue whether a thing exists or is real, we declare our thesis as a question of fact. We will find that developing our main headings to establish theory and practice will be wise. ("Cigarette smoking causes lung cancer"; "Extrasensory perception is a fact.")

When we argue whether a thing is good, beautiful, dependable, we state the thesis as a question of quality, e.g., "Television is good entertainment"; "Modern art is ugly"; "The sales tax is unfairly discriminatory." We will find that using criteria as main headings will serve well, e.g., "U.S. compact autos provide fine transportation" (thesis) and quality, price, service, safety, beauty (main headings).

When we argue whether a thing is better or worse than, larger or smaller than, something else, we are stating the thesis as a question of degree, e.g., "U.S. compact autos are superior to foreign-made." Again we will be well-advised to develop main headings as criteria, e.g., "Radio news coverage is superior to television's" (thesis) and speed, accuracy, comprehensiveness, clarity (main headings).

When we argue whether something ought or ought not to be done, we state the thesis as a question of policy, e.g. "We should fluoridate the public water supply"; "We must stop the military conflict in Southeast Asia"; "The United Nations should not admit Red China to membership." Main headings here should establish problem, damage, and solution, e.g., thesis: "We should support programs of planned parenthood in all developing nations"; main headings: "1. The problem of world overpopulation is acute. 2. Dire consequences are starvation, grinding poverty and political exploitation. 3. Expansion of birth control programs is a practical and desirable solution."

Transitions

Structure of the speech should emerge boldly. If the listener can visualize the framework he can help the speaker fit the component parts together in their intended relationships. Nonetheless there should be smooth transitions that tie part-to-part and part-to-whole. The best transition is a partial summary, e.g., "Thus we see there is a critical problem of overcrowded classrooms. Secondly, let us consider the consequences while this problem continues . . . ." Other transitional devices include enumeration (e.g., "Secondly, consequences"), questions (e.g., "Next we may ask: who is affected by this situation?"), directional phrases (e.g., "Let us move then"), audio-visual aids (e.g., "Consider now, please, this portion of the display").

MODEL OUTLINE

The following is a model outline, employing the recommendations above, but not including the actual supporting particulars (specifics) that flesh out the skeleton.

I. Introduction
   A. Icebreaker
      1. Reference to audience's (Olympia Civic Association's) contributions to mental health programs
      2. Reference to the speaker's own service with the Mayor's Committee
      3. Reference to the day's news item on the Committee's proposal
      4. Case history of John D., whose rehabilitation was botched by archaic mental health services
   B. Preview
      1. We must all help in establishing the Olympia Community Mental Health Center
         a. Problem of out-dated mode of treatment
         b. Damages to patients, families and community
         c. Workability, desirability and bonuses of Committee's Plan

II. Body
   A. We all must help in establishing the Olympia Community Mental Health Center
      1. Problem of antiquated approach to treating mental and emotional illness
         a. Olympia facilities are antiquated ("specifics")
         b. Olympia modes of treatment are consequently archaic ("specifics")
      2. Damage
         a. Patients suffer longer and more intensely than necessary ("specifics")
         b. Family is distraught and inconvenienced unnecessarily ("specifics")
         c. Olympia taxpayers and citizens generally bear the brunt ("specifics")
      3. Solution
         a. Mayor's Committee's proposed plan to implement Community Mental Health Center is practical, dealing with problem at its roots ("specifics")
         b. Plan is desirable, consistent with highest precepts of community action for local problems ("specifics")
         c. Plan offers several "extras," bonus advantages ("specifics")

III. Conclusion

    A. Summary

        1. We must all move directly and speedily to establish the Olympia Community Mental Health Center

            a. The problem of outmoded treatment is a civic disgrace

            b. The consequences touch every Olympian, certainly the community leaders here assembled

            c. Support of Olympia Civic Association members will help implement Committee's eminently practical and highly desirable plan.

    B. Haymaker

        1. Recall case of "John D."? Never again need this tragedy occur if we will act now.

From the foregoing it can be seen that the heart of this outline is the schema: central idea and main headings. The speaker will "tell 'em what he's gonna tell'em, tell'em, and tell'em what he told'em"—preview, body, and summary. Then to this basic pattern he adds an icebreaker to begin, and a haymaker to conclude. The purposes of the icebreaker are two: (1) to call attention to, and arouse interest in the speaker and his topic; and (2) to create common bonds and warm rapport between speaker and audience.

Chief icebreaker items are narratives (preferably of the case history type); references to the audience, topic and/or occasion (latter includes "outside world," e.g., news of the day); humorous anecdotes; participation, such as show of hands, rhetorical questions; sensational "shocker" statements; definitions; quotations of Scripture, maxims, poetry; audio-visual aids, and the like.

If time is plentiful the speaker may wish to use several of these items to arouse interest and build rapport. Perhaps the best icebreaker is the case history type of narrative. It attracts attention (we never outgrow the magic of "let me tell you a story") and arouses interest. Properly selected it creates mutual ties among speaker, topic, audience and occasion—definitely identifying the speaker with topic—and clarifies the talk's theme.

The purposes of the haymaker are to bring the talk to a climactic finale, and for the speaker to land his final blow for his central idea. (Ancient orators made much of the *peroration* in which the speaker made his final eloquent plea for his central idea.)

The speaker may use for his haymaker many of the selfsame items he uses for the icebreaker: quotation, rhetorical question, humor, participation. It is particularly esthetically satisfying if the haymaker can revert back to the icebreaker, bringing the talk fullcircle. Possibly the best combination, therefore, is, for an icebreaker, a case history type narrative that illustrates the talk's central idea, and, for a haymaker, another reference to that narrative, possibly completing the story or bringing it up to date.

ANIMATED CONVERSATIONALITY

Can you recall a recent experience when you went all out in friendly persuasion? You wished to persuade some friend of yours to a point of view or action not for your good, but for his good as you saw it. These things were happening—all intuitively: You brought into play every reason, contention, emotional appeal, instance, description, story, comparison, quotation, figure, and statistic that would build your case. You thus employed all the substance or *content* at your disposal.

Secondly you structured your persuasion. You may have said, for example, "All right, we are agreed up to here, are we not?" Then you would venture off into no-man's land, penetrating as deeply as you thought you could before experiencing rebuff. Then you would fall back and regroup, consolidating your gains, then venture off on another tack into no-man's land. Thus you were structuring, adding *organization* to your persuasive armamentarium. Thirdly, your personality ran its gamut and all the techniques of effective presentation came into play as you pled your case.

You were alternately friendly and stern, forceful and humble. Your voice ranged from shouting to whispering and the inflections varied persuasively. Your enunciation was crisp, biting out the syllables of key words with telling precision. You moved about freely, sometimes towering above your friend, sometimes almost on bended knee before him. You gestured freely. Your face was expressive, characterized chiefly by alertness and a friendly smile. Your eyes rarely left those of your friend as you studied and adapted to his responses. Your language was eloquent; you expressed yourself dynamically in compelling words, phrases and sentences.

In short, you were intuitively bringing into play every facet of personality and every aspect of *delivery* (psychological set, voice, articulation, bodily expression and language) that would enhance your persuasiveness. And equally important, you were totally unselfconscious as you immersed yourself in the project of *eliciting the desired response,* winning your friend over to believe and act as you know best for him. These are the selfsame things that should characterize our platform presentations: a lively, communicative personality; a rich, varied vocal expressiveness, with accurate pronunciation and distinct enunciation; bodily expression that is plentiful, meaningful and spontaneous: movement about the platform, stance, gesture, facial expression and eye contact; and language that is accurate, vivid, appropriate for the conceptual and vocabulary level of the listeners, action-oriented and rich in imagery.

When our speaker takes the platform we wish him to achieve the following:

1. A lengthy focal or initial pause, with a friendly facial expression (preferably a smile) as he looks out over the audience. This pause enables listeners and speaker to settle down in preparation for their respective "duties," and also builds suspense.
2. A rather full, and certainly genial and spontaneous salutation: "Thank you, Program Chairman Ellery Webb, for a sparkling sendoff; Mr. President Montgomery, Reverend Young, Judge Cloud, officers, guests, and members of the Olympia Civic Association." The most

important parts of the salutation are the acknowledgment of the introduction and addressing the members by their organization's name. The speaker's salutation can virtually simulate his response if he were being introduced to these folks around a living room in a social setting.

3. "Parry and thrust" ad lib remarks to achieve a smooth transition into the text of the talk itself. At best these remarks will call attention to the speaker and his topic, arouse interest in them, and create common ground and rapport among speaker, audience, and topic. References to the audience, the occasion (including news of the day), the speaker himself, and the topic all can be effective.

4. Impressive presentation of the talk itself: "situation well in hand" authority; "think the thought" involvement; "elicit desired response" commnicativeness; "persuasive vitality" in vocal expressiveness (with crisp enunciation); "plentiful, meaningful, spontaneous" physical expressiveness; and felicitous language, alive with action and rich in imagery.

5. Triumphant finale: knowing his closing sentences "cold," our speaker brings the talk to a resounding climax. He concludes with a terminal pause, holding eye contact, and avoids (as he would the plague) limping off on the weak crutch of "Thank you."

Bibliography

1. "Action Guide: How to Write Effective Business Reports," Bureau of Business Practice, 1969.
2. Adams, Stacy J. *Interviewing Procedures* (Chapel Hill, NC: The University of North Carolina Press, 1958).
3. Anderson, C. R., A. G. Saunder, and F. W. Weeks. *Business Reports* (NY: McGraw-Hill, 1957).
4. Babbie, Earl R. *Survey Research Methods* (Belmont, CA: Wadsworth Publishing Company, Inc., 1973).
5. Baker, William H. "Report Evaluation Form." Class handout in Business Education 320, Brigham Young University, Provo, Utah, 1975.
6. Balsley, Howard L. *Quantitative Research Methods for Business and Economics* (NY: Random House, 1970).
7. Bennet, James C. "The Communication Needs of Business Executives," *Journal of Business Communication* (Spring, 1971).
8. Berenson, Conrad and Raymond Colton. *Research Report Writing for Business and Economics* (NY: Random House, 1971).
9. Bergwerk, Rudolpf J. "Effective Communication of Financial Data," *The Journal of Accountancy* (February, 1970).
10. Bingham, Walter Van Dyke and Bruce Victor Moore. *How to Interview* (New York, NY: Harper and Brothers, 1959).
11. Boer, Germain. *Direct Cost and Contribution Accounting: An Integrated Management Accounting System* (New York: John Wiley & Sons, 1974).
12. Bormann, Ernest G., et al. *Interpersonal Communication in the Modern Organization* (Englewood Cliffs, NJ: Prentice-Hall, 1969).
13. Bowman, Garda W. "What Helps or Harms Promotability," *Harvard Business Review* (January-February, 1964).
14. Boyd, William P. and Raymond V. Lesikar. *Productive Business Writing* (Englewood Cliffs, NJ: Prentice-Hall, Inc., 1959).
15. Bradburn, N.M. "Selecting the Questions to be Asked in Surveys," *Monthly Labor Review* 93 (January, 1970): 27-9.
16. Brown, Leland. *Effective Business Report Writing* (Englewood Cliffs, NJ: Prentice-Hall, Inc., 1963).
17. Bureau of Business Practice, Inc. "Action Guide: How to Write Effective Business Reports," 1969.
18. Clover, Vernon T. *Business Research* (Lubbock, TX: Rodgers Litho, Inc., 1959).
19. Compton, Norma H. and Olive A. Hall. *Foundations of Home Economics Research* (Minneapolis, MN: Burgess Publishing Company, 1972).
20. Cook, David R. *A Guide to Educational Research* (Boston: Allyn and Bacon, Inc., 1965).
21. Coonrad, Harold A. and Lloyd Garner. "Writing the Report of a Major Investigation" (Oklahoma State University, unpublished, 1964).

268

22. Dawe, Jessamon. *Writing Business and Economics Papers* (New Jersey: Littlefield, Adams and Co., 1965).
23. Dawe, Jessamon and William Jackson Lord, Jr. *Functional Business Communication* (Englewood Cliffs, NJ: Prentice-Hall, Inc., 1968).
24. deMare, George. *Communicating for Leadership* (NY: The Ronald Press Co., 1968).
25. Devlin, Frank J. *Business Communication* (Homewood, IL: Richard D. Irwin, Inc., 1968).
26. Dewey, John. *How We Think* (Boston: Heath, 1933).
27. Douglass, Paul. *Communication Through Reports* (Englewood Cliffs, NJ: Prentice-Hall, Inc., 1957).
28. Drake, Jerry E. and Frank I. Millar. *Marketing Research: Intelligence and Management* (Scranton, PA: International Textbook Co., 1969).
29. Dugdale, Kathleen. *A Manual on Writing Research* (Bloomington, IN: Kathleen Dugdale, 1962).
30. Evans, Bergen and Cornelia Evans. *A Dictionary of Contemporary American Usage* (NY: Random House, 1957).
31. Fielden, John. "What Do You Mean I Can't Write?" *Harvard Business Review* (May-June, 1964): 144-152.
32. Foy, Fred C. "Annual Reports Don't Have to Be Dull," *Harvard Business Review* (January, 1973): 49-50.
33. Garrett, Annette. *Interviewing: Its Principles and Methods* (New York, NY: Family Service Association of America, 1942).
34. Gorden, Raymond L. *Interviewing Strategy, Techniques and Tactics* (Homewood, IL: The Dorsey Press, 1969).
35. Gunning, Robert. *The Technique of Clear Writing* (McGraw-Hill Publishing Co., 1968).
36. Hammer, D.P. "Questionnaire Guide Lines," *Library Journal* 93 (September 15, 1968): 3059.
37. Hawkins, David F. *Financial Reporting Practices of Corporations* (Homewood, IL: Dow Jones-Irwin, Inc., 1972).
38. Hay, Robert D. *Written Communications for Business Administrators* (NY: Holt, Rinehart & Winston, Inc., 1965).
39. Hillway, Tyrus. *Introduction to Research* (Boston: Houghton Mifflin Co., 1964).
40. Himstreet, William C. and Wayne M. Baty. *Business Communications: Principles and Methods* (Belmont, CA: Wadsworth Publishing Co., Inc., 1973).
41. Hines, George H. "Courses Recommended for Business Students by Managers and Educators: A Cross Cultural Study," *The Journal of Business* (December, 1971).
42. "How to Organize Letters, Reports, and Staff Studies," *Writing Guide for Naval Officers.*
43. Ironman, Ralph. *Writing the Executive Report* (London: Cox and Wyman Limited, 1966).
44. James, Don L. and Ronald L. Decker. "Does Business Student Preparation Satisfy Personnel Officers?" *Collegiate News and Views* XXVII (Spring, 1974).
45. Janis, J. Harold. *Writing and Communicating in Business* (NY: Macmillan Publishing Co., Inc., 1973).
46. Jelley, Herbert M. "Preparation of Dissertation Proposals" (Oklahoma State University, unpublished, 1973).
47. Kelley, Truman L. *Scientific Method: Its Function in Research and in Education* (NY: Macmillan Co., 1932).
48. Kendall, Patricia L. *Conflict and Moods* (Glencoe, IL: The Free Press, 1954), pp. 103-122.
49. Kish, Leslie. *Survey Sampling* (NY: John Wiley & Sons, 1965).
50. Knapp, Mark. *Nonverbal Communication in Human Interaction* (NY: Holt, Rinehart and Winston, 1972).
51. Lee, C. P. *Library Resources* (Englewood Cliffs, NJ: Prentice-Hall, Inc., 1971).
52. Lesikar, Raymond V. *Report Writing for Business* (Homewood, Illinois: Richard D. Irwin, 1964).
53. Lewis, Phillip V. "Communication Competency and Collegiate Schools of Business," *Collegiate News & Views* XXXIII (Winter, 1975-76): 15-16.
54. Lewis, Phillip V. *Organizational Communications: The Essence of Effective Management* (Columbus, OH: Grid Publishing, Inc., 1975).
55. Lewis, Philip V. "Presenting the Formal Report to Management," *Administrative Communication—A Survey* (Stillwater, OK: OSU Press, 1972): 301-304.
56. Lopez, Felix M., Jr. *Personnel Interviewing—Theory and Practice* (NY: McGraw-Hill Book Co., 1965).

57. Lull, P. E. "What Communication Means to the Corporation President," *Advanced Management* (March, 1955).
58. Mambert, W. A. *Presenting Technical Ideas: A Guide to Audience Communication* (NY: John Wiley and Sons, Inc., 1968).
59. Martin, M. P. "Making the Management Report Useful," *Journal of Systems Management* 24 (May, 1973): 30-37.
60. McGrath, J. H. *Research Methods and Designs for Education* (Scranton, PA: International Textbook Co., 1970).
61. McGuire, E. Patrick. *Salesmen's Call Reports* (NY: The Conference Board, 1972).
62. Meyers, Cecil H. *Handbook of Basic Graphs: A Modern Approach* (Belmont, CA: Dickenson Publishing Co., Inc., 1970).
63. Monroe, Alan H. and Douglas Ehninger. *Principles of Speech Communication* (Glenview, IL: Scott, Foresman and Co., 1975).
64. Moyer, C. A. and R. K. Mautz. *Intermediate Accounting—A Functional Approach* (New York: John Wiley & Sons, Inc., 1962).
65. Murphy, Herta A., and Charles E. Peck. *Effective Business Communications* (NY: McGraw-Hill Book Co., 1969).
66. Nadean, Ray E. *A Basic Rhetoric of Speech-Communication* (Reading, MS: Addison-Wesley Publishing Co., 1969).
67. Oppenheim, Abraham Naftali. *Questionnaire Design and Attitude Measurement* (NY: Basic Books, Inc., Publishers, 1966): 24-80.
68. Parten, Mildred Bernice. *Surveys, Polls, Samples: Practical Procedures* (NY: Cooper Square Publishers, Inc., 1966): 157-219 and 386.
69. Pattillo, James W. "Communication Through Reports," *Management Accounting* (October 1969): 19-22.
70. Powell, J. Lewis. *Effective Speaking—An Acquired Skill* (Washington D.C., BNA Inc., 1972).
71. Rankin, Paul T. "Listening Ability," *Proceedings of the Ohio State Educational Conference* (1939): 172-183. In Ralph G. Nichols and Leonard A. Stevens. *Are You Listening?* (NY: McGraw-Hill Book Co., Inc., 1957).
72. Rathbone, Robert R. "A New Approach to Effective Writing," *Journal of Technical Writing and Communication* (July, 1972).
73. Reiter, Michael J. "Reports that Communicate," *Management Services* (January-February, 1967): 27-30.
74. Robinson, David M. *Writing Reports for Management Decisions* (Columbus, OH: Charles E. Merrill Co., 1969).
75. Rummel, J. Francis and Wesley C. Ballaine. *Research Methodology in Business* (New York: Harper and Row, Publishers, 1963).
76. Sanford, William P. and Willard H. Yeager. *Effective Business Speech* (NY: McGraw-Hill Book Co., Inc., 1960).
77. Schneider, Arnold and William Donagy and Pamela Newman. *Organizational Communication* (New York: McGraw Hill Book Co., 1975).
78. Selltiz, Claire, Marie Jahoda, Morton Deutsch, and Stuart W. Cook. *Research Methods in Social Relations* (NY: Holt, Rinehart and Winston, 1967).
79. Shidle, Norman. *The Art of Successful Communication Through Business Reports* (New York: McGraw Hill Book Co., 1965).
80. Shurter, Robert L. *Written Communication in Business* (NY: McGraw-Hill Book Co., 1971).
81. Shurter, Robert L., J. Peter Williamson, and Wayne G. Broehl. *Business Research and Report Writing* (NY: McGraw-Hill Book Co., 1965).
82. Sigband, Norman B. *Communication for Management* (Glenview, IL: Scott, Foresman and Co., 1969).
83. Sigband, Norman B. *Communication for Management and Business* (Glenview, IL: Scott, Foresman and Co., 1976).
84. Simmons, Harry. *Executive Public Speaking Techniques* (Philadelphia, PA: Chilton Co., 1959).
85. Simons, Rollin H. "Skills Businessmen Use Most," *Nation's Business* (November, 1960).
86. Sklare, Arnold B. *Creative Report Writing* (NY: McGraw-Hill Book Co., 1964).
87. Swift, Marvin H. "Clear Writing Means Clear Thinking Means . . . " *Harvard Business Review* (January-February, 1973): 59-62.

88. Tubbs, Stewart L. and Sylvia Moss. *Human Communication—An Interpersonal Perspective* (NY: Random House, 1974).
89. Turabian, Kate L. *A Manual for Writers of Term Papers, Theses, and Dissertations* (Chicago: The University of Chicago Press, 1973).
90. Tuttle, R. E. and C. A. Brown. *Writing Useful Reports* (NY: Appleton-Century-Crofts, Inc., 1956).
91. Vardaman, George T. and Patricia Black Vardaman. *Communication in Modern Organizations* (NY: John Wiley and Sons, Inc., 1973).
92. Vincent, Clarence E. "Personnel Executives Examine the College Graduate," *Collegiate News and Views* XIX (March, 1966).
93. Wagner, Harvey M. *Principles of Operation Research* (Englewood Cliffs, NJ: Prentice-Hall, Inc., 1969).
94. Weeks, Francis W. "A Check List for Writing Effective Reports," *The ABCA Bulletin* 33 (November, 1970): 17-18.
95. Wells, Walter. *Communications in Business* (Belmont, CA: Wadsworth Publishing Co., 1968).
96. Wilcox, Rodger P. *Oral Reporting in Business and Industry* (Englewood Cliffs, NJ: Prentice-Hall, Inc., 1967).
97. Williams, John W. "The Interview" (University of Nebraska, unpublished paper, 1974).
98. Wolf, Morris P. and Robert R. Aurner. *Effective Communication in Business* (Cincinnati, OH: South-Western Publishing Co., 1974).

Index

272

Random sampling, 45
Readability, 89-91
Readings, 183+
Reasoning procedures, 19-20
  deductive, 20
  inductive, 19
Recognition, 72
Recommendations, 84-85, 105
Recording information, 73
Reliability, 46-47
Reports
  accounting and financial, 6
  analysis of, 45-46
  classification of, 4-13
  content of, 145-146
  definition of, 3-4
  external, 5-6
  formal, 9
  horizontal, 5
  informal, 9
  informative, 7
  internal, 5-6
  interpretive, 7-8
  language style, 144
  letter, 11
  long, 9, 11-13
  mechanics of, 145
  memorandum, 10
  miscellaneous considerations of, 146
  nature of, 4
  organization of, 96-98, 143
  personnel, 6
  presentation of, 145
  requirements of, 26
  sales, 6
  short, 9-11
  writing, 89-98
Research
  basic and applied, 17
  business and economic, 18-19
  characteristics of, 16
  definition of, 15-16
  descriptive, 17
  experimental, 48-49
  functional, 18-19
  historical, 16
  industrial, 19
  institutional, 19
  motivation, 17
  observation, 47-48

Research (*continued*)
  operations, 17-18
  primary, 42-49
  proposal for, 51-58
  related, 54-55, 58
  scientific, 18
  secondary, 41-42
  survey, 42
Responses
  inaccurate, 77-78
  irrelevant, 77
  nonresponse, 78
   oververbalized, 78
  partial, 77

Sales reports, 6
Sampling, 44-47
  point, 46
  quota, 45-46
  random, 45
  reliability, 46-47
  stratified random, 46
Secondary research, 41-42
Semantic decoder, 24
Semantic encoder, 24
Semantic noise, 24
Sentence construction, 91-93
Short reports, 10-11
Speaking position, 160
Statistical measures, 84
Stratified random sampling, 47
Survey research, 42
Sympathetic understanding, 72
Synopsis, 136-138

Table of contents, 135-136
Table of illustrations, 136
Tables, 84, 117-120
Telephone interviews, 43
Title fly, 133-134
Title page, 134
Tone, 94
Trauma, 72

Unity, 95

Vertical reports, 5

Writing, 89-98, 103-108